INLET

BUTE INLET

TOBA INLET

JERVIS INLET

N

urlow
nd

Stuart Island

Surge Narrows
Redonda Islands
Read Island

Cortes Island
Squirrel Cove

Cove

Cortes Bay

Manson's Landing

Powell River

HOWE SOUND

Whaletown

Comox

Vananda
Texada Island

Garden Bay
Pender Harbour

VANCOUVER

Lasqueti Island

False Bay

STRAIT OF GEORGIA

L A N D

VICTORIA

God's Little Ships

God's Little Ships

A HISTORY OF THE COLUMBIA COAST MISSION

MICHAEL L. HADLEY

HARBOUR PUBLISHING

Published by
Harbour Publishing
P.O. Box 219
Madeira Park, BC Canada V0N 2H0

Published with the assistance of the Canada Council and the Government of British Columbia, Cultural Services Branch

Cover painting by Michael Dean
Cover design and maps by Roger Handling, Terra Firma
Edited by Daniel Francis
Page design and composition by Vancouver Desktop Publishing Centre
Author photo by David L. Hadley
Printed and bound in Canada

Photo credits: Page 19, BC Archives and Records Service 37778. All others courtesy Provincial Synod Archives, Vancouver School of Theology, UBC, Vancouver, and Diocesan Archives, Christ Church Cathedral, Victoria.

Canadian Cataloguing in Publication Data

Hadley, Michael L.
  God's little ships

  Includes bibliographical references and index.
  ISBN 1-55017-133-X

  1. Columbia Coast Mission—History. 2. Missions, Medical—British Columbia—History. 3. Boats and boating in missionary work—British Columbia. 4. Anglican Church of Canada—Missions. I. Title.
BV2815.B7H32 1995   362.1'2'09711   C95-910738-X

To the Old Timers and the Absent Ones:
those who served and those whose lives were changed

Contents

Preface

WHEN THE MAVERICK MISSIONARY PIONEER John Antle founded the seagoing Columbia Coast Mission in 1904, he set events in motion that helped change the face of British Columbia's coastal society in remarkable and subtle ways. A deep-sea navigator and yachtsman, the crusty Newfoundland priest took up threads of the Grenfell Mission of Labrador and wove them into a unique pattern specially adapted to the needs of Canada's Pacific Coast. A glad, bold, even brash organization in its halcyon days, his Mission could be as rough cut and unconventional as the tough, unschooled individuals it served. Motivated by an abiding faith, "Rev. John," as he was known, took his inspiration from the Social Gospel as a means for social reform and labour justice. It was a unique exercise in practical Christianity.

Sending out its ships in all weathers, this Mission of the Anglican Church delivered medical care to isolated logging camps and settlements, established its outpost hospitals and clinics, and nurtured an essentially nonsectarian spiritual life. If the expression had been current at the time, the undertaking would have been called an ecumenical ministry. The Mission patrolled a maritime parish of over twenty thousand square miles, and by sharing a wide-ranging fellowship with everyone, fostered a sense of community that cut across all boundaries.

The success of the venture could never be measured by any statistical means such as the number of religious services or the amount of cash flow. These criteria were not germane to the founders. Instead, they stressed practical aid over proselytizing and liturgical flair: church Service over Church services. All members of the Mission saw themselves as the leaven in the bread of an evolving society. John Antle's successor as superintendent of the Mission, Alan Greene, captured the essence of this transformational role while steaming upcoast in 1944 and meditating on the Mission's influence and work:

> Yes, the channels are full of memories. Memories that make one feel there is such a field for the ministry of the Church through its itinerating missionaries. The *Rendezvous,* as could the [hospital ship] *Columbia,* might tell of endless missions over a period of years that have left an indelible impression on the minds of those whose lives are so deeply intertwined with the frontier life of this Coast.

In a very profound sense, this was a mission engaged in the process of secularization. This meant living as the vanguard of change, laying the groundwork for reform and, in the long haul, putting oneself out of a job.

The BC coast and the Columbia Coast Mission have marked my own life as well. Born in Campbell River almost sixty years ago to a "mission family" of pioneers, I grew up amidst the lore of the sea and the church. My family experienced the isolation and loneliness, as well as the special challenges and fellowship of life in such outposts as Alert Bay, Merry Island and Pachena Point. Tales of "the potlatch," of Indian burial practices and dances, of infrequent supply ships like the *Maquinna,* triggered my childhood imagination. So too did yarns about the Department of Transport's wireless service in which my father worked. Anecdotes about loggers and lightkeepers, mission ships and mountebanks, fishermen and priests conjured up a marvellous world of pluck and adventure. Influenced by two seafaring uncles from Newfoundland who served in BC waters as skippers with the Department of Fisheries and with Union Steamships, I first went to sea aboard the Union's passenger–freighter *Cardena.* Messed in the fo'c'sle as dayman and apprentice helmsman, I lived with Chinese cooks and donkeymen, wipers and drifters. Each voyage to remote ports of call like Namu, Bella Bella, Bella Coola, Minstrel Island and Alert Bay seemed to cast a spell from which I never escaped; nor have I ever wanted to.

During later years with the navy, I again explored the coast in a variety of ships, at one stage even as a young skipper in command of the coastal vessel HMCS *Porte Quebec*. I first sailed between Victoria and Desolation Sound in my twenty-three-foot sloop *Patmos*, and in recent years my wife Anita and I have followed the wakes of the Columbia Coast Mission ships in our thirty-two-foot sloop *Peregrine*. Though preoccupied all this time with writing and publishing naval history, I reflected on the BC coast and the Columbia Coast Mission. What could we know about that enterprise that had touched so many lives?

In the course of researching this fascinating topic, I realized that any hope for a thoroughgoing, scholarly history of the Columbia Coast Mission was simply expecting more than the lean and often fragmentary evidence could deliver. Indeed, many old yarns and supposedly canonical events had gone through so many variations in the telling as to make their original version unrecognizable. But I could still tell a solid story—even an authoritative one—and capture what the Mission was about. In doing so, the largely anecdotal material underwent rigorous selection in my hands. In the process, I experienced the same twinges of regret as Cecil FitzGerald in 1965 when he edited the Diamond Jubilee folio of the Mission's journal *The Log*, marking sixty years of service:

> Would that it were possible to name all those who gave their service to this work. But the list is too stupendous. Moreover, to name a few of these persons would be virtually impossible, for who can judge whether one man's ministry has been greater than another's?

In writing this history of the Columbia Coast Mission, I have concentrated more on the contours and substance of the venture than on the full network of human occasions and broad cast of characters that populated its scenes. I have singled out representative individuals and central events in order to elucidate a social process and its impact on individuals and locales. To have done otherwise would have overshadowed with distracting anecdotal detail the very profile in which the Mission's identity and achievement lies.

This then is the story of the men and women of the Columbia Coast Mission, and of the ships in which they plied the coast. It is an account of a dedicated few who lived the Gospel which they took into the remote regions of the coast. It is ultimately the story of a vision of ministry which, at its close, seemed to have had its day, yet which many still believe did not merit demise, but transformation.

Acknowledgements

THIS ACCOUNT OWES ITS EARLIEST ORIGINS to stories heard in childhood and early youth, told by people who had experienced the Mission ministry. I acknowledge Norman Hadley, wireless operator at Merry Island, Alert Bay and Pachena Point, and his wife Winnifred—my parents; Cecil FitzGerald, engineer on the hospital ship *Columbia*, and his wife Grace, nurse at St. George's Hospital—my godparents; Doug Dane, lightkeeper at Ballenas Light Station, and his wife Bessie, nurse at St. Mary's Hospital, Pender Harbour—who brought the youngsters movies and good times. They and their community of friends turned such names as John Antle, Alan Greene, Bathurst Hall, Ed Godfrey and *Columbia* into household words.

My good friend John Lancaster encouraged me to research the topic, and the Board of the Columbia Coast Mission has given such support as was needed to complete the work.

I thank Doreen Stephens of the Provincial Synod Archives, Vancouver School of Theology, without whose assistance I could not have navigated through the records which sometimes buried the story. I appreciate as well the assistance of Elizabeth Hyde and Mary Barlow, Diocesan Archivists, Diocese of British Columbia, Victoria. Catherine Greene Tuck kindly provided occasional letters from her private collection. Dallas Brock, imaginative organizer of the Mission Boats Homecoming in Pender Harbour in August 1994, helped evoke a special legacy.

For their critical reading of the original manuscript, I thank

Chief Frank Calder of the Nisga'a, the Reverend Ivan Futter, and Archdeacon John Lancaster of the Columbia Coast Mission Board. My wife Anita Borradaile Hadley, who shared in explorations of the Mission territory in our sloop *Peregrine* and vetted early drafts, has been instrumental in bringing this story to press. We are both indebted to the late Reverend Rollo Boas and his wife Kay, whose hospitality during our visits to Whaletown showed us how the Columbia Coast Mission was lived.

Publication has been supported by a grant from the Board of the Columbia Coast Mission.

Introduction

THE WEST COAST SURF SURGES against the rocky shores of Vancouver Island, pounding its way into still uninhabited reaches of Canada's westernmost sea frontier. On full flood it sweeps northward around Cape Scott into Queen Charlotte Sound, thrusting ever southward into the increasingly constrained waters of Johnstone Strait. Some three hundred miles farther south, this same flood sweeps southeastward around Vancouver Island into Juan de Fuca Strait, then northward through Haro and Georgia straits until its mass wells up through a vast network of deep-sea passes and converges against the southbound flood. Here at the meeting of waters are concentrated some of the greatest natural hazards a mariner can encounter: narrow passes, overfalls, whirlpools and twelve-knot tide races. Dashing, twisting and turning, powerful ebb currents withdraw the sea's embrace—revealing threatening rocks during the tide's eighteen-foot drop—and with only a few minutes slack water, simultaneously reverse the surge both northward and southward to the open ocean from whence it came.

This land has been inhospitable to all who could not learn its ways. Yet its richness—forests, fisheries, minerals, immense rugged beauty and solitude—continues to beckon. For over two hundred years it has drawn explorers, adventurers, entrepreneurs, settlers and missionaries. It is a land marked as much by grand enterprises and human success as it is by broken ventures and failed dreams. Today, cities and thriving businesses form a discordant counterpoint to the ghost towns and decaying Indian villages whose silent witness recounts an unspoken narrative of obsolescence or failure, loneliness and despair.

Human intrusion into this wilderness has left its traces. One finds them in the Indian rock paintings of Gorge Harbour, and the abandoned farms, canneries and logging camps of Bute Inlet and Redonda Bay. Mariners encounter yet another legacy as they plot their course on nautical charts, where place names evoke a haunting past from the mists of memory. Quadra, Maurelle and Vancouver Islands recall the Spanish and British explorers who first surveyed these waters in the eighteenth century, while Discovery Passage, Sutil Channel and Sonora Island echo the passage of their stout sailing craft. The charts hearken back to other wayfarers as well: explorer-artists (Cordero Channel); early settlers and pioneers (Hadley Bay, Mansons Landing, Waddington Channel); nineteenth-century surveyors and Royal Navy gunboats (Seymour Narrows, Plumper Point); and Hudson's Bay trading vessels (Otter Cove, Beaver Point). A host of names recalls the Royal Navy's indebtedness to its imperial past (Nelson Island, Jervis Inlet) and its nostalgia for home (Epsom Point). That isn't all. Both the old world and the new have left their contrasting spiritual legacies on coastal geography: from the poignant presence of the coast's Native peoples (Skookumchuck Narrows, Yuculta Rapids and Okisollo Channel) to the work of Christian missionaries (Church House, Hospital Bay).

These once untracked waters, first inhabited by First Nations groups such the Kwagliuth, Homalco, Nisga'a, Tsawataineuk and Tshimshian, are now familiar territory to generations of coastal mariners and yachtsmen. With excellent navigational aids—charts and tide tables, VHF radio, Loran, GPS and echo sounders—and with access to marinas and supply bases, well-found and well-skippered vessels can brave the alluring and forbidding BC coast with confidence. Indeed, today's mariners reap the rich legacy of coastal exploration and growth.

Varied talents opened up this land. In the years 1791–93, the expeditions of Juan Francisco de la Bodega y Quadra and George Vancouver marked the first European surveys of the coast. Under sail and oar, their small ships challenged even the flood currents and swirls of Arran Rapids, their crews hauling the boats by rope from shore when the current became too strong. British Admiralty surveys—under sail, oar and steam—embarked from Esquimalt throughout the nineteenth century. Settlers and speculators, miners and charlatans, saloon-keepers, prostitutes and tin-horn gamblers followed in their wake. Coastal passenger service between frontier sites commenced in the 1890s. Beginning with Union Steamships, and later joined by vessels of the CPR and CNR, these voyages forged new economic and social links among pioneering communities.

In time, the coast and its people attracted seagoing pastors. Since the gold rush of 1858, British Columbia and Vancouver Island had been well known to British missionary societies. But they had focussed on inland communities and neglected the southern coast. Individual initiatives by visionary pastors changed all that. The Roman Catholic Church had founded the shore-based Nootka Mission in 1874 on the west coast of Vancouver Island, but not until 1950 did its missionaries put to sea. For thirteen years the *Sea Queen* operated out of Friendly Cove until 1963, when the *Star of the Sea* took up the sea-going ministry. She served a three-hundred-mile area covering Simoom Sound, Alert Bay, Bella Bella, Bella Coola, Sointula, Minstrel Island, South Bentinck, Namu and Klemtu. In 1884 the Methodists launched their seventy-one-foot steamboat *Glad Tidings*, which sailed the northern coastal waters until wrecked by marine accident in 1903. She was the first of many Methodist, and later United Church, mission boats on the coast. By 1927 the United Church was operating five mission ships in as many different zones: *William Oliver* (Alert Bay), *Edward White* (Cape Mudge), *Broadcaster* (West Coast), *Sky Pilot* (Vananda) and the *Thomas Crosby*. The nonsectarian Shantyman's Missionary Society, founded in 1903, first travelled by canoe until acquiring seaworthy vessels. Many of them bore the name *Messenger*. In 1937 the Shantymen established the first West Coast hospital, at Esperanza, some seventy-miles northwest of Tofino.

Isolated Anglican ventures in marine mission during the last decades of the nineteenth century gave a foretaste of greater things to come. From 1880 until 1892 the steam vessel *Evangeline* tried to cover the far northern coast of BC. Rising operating costs forced her sale and a continuation of the mission by canoe. Not until 1912 could the church launch another vessel for northern coastal mission in the Diocese of Caledonia: the forty-five-foot *Northern Cross*. All this was but a prelude to the major undertaking that established the Columbia Coast Mission in 1904, and committed it to a course that would not alter until new technologies ended the coastal marine mission in 1969.

The roots of the Columbia Coast Mission reach back to the early days of coastal mission work in Newfoundland, where the Reverend John Antle lived from 1865 to 1897, learning the ways of the sea and responding to the needs of isolated fishing communities. As alien as this territory might seem to the founding of a seagoing mission on Canada's West Coast, Newfoundland was nonetheless the matrix of his formative experience. Places like Conception Bay, Spaniards Cove, Harbour Grace and "the Labrador," as fishermen called the barren northern coast, prefigured Antle's great venture in British Columbia. Though remote from one another, these two great coastal regions had much in common: their ruggedness, isolation and the self-reliance of their people in adversity. Antle would have pushed the analogy even further, and spoken of their overt need for pastoral and medical care, as well as for social change. Professing a practical faith, he committed himself while still a youth to what he later termed "the high and holy calling of a priest of the Church of God."

John Antle was a maverick. Had he not been, he would not have realized his dream: the establishment in a few short years of seven mission ships and five mission hospitals on the BC coast. His territory, and that of his successors, covered some twenty thousand square miles of land and sea. He launched the Columbia Coast Mission by undertaking an exploratory voyage from Vancouver to Alert Bay and back: five hundred miles in his home-built, sixteen-foot sailboat *Laverock* with only his nine-year-old son as crew. He completed his commission in 1939 at the age of seventy-four by bringing yet another vessel to the fleet: the seventy-foot yawl-rigged *Reverie*, which he skippered thirteen thousand miles from Falmouth, England, to Victoria via the Panama Canal. Asked how he had coped with the sometimes violent storms on war-threatened waters, he replied: "You may argue as you like, but there is an answer to prayer." Prayer was a major theme in his life.

His exploratory trip in 1904 triggered rapid change. The wake of the little *Laverock* was followed a year later by Antle's sixty-foot *Columbia I*; then the hundred-foot *Columbia II* in 1910, the *Governor Musgrave* in 1911, the *Makehewi* in 1919, the *Rendezvous* in 1924, the *John Antle* (ex-yacht *Syrene*) in 1933 and *John Antle II* (ex-seiner *Florida V*) in 1936. As the fleet and its routes expanded, so too did shore-side medical care and solace in the mission hospitals: at Rock Bay in Discovery Passage (1905), Vananda on Texada Island (1907), Alert Bay on Cormorant Island (1909), Columbia Hospital at Carriden Bay (1920) and St. Mary's Hospital at Pender Harbour (1930). The links among these hospitals were the ships of the mission, and the faith of their skippers. The foundation stones of the Columbia Coast Mission were John Antle, Heber Greene and Antle's successor, Alan Greene. These men devoted virtually their whole career—their "calling," as they would have expressed it—to the Mission.

What did it mean to become chaplain–skipper of one these ships? The Reverend Rollo Boas explained it to me:

> Unlike moving from one parish or mission to another, becoming the chaplain–skipper of the *Rendezvous* was saying to me: "Here is your means of transportation and living quarters as you go out into your patrol area. You will visit every port, village, isolated dwelling in between Savary Island to the south, Greene Point Rapids to the north, all the inlets and reaches of the sea into mainland Canada. Your westerly boundary is Quadra Island and those living on the shores of Discovery Passage. There is no parish list, no routine of services to be followed. You are on your own."

This, then, was the world of "God's Little Ships," as journalist Gilean Douglas described it in the *Vancouver Sun Magazine* in 1951. Their task involved more than taking the Social Gospel into the remote regions of the coast—though that was much. In the quaint incisiveness of an older vernacular, it involved a cure of souls, a mission of faith. In Douglas's words: "They have been christening, marrying, burying, preaching and performing their thousand and one other jobs by the tides off coastal British Columbia for forty-six years." Over twenty years later, novelist Margaret Craven captured the scene in her best seller, *I Heard the Owl Call My Name*:

> Up and down the straits. In and out the lower inlets in a mild chop, in a moderate chop, in a gale. The tide-book open by the compass because you came with the tide, you went with the tide, you waited for the tide, and sometimes you prayed for the tide. Check the oil pressure and the shaft bearings. Pump the bilge. Watch for the drift logs. Count the lights on the masts of the tug boats that showed the size of their booms.

The territory of the Mission was daunting: from the Sechelt Peninsula in the south to the top of Kingcome Inlet in the north; from halfway up Vancouver Island in the west to the very ends of Bute and Jervis Inlets in the east. It covered thousands of miles of coast, many of them uncharted in the early days and most without navigation aids until later years. Indeed, the pioneer days of coastal pilotage are still of recent memory. Again, Gilean Douglas put the task in perspective in 1951:

> The three mission boats and one hospital ship of the mission travel the waterways between Halfmoon Bay, just above Vancouver City, and Cape Scott, some 250 more miles north, off the tip of Vancouver Island. Four little ships battling skookumchucks ... Bute winds, Qualicums, Squamish squalls—and that sea of inertia and materialism which is encroaching with such deceptive calm upon our continent of the spirit.

CHAPTER I

Maverick Minister:
The Antle Vision

SEAFARING WAS THE OBVIOUS CHOICE of profession for the coastal men of Newfoundland where the founder of the Columbia Coast Mission grew up. John Antle had known boats from his earliest days. Born in 1865, he had watched square-rigged sealing vessels from many countries working their way in and out of ice-strewn harbours. He eventually sailed before the mast with his father, who skippered a barquentine out of Harbour Grace. Antle's father intended his son to follow this tradition, and planned to send him to the nautical school in St. John's. From the family's point of view, this would have been natural, perhaps even providential. But young John had a mind of his own and refused to go to sea on his father's terms. "What, then, are you going to do?" his father asked. "I'm going to teach school and then I hope to enter the ministry." "Who's going to pay for all this?" the father testily enquired. "Not you," retorted young John.

Abrupt, direct and uncompromising, Antle displayed a self-determination that at first seemed ill considered. Yet his approach revealed the beginnings of both a vision and a leadership style rooted in a profound compassion. At age seventeen, he resolved to place no further burden on his father for training and education; he regarded himself a man and would see to matters on his own. Although he did go to sea as his father wished, he did so in response to a call much deeper and more spiritual than hunting seal and catching fish. While taking up the profession of seafaring, he was becoming, in the biblical phrase, "a fisher of men."

The rough notes of John Antle's unpublished memoirs reveal a reflective, tough-minded man who enjoyed the challenges of life. Before his eighteenth birthday, he had taken a job as teacher and catechist on the northern coast of Newfoundland. Of that early period he later wrote: "I learned the hard way to stand on my own feet and make my own decisions." He always sought new tasks, even launching himself into a sailing mission along some forty miles of the Strait of Belle Isle to visit his charges. Bleak, barren and sparsely populated, the region offered little solace. From there he moved to Conception Bay as teacher and lay reader. Throughout his life he felt indebted to the friends and families of Christ Church, Newfoundland, for "rubbing off the hard corners of my character and manners, and otherwise perfecting the groundwork fitting me for the high calling" of pastor. It was not so much the intellectual challenge of theological study that attracted him; he had little patience with abstractions. Nor did he have much patience with those who saw the ministry as a sinecure. What mattered was the Social Gospel that sought practical solutions to human problems. Time and again he touches these themes in his memoirs: his work during the smallpox epidemic at the town of Island Cove; his caring for the diphtheria victims in Harbour Grace, before returning to theological studies at St. John's College in the provincial capital; his polite disdain of expatriated English candidates for the priesthood who seemed ill suited and ill motivated for their tasks.

Ordained a deacon in 1890, Antle moved to Greenspond, a large parish extending some seventy-five miles along the northern shore of Bonavista Bay. The vicar, it turned out, was not himself a sailor and could only visit throughout his parish infrequently. "As a matter of fact," Antle later recalled, "the parish was so unwieldy that even a good boatman, as I afterwards found, could not minister to it efficiently." Here he acquired the small sailboat *Nettie*. She was a lakeboat unsuited for the coastal waters. Greenspond, a remote unschooled community, matured him:

> In this place I learnt much of life from ignorant people who had read deeply in the book of life. They were all fishermen, more or less well-to-do. They skippered

their own craft, and some of them skippered sealing
steamers . . . all of them seal killers and the most interesting of all the common fishermen, whose fathers and
grandfathers were fishermen before them. They were a
church-going, God-fearing people. To the outsider rather
superstitious.

This supposed superstition offered him insight into spiritual dimensions—some might even say psychic dimensions—which he had
not yet met. His memoirs recount stories of those who in Newfoundland parlance "went to the ice" on the seal hunt, and whose
families literally "prayed them home." "Looking back today over
fifty years," Antle recalled, "I know how possible it is for simple
hearts to catch faint echoes of the beyond, denied to the highly
educated and even to the man of science." This tension between
the intellectual and the existential informed much of his later
pastoral life.

His next sailboat, *Acolyte*, was built to serve Antle's ministry
and to extend both his range and his endurance. Based on plans
supplied by the United States Fishery Commission, this "wonderful
seaboat," as Antle described it, took him far. He sailed with her
through "the choppy sea outside the narrows," worked along the
coast, and even reached out to the drifting pack ice that pressed
off the coast of Newfoundland in early spring. Warned by his
bishop to consider "more caution and the avoidance of foolhar-
diness," Antle took his taut vessel and crew of three wherever his
pastoral duties called. One venture in the ice pack almost cost
him his boat, another his life. As an old fisherman observed when
Antle finally left the parish: "Well, parson, we've never had a gale
on this coast that you haven't been out in." In such conditions
he developed his concept of parish. For him, it was not an area
within ecclesiastical boundaries, but the place of the ancient "ecclesia"; it was the community wherever it lived and moved and had
its being—settlements ashore, dories and schooners at sea, fishermen
in outports far from home.

Ordained to the priesthood in 1892, John Antle was posted to
Catalina where he again extended his parish by undertaking seagoing mission. In spring and fall the harbours filled with schooners.

Fishermen, he found, were a conservative lot; though accustomed to attending church, they never did so when in the outports far from home. They found their working clothes ill-suited to the occasion, and no one had tried to persuade them otherwise. Antle's solution was simple: he founded The Church Harbor Crew to bring the church to the fishermen. Scattered over the Grand Banks throughout the week, the fishing vessels tried to make a port for the weekend, where Antle's *Acolyte* dropped in on them. Much later he recalled how "in the little boat flying the Church flag, St. George's red cross on a white ground [he] called on every vessel in the harbor every Saturday." This flag was the prototype of the one later flown by the Columbia Coast Mission.

In the summer of 1897 Antle resigned the Parish of Catalina and moved to Toronto, intending to take a Bachelor of Arts degree at Trinity College. Little is known of his brief time there. It seems, however, that an eleventh-hour decision by his home diocese had deprived him of the money he had been promised, and which he desperately needed to pursue his studies. Feeling forsaken by the Newfoundland church, he moved west to join his wife who was visiting her parents on a ranch near Seattle. (Very little is known about Antle's wife, who separated from her husband in late 1910.) Antle thus began a new ministry on the Pacific coast.

The experience of being left stranded in Toronto strikes another theme that weaves its way through his later ministry on the BC coast: the conflict between "good business" and the moral imperative to support ministry. Antle later recalled the "bolt from the blue" that had deprived him of his funds for study: "It was a sharp piece of business for which the diocese was not so much to blame as [was] the head of its business affairs who had absorbed in his career more business methods than was good for one who put Reverend before his name."

Years later he would encounter similar characters when dealing with his Columbia Coast Mission board. Some members proved more comfortable investing in the markets—or at least in bricks and mortar—than in the "living stone" of an essentially spiritual enterprise.

In the meantime, Antle was gaining frontier experience in the rough mining town of Roslyn, in Kittitas County, Washington. If he had had any high ideas about ministering to westerners, this experience brought him down to earth. Underscored by labour strife and racial tensions between white and black miners, the harsh gunslinging mentality of his three-thousand-soul territory made him "hit the ground harder there than at any other time in [his] whole life." It made him confront a social reality more committed to individualism and free enterprise than anything he had ever encountered on the Atlantic coast. Not that these attitudes were in themselves wrong, but they seemed to exclude concern for the interests of others. Nor was western culture necessarily hostile to his pastoral message; he would readily have grappled with a challenge like that. What got him down was the sheer indifference to his message. The culture of Roslyn lacked the spiritual centre which had defined the life of even the remotest outpost in Newfoundland. "In Newfoundland," he later wrote in his autobiographical sketch, "I had never met an unbeliever. Here no one seemed to have any religious faith. The churches were small and of little influence." Yet for all its disappointments, his seven-month sojourn in Roslyn proved salutary for his future career. Ultimately, it was not only the social atmosphere that made him want to move on, but the geography as well. As he recalled: "It was in mountainous country, snow peaks visible all around, and to one from the sea, it was a prison. I felt absolutely stifled."

Offered a church in Anacortes, Skagit County, Antle accepted with little persuasion. Situated since 1876 near the northern tip of Fidalgo Island (Puget Sound), Anacortes had once been a boom town of some ten thousand inhabitants. Plans to develop it as the western terminus of the US transcontinental railway had already collapsed by the time Antle arrived in 1898. He found a strangely beautiful ghost town of only sixteen hundred inhabitants: "There were fine houses standing unoccupied and large hotels being used as rooming houses. Many of the streets were grown over with grass and bushes. All hope of the railroad had been lost." Extending beyond the four small established churches in Anacortes, Mount Vernon, Burlington and Hamilton, his sprawling parish also embraced the alluring San Juan Islands. Yet, island dwellers could be as two-fisted as those in the mining town of Roslyn. His parish outposts were, perhaps, more in need of civilizing than any place he later met along the rugged BC coast.

Antle's experiences in Washington triggered lasting reflections on the relationship between freedom and law, between self-determination and moral duty. Nowhere did this seem more graphically displayed than in the American insistence on individual freedom and on the perceived right to take the law into one's own hands. He never forgot conducting a funeral in "a small cemetery well back in the timber" for a man who had been shot to death—and whose gun-toting murderer attended the graveside service. Acquitted after a brief trial, the accused went free. As Antle recalled: "The citizens of Mount Vernon . . . were obviously delighted with the verdict which freed the man despite the general belief that he was guilty of the crime. They were sentimental in their desire to have the man escape the consequences of his actions." Later that year, the same gunman beat the sheriff of Mount Vernon to the draw, marched him down the street in broad daylight with hands high, then burst into a local law office and murdered one of Antle's staunchest supporters. Angered by these incidents, Antle preached his next sermon against the legal and social system. At least one parishioner cautioned him that as a non-American he should keep such opinions to himself. Never did he feel more an outsider than on that day. It was one of many incidents that made him want to return to a culture whose ethos he shared: "I had an increasingly strong desire to get back under the British flag, so pointed out to [my] Bishop . . . that I never could become a United States citizen and therefore would be handicapped in church work." Yet his experience in the United States triggered the formulation of a concept of mission that prefigured elements of his later work on the BC coast.

While visiting patients at St. Elizabeth Hospital in the small town of Sedro, he came across loggers who had been injured in the woods—some of them seriously. It was startling to discover among these woodsmen many former professional men who "had gravitated to the simple life via the whisky road." Alcoholism was not an unusual disease in isolated outposts of the forest industry. Nor was it unusual to find professionals from the East who had "hit the skids" even before arriving at the coast where they hoped to lose themselves. It was in just such straits that Antle later found the first surgeon for the Columbia Coast Mission, cutting cordwood in Halfmoon Bay. But what impressed Antle about the hospital in Sedro and elsewhere in Washington was that the Episcopal Church took its work with alcoholics seriously—even enthusiastically. These early experiences led to his first plan for a string of hospitals in the Puget Sound district, and a mission boat to keep in touch both with them and the men in the camps. He submitted the plan to his bishop, only to have it turned down by "a very conservative executive committee."

Once released from his obligations in Anacortes, Antle moved to Vancouver, BC, which he had already visited on a number of occasions. In December of 1899, he became the first rector of a parish in Vancouver's new district of Fairview. As he recalled in his memoirs: "Houses were scattered among the trees; Broadway was farthest south and after that was the tall timber, with Granville Street as a carriage road leading to [the fishing village] of Steveston" on the Fraser River. The parish of Holy Trinity Church, which he proceeded to build from the ground up, afforded him an urban stability which soon made him restless. He could never stay in one place—particularly a quiet one—when there was so much pastoral work yet to be done. Although his parish had its own special needs and challenges, it was already becoming well established. Indeed, compared with the marginal living of upcoast settlers and loggers, it was well off. With his love of the sea, and his concern for the socially deprived, it was inevitable that Antle would be drawn to these remote coastal people.

One day in the fall of 1903, Antle's memoirs record, the coastal steam vessel SS *Cassiar* arrived in Vancouver from its regular route on the so-called "logging run." Known affectionately in the trade as "the loggers' palace," the two-year-old Union Steamship vessel was one of the principal links among the many outposts on the coast. On that particular day, she arrived in port with four dead men aboard, victims of careless logging and no recourse to medical aid. One of the loggers had died on board while being brought to hospital. In reporting the tragedy, however, the newspapers made no mention of the victims' names. "Better class" passengers were worthy of note, but loggers belonged to a nameless class who became even more anonymous in death. While settled travellers arrived by ship and went to their homes, loggers away from camp had only the rooming houses and bars of boomtown Vancouver for their rest. Here they were soon parted from their pay. For many, the Reverend Rollo Boas later recalled, "the saloon became a revolving door—in sober and flush, out drunk and broke." This "swashbuckling, rip-roaring habit of the logger, the miner, the pioneer," as one of Antle's first mission doctors, J.H. MacDermot, surmised in 1935, had natural and correctable causes. In 1904, however, "there was nothing in their lives to sublimate these perhaps irregular and even dangerous instincts." It was the disturbing mix of anonymity, vulnerability and the potential futility of these pawns of the logging trade that moved Antle to take action.

As Antle reflected later: "Four thousand men in the camps, working in the most dangerous calling in Canada, and the nearest doctor from fifty to three hundred and fifty miles away. What was to be done?" In a series of moves no longer traceable in any detail, Antle established a joint committee of the Dioceses of Columbia and New Westminster which ensured support from the large mainland diocese and its counterpart on Vancouver Island. Thus reinforced, he set forth to investigate conditions among the loggers on the coast.

Antle's first journey of exploration began with great simplicity: it consisted of a man, a boy, a homemade boat and a one-hundred-dollar grant from the church. The money bought an innovative piece of modern technology: a Springfield three-quarter horsepower "Bull Pup" outboard gas engine. Antle mounted this "infernal combustion" engine on the sixteen-foot racing dinghy *Laverock* he had built two years earlier in his back yard. (He took the name from the church ship at Newfoundland on which he had occasionally served as chaplain.) Then, according to his colloquial note, "on 1st of June [1904] with my little son [Victor], a lad of nine years as crew, at 5 o'clock in the evening we hoisted our sails and cranked our engine and headed 'North by West in the Sunlight.'"

The journey took them five hundred miles from Vancouver to Alert Bay and back, visiting twelve logging camps and twelve settlements en route. In the logging camps Antle focussed primarily

John Antle and his wife in their sixteen-foot Laverock in 1901. This is the vessel in which Antle and his nine-year-old son journeyed from Vancouver to Alert Bay and back in 1904 in order to scout out the opportunities for establishing missions.

on the foremen, engineers and leaders in order to sound out their views on his project; most, it turned out, supported him. Whenever possible he conducted church services in the camps and led prayers in the homes of isolated families. Working their way northward, camping at night or sleeping in their anchored boat, Antle and his son passed from Bowen Island, up the Sunshine Coast to Merry Island, rounding from there into Malaspina Strait, marvelling as they went at "the pristine beauty" of the site that was to become the mill town of Powell River. Each aspect of the voyage harboured its challenges and fears. Tide tables and detailed charts were not yet available. Guided only by a small-scale general chart of Vancouver Island, and by local information on camps and havens, Antle decided not to follow the mainland coast into Desolation Sound, but to cross over to Discovery Passage where the main steamship routes ran. At every stop, the *Laverock* and her crew met people who eventually formed the network of the Columbia Coast Mission. It was raw culture: the cordwood camp in Halfmoon Bay; the Hastings Mill Company's camp run by Jim Springer near the Indian village of Sliammon; or the watering hole of Lund founded by the Thulin brothers whose general store allegedly began with a side of bacon and bottle of whiskey. The *Laverock's* venture under Bull Pup and sail had now set many coastal people wondering. As the Cape Mudge lightkeeper told Antle: "I mind the day when first you kemm roond the Cape. Y'r sail was up but it was no pullen' and yet ye gaed alang at a guid rate. I was fair surprised till someone tell't me aboot the contraption called the gasoline engine, and then I kenn'd all aboot ye."

After a stop at Quathiaski Cove on Quadra Island where he found more church families than anywhere else in the district, and where he would soon establish his Mission's operating base, Antle prepared to sail farther north. It had been an encouraging visit. A cannery was under construction, and the family of Indian Agent Reginald Pidcock was already the focal point of a nascent community. But Antle could not tarry. "Keyed up with many and weird tales of the roaring whirlpools," his record shows, "we summoned all the fortitude we possessed [for the] long dreaded gateway to the land of the 'big sticks' and the 'timber wolf.'" That was how he described the daunting entrance to Seymour

Narrows, beneath which lay the vicious pinnacles of Ripple Rock. Some 112 years earlier, Captain George Vancouver had explored this dangerous passage and described in his journal this same tide rushing "with such immense impetuosity as to produce the impression of falls considerably high." From a viewpoint on Maude Island, the two Antles stood fascinated by the roaring, surging upswellings below their feet. Late for slack water, they rode the ebb current northward up Discovery Passage to the logging camp at Rock Bay. Situated in the lee of Chatham Point, at the junction of Discovery Passage and Johnstone Strait, it was a natural focal point for the logging industry. Before long, it would also prove a focal point for pastoral care. It was here that John Antle would one day establish his first hospital.

That first Sunday at Rock Bay was memorable. While liquor flowed freely in the camp saloon, Antle learned the futility of attempting to convert disinterested loggers by the sheer weight of rhetoric and the imposition of moral law. Having grown up in church-minded communities, he himself had once been "like many young and ardent clergymen [who] knew only one cure for all conditions, and that was to hold a service." Although Divine Service would always have its place in his missionary work, he would recognize that the "less than adequate Anglican service" of that Sunday marked a turning point in the direction of his ministry. Leaving exhortation aside, he briefed the loggers on his plans to meet their immediate needs: a hospital, a doctor, a boat and social services. His practical vision rallied the support of those who heard him. Some allegedly carried him on their shoulders to the bar— where he declined the drink and took a pipe of tobacco instead. But could anyone have really foreseen the implications of the dream? Many years later, Antle confided to his journal:

> For could I have known the disappointments, the heart-break, the hell, that I was to endure in making the idea which was slowly forming in my mind a reality, would I not have gone back to my parish in Vancouver and forgotten all but a very thrilling holiday?

Leaving Rock Bay, *Laverock* pressed northward to Big Bear River

and Camp 0, owned and operated by the Hastings Mill Company
of Vancouver. Storms en route to Kelsey Bay turned Johnstone
Strait into what Antle described as "a boiling cauldron" churned
up by conflicting winds and tide. It was a phenomenon he repeatedly encountered in subsequent years. Seeking shelter, Antle
met two unemployed adventurers in an almost derelict sloop, heading to Rivers Inlet in search of work. Sharing his supplies while
they rode out the storm at anchor, Antle described his plans for
mission and social reform. This chance meeting of two wayfaring
sloops was precious in Antle's recollections. From it he received
his first private donation to the Columbia Coast Mission Fund.
The money arrived later via "coastal telegram," passed from hand
to hand, from cannery to camp, and eventually to the diocesan
door in Vancouver. The gift of five dollars amounted to 10 percent—a full tithe—of what the donors had paid for their boat.

After reaching Alert Bay with its cluster of habitations, its church
mission school, Indian village and BC Packers cannery, Antle began
working his way south. But the state of the Indians' health and
their lack of medical resources troubled him deeply. Whatever else
church and government had done in the name of religion, education and training—and he was not always convinced either party
had done right—they had, in his paternalistic phrase: "made no
provision for the physical health of their Indian wards." He was
dismayed at the sight of emaciated, tubercular-looking, occasionally
crippled children. Antle remembered such sights years later in Ottawa when urging the minister responsible for Indian Affairs to
provide the Indians with a hospital and doctor. For the moment,
however, he was establishing his own links and casting the net of
mission ever wider. From Alert Bay his route led to Port Harvey,
then with fair winds to Port Neville and Navvy Jack's Camp about
halfway up the harbour where the two Antles spent their Sunday:

> We went ashore with the thought of [holding a church]
> service. Hesitatingly we made the suggestion to the crew
> in the bunk house. All agreed except two young men,
> apparently late arrivals from the Old Country . . . The
> service proceeded, not perhaps in cathedral style, yet with
> all the essentials necessary to the physically tired, whose

minds and spirits unconsciously sought that rest and refreshment to be found in otherworld[ly] things.

Such poignant informality was a model for years to come. From
there the journey continued in squalls through Sunderland Channel,
Whirlpool Rapids, Greene Point Rapids and eventually to Shoal
Bay on East Thurlow Island, at the junction of Cordero Channel
and Phillips Arm. In following this course Antle unwittingly established the routes of his seagoing mission.

The deserted settlement of Shoal Bay had once been a boom
town with as many as three hotels. It had thrived on the business
brought its way by a mining company with claims in nearby
Frederick Arm. When the company went broke, the whole town-
site had sold for $1,400. Only one hotel was open when Antle
arrived. With no sense of desolation, he sailed to the logging
camps in Frederick Arm, again promoting his concept of a loggers'
mission both on the coast and in Vancouver itself. Bunkhouse
gatherings provided him with ample evidence of the need for just
such a mission: tales of loggers with frightful injuries and little
hope of medical care. "The frequent mound marking the lonely
grave along the Coast . . . bore silent witness to the truth of the
statements."

The next and most difficult leg of the homeward journey lay
through the powerful whirlpools and eddies of the Yuculta Rapids,
the "Yoo-cla-taws" in local parlance. As is still common practice
among mariners today, Antle was anxious to pass the rapids at or
near slack water in order to be well through before the current
changed. But his pastoral zeal overrode his nautical sense when
he accepted a camp foreman's invitation to tarry over breakfast.
The temptation to promote the mission was too great, and Antle
allowed the time for safe passage to slip by. The incident illustrates
the tension underpinning the instincts of pastor and seaman that
dwelt within every skipper–chaplain in the Mission. By the time
Antle eventually set sail and cranked up his three-quarter-horse-
power engine, powerful natural forces had gripped the sea:

> . . . arriving at the rapids, we were to regret that en-
> joyable meal. The rapids were running very strong in

the flood. How strong we did not know, and its crooked course being over two miles, it was impossible to see . . . Soon we began to see the whirls and turmoil beyond Dent Island . . . If there is anyone who thinks he can steer clear of the whirlpools of this rapid in a strong floodtide, he has my permission to try. We skimmed along the edge of several big [whirlpools], looking dread into their funnel-like depths, [until] finally we crashed to the bottom of [a huge one] against a chunk of wood, which shook every timber in the little ship. The boy was yelling at the top of his voice . . . while I, less articulate, but just as scared, wondered how far down we should go. But to our great surprise and relief [we found ourselves] suddenly on a flat surface, the engine and sail still doing business. Verily, there is a Providence who takes care of children and fools, and both were in that boat.

Antle's self-deprecating description is apt; whether braving the elements in deep-sea crossings, or trusting the ability of an alcoholic to fight the disease and regain a useful role in society, he remained a "Fool in Christ" all his life.

On return to Vancouver—"from Buccaneer Bay to Vancouver in a howling westerly"—Antle submitted to the Dioceses of New Westminster and Columbia a detailed report of his voyage. He had identified the scope of his proposed mission, and had grasped the potential of Quathiaski Cove, Cortes Island and Shoal Bay as possible centres for the venture. He had solicited positive responses from a broad range of settlers and loggers, and had recognized the failure of "traditional religion" either to influence the loggers' working conditions, or to make even the slightest impression on their isolated lives. He reiterated a classical principle of mission: "in order to bring the Church into contact with these men the work must be largely social at first, and this will open the way for all she may wish to do and teach." According to Antle, "social service" meant three things: the provision of hospitals and medical aid, a circulating library, and a monthly magazine. The library would supply "healthy literature, books, magazines and newspapers"; the monthly magazine would become the "voice of the camps to each other [and] the voice of the Church to the men"; and the hospitals would provide "competent surgical aid within reach of the camps," at the time only available in Vancouver. A good boat was the linchpin in all these operations, and Antle knew what he needed: a sixty-foot vessel with ample sleeping quarters for a crew of three and a main cabin large enough to accommodate twenty-five or thirty persons.

All these things eventually came to pass. But at the time, Antle urged the dioceses not to delay. To his mind the project had already gained such momentum in Vancouver and Victoria, and such expectations up the coast, that "delay will mean disappointment to all." In particular, delay would leave the challenge open to some other denominations "not as well equipped as our own." In those pre-ecumenical times, churches saw themselves in competition with one another, thereby missing the opportunity of pooling their scarce resources. Mutual respect would grow as their lines of contact developed. But the nascent Columbia Coast Mission of 1904 needed a good leader. Antle urged that the chief missioner be "a man of tact and resource" in order to bring the coastal inhabitants "under the influence of the Gospel of Jesus Christ." Small wonder, then, that for so exacting an undertaking the diocesan committee chose John Antle himself.

The choice proved prescient, despite Antle's frequent lack of tact. Indeed, experience would show that Antle was not only the right man to begin and sustain the early venture, but the best leader to train his successors. As the Reverend Alan Greene recalled in conversations after retiring in 1959:

> [Antle] was very down-to-earth. And you couldn't pull over any nonsense or anything that was unreal with him. He was a realist from start to finish. You had to be dead honest in your ministry or he had no use for you. He was an out-spoken, blunt, clean-thinking Newfoundlander. He wanted you to be practical. He wanted you to show physical courage. He looked for common sense in the matter of your approach to religion, 'cause he'd

The Reverend John Antle (1905) in the uniform of the Columbia Coast Mission.

shown great wisdom in his presentation of the religious side of the mission work . . . He was a man of great force of character. Quiet, dignified, but absolutely to the point and kindly.

Dr. J.H. MacDermot, who served at the Mission's hospital at Vananda in 1907–08, described him as "a delightful companion; not talkative, but friendly, and always ready to talk about his work and about boats." He was, MacDermot wrote, "a strong, wise, gentle man with a strong sense of humour, and without fear."

The committee of the Diocese of New Westminster adopted Antle's plans with little objection. However, the diocesan authorities in Victoria were much less forthcoming. The executive committee of the Diocese of British Columbia summoned him twice to explain what appeared to be a needlessly extravagant plan. Dissenting members deemed it far too expensive to provide a mission boat to serve the coastal communities. Even among those in favour, opinions and depth of vision varied. One member—who obviously had his own boat to sell—went to great lengths in detailing the rigging and equipment one would need to outfit a thirty-foot motorboat with auxiliary sail. A second struck upon the idea of buying an old sealing schooner in Victoria harbour. Yet another suggested the cheapest solution: a rowboat that could be drawn up onto the beach at night, with the missionary, of course, sleeping beneath it. At this point, the committee must have discovered another side of Antle's character; as Alan Greene said, he could be "fierce in his denunciation of anything hypocritical or unreal." Not concealing the scorn he felt for the ideas of men who demonstrated not the slightest conception of what the Mission would entail, Antle bluntly reiterated his needs: a well-found, seaworthy powerboat with accomodation for a small crew, including chaplain–skipper, and space for medical consultation and basic surgery. Antle curtly rebuked them—"I am not a cheap man and I will not touch a cheap outfit"—and left the meeting. Next day the committee accepted his plan in its entirety, and subsequently appointed him delegate to the annual meeting in Toronto of the Missionary Society of the Church [of England] in Canada (MSCC), with instructions to apply for a grant to build the mission boat. Thus began the first of many fund-raising trips to eastern Canada. After a rather frosty initial response to his proposal, the MSCC eventually agreed to grant him $2,500 to build and maintain the first mission boat.

A boat in those days was a special kind of cultural artifact. For the missionary, it provided not only the vehicle for delivering the Social Gospel, but also the means for authenticating his credentials. As the Reverend Alan Greene later recalled:

> . . . the boat gave you an entree amongst men that nothing else could have. They appreciated the physical adventure and risks that it involved. They gave you credit for being a man, in spite of your youth, and that boat was my entree, was my visiting card that got me

into tough spots. Because they knew that I was a fairly capable boat man, and weather conditions had no fears for me . . . If I had arrived there on foot, it would have been different. But a boat was the only means of communication for the whole country. The highway for everybody was the sea, except for a few little island roads and trails. You were a part of the fraternity of seamen that were the light of that part of the coast. Everything depended on boats.

On 4 April 1905, the Columbia Coast Mission's first boat, the sixty-foot *Columbia I* was launched from Wallace Shipyards in False Creek, Vancouver. Powered by a 20 hp Union gasoline engine, she embodied the hopes not only of Antle and the medical doctor, W.A.B. Hutton, but of the diocese as well. The launching was attended by Archdeacon Pentreath and other Vancouver clergy, by choirs and about a thousand guests. On completion of trials, *Columbia I* arrived in Victoria on the April 28 to be dedicated by Bishop Perrin. Here too, choirs, clergy and the lieutenant-governor of the province joined the celebration. Following the ceremonies, *Columbia I* offered a familiarization cruise to selected guests, including Captain John T. Walbran of the dominion government survey vessel CGS *Quadra*, whose book *British Columbia Coast Names* appeared the following year. A mariner with unparalleled knowledge of the region, Walbran was intrigued by the vessel's unusual "combination of Sky Pilot and gasoline engine," both new to coastal waters. Quite frequently, Antle would have to bear criticism on both counts during his voyages up the coast: a parson in "a man's world" driving a cantankerous contraption noted for bringing out the worst in its owner. Others quipped that the engine provoked bouts of cursing and would soon disqualify even Antle himself for the ministry. Indeed, Antle recalled the mission boat's first voyage up the coast as essentially a struggle with the gasoline engine:

> We learnt, Dr. Hutton and I, by long hours of hard work, to know the idiosyncrasies of this particular engine and with knowledge of it came power over it, so that

The first Columbia, a sixty-foot vessel driven by a 20-hp Union gasoline engine. Built in 1905, she was sold in 1910.

> we were able to get from place to place with speed and convenience, and notwithstanding the sneers of the steamboat men, kept our appointments and made our dates with marvellous accuracy. We kept in touch with eighty-four camps, towed [floating] camps from place to place, and, proudly we say it, towed to safety three broken down steam vessels . . . and I am still in the Ministry.

Even fifty-five years later, a seagoing chaplain would chant in mock despair, "engines, engines, engines—a Missionary should have a special saint to teach him patience with engines."

In 1905, mariners spoke of their power-driven vessels as "sailing" or "steaming" along the coast—as they do today. Thus after her dedication in Victoria, *Columbia I* "sailed" out of harbour and "steamed" to Nanaimo where volunteers installed two hospital cots in the sickbay. Then, in Antle's words: "back to Vancouver to give the little vessel the final touches [before] her first voyage into the comparatively little known region of the giant fir, and the men who handled them, known among themselves as the 'timber beasts.'"

A cryptic entry in the ship's log for 9 May 1905 barely hints at the deeper meaning it records: "Left Vancouver for the Mission District at 5 p.m." Antle had always maintained that he would set forth the very minute the vessel was ready. That moment had now come. Months of promoting and planning, of encouraging others and not losing heart himself, of holding fast to a dream while grappling with the practicalities of making it come true—all this had converged in the building and launching of his seagoing mission. Then followed the exacting seamanlike tasks of readying a vessel for her maiden voyage—equipping, fine tuning, storing and making secure. At last, came the exhilaration and satisfaction of being, in the naval phrase, "in all respects ready for sea." As Antle wrote in his journal, that "final break with the old life had [now] come, and one had to step briskly forward despite many qualms." He was a missioner in haste whose first hospital would open in just two months time. On this day in May, the Columbia Coast Mission commenced a more than sixty-year commitment to the loggers and settlers of the BC coast.

CHAPTER 2

Launching a Dream:
The Early Years

JOHN ANTLE WAS NOT ALONE in grasping the full meaning of that "final break with the old life" which his journal records. Association with the Mission project also marked a turning point in the life of his lay partner, Dr. W.A.B. Hutton. A debilitating dependency on alcohol had ruined Hutton's promising medical career, first in Manitoba, then in Washington State. Eventually, he had found uneasy refuge as a woodcutter on an isolated coastal lot. The lighthouse keeper on nearby Merry Island knew him and his story and, having judged Hutton's character correctly, recommended him to Antle as the ideal physician for the medical mission. "Success [had] rather overwhelmed this exceptionally fine and clever man," Antle confided in his memoirs, "and fate eventually landed him at Half-Moon Bay where it proved my good fortune to get in touch with him."

The casualness of these lines masks a deeper reality, for the record leaves little doubt that, as far as Antle was concerned, "fate" and "fortune" played little part in what transpired. He preferred "providence" and "grace" to describe such events. Be that as it may, Hutton, the former alcoholic, at last had found the courage and will to turn his life around. All who met him on the coast sensed his inner worth. Brought to Vancouver to stay with Antle during the completion of *Columbia*, he quickly assumed his part in realizing the mission's aims. Bringing commitment and medical skill, Hutton proved invaluable.

Columbia was setting set off on her maiden voyage a mere eleven months after Antle's adventuresome departure in *Laverock*. Once again he departed "North by West in the Sunlight." This time crew and craft were quite different. Hutton's fascination with the ship's machinery turned him into somewhat of a marine engineer. "The Union gasoline engine with which the vessel was equipped became his special pet," Antle recalled years later. "And, though no mechanic, he developed an ability to operate it which left little to be desired. Many a stormy night, when the wind blew and the currents were strong, he tooled the little machine along while he kept an eye on a patient or two en route for the hospital. On arrival there was no waiting for morning. The patients [we had] brought in, and the patients [already] waiting [for him] at the hospital, were at once attended to."

Thus it was that the two men, skipper–priest and engineer–doctor, took *Columbia* on her earliest voyages of mercy. In their first year they maintained links with some sixty-eight camps. They provided medical service wherever needed, carried books and magazines for distribution, and even towed floating camps to new locations. First aid in the camps was crude, and it fell to the Columbia Coast Mission to provide first aid kits wherever loggers worked. These were frequently cobbled together by packing cookie tins with basic medical gear. "All this and more," Antle's journal reveals, "had to be forced home to the consciousness of the logging operators." Indeed, the industry's social conscience took a long time forming. Logging accidents were frequent and often nasty: one man suffered head injuries caused by falling timber; another a smashed knee; yet another was run over by a logging train. Hutton freed himself for surgery by training Antle to act as anaesthetist. If accident victims had depended solely on the weekly steamer—which logging companies seemed to regard as normal— many men would simply not have pulled through.

One pioneer recalled the rugged life in the mines and forestry camps in the years before upcoast hospitals were built:

> Mining was rough and they did not have the safety first precautions imposed on the trade by government regulations. Men were expendable, you could always get

someone else to replace those that were crippled or killed—In those days it was the Church with its love for Humanity that took care of the flotsam and jetsam, an unending task . . . But that was life in those days.

I, like many others, had a stump ranch and worked part time in logging camps—ten to twenty men in a bunkhouse with a big pot-bellied stove in the centre. We worked all day rain or fine and no place to dry your clothes and only cold water in tin basins for washing (no showers) everything was very crude and in many camps very little contact with the outside world, men were cut off from their families for months on end. But in an emergency people would invariably try to contact the mission boat through their local store. There were no doctors up the coast except later at Powell River and of course in the coast mission, and the average person depended almost entirely on the mission. In any case most people could not afford to pay for a Doctor.

Another measure of the frontier character of the coast may be gleaned from navigation records of these early days. Though coast-wise shipping was moving into a competitive phase, with commercial coastal and deep-sea vessels of many types plying local waters, surveys had not kept pace. With each voyage, seafarers were discovering for themselves the ways of the coast and unlocking its secrets. Navigators still depended largely on sketchy surveys conducted by British naval vessels during the nineteenth century. The first Dominion Hydrographic Survey of the BC coast was conducted in Burrard Inlet in the port of Vancouver, in 1861. Not until 1907 did the Dominion hydrographer open a BC office in Victoria. In 1908 Lieutenant P.G. Musgrave commissioned the Canadian Government Ship CGS *Lillooet* for hydrographic surveys; he was succeeded in command in 1920 by Commander H.D. Parizeau. The issuance of new hydrographic charts was always worrisomely behind schedule. The sole survey vessel on the coast, CGS *Lillooet*, worked only six months of the year. Surveyors put to sea just after Easter and returned to Victoria the following October to assist cartographers in preparing charts of the areas just surveyed. Though much had been accomplished in marine surveying by the early 1920s, the overtasked vessel remained the sole survey ship well into the 1930s. Even by 1920 there was still no adequate chart of the rich fishing grounds on the west coast of the Queen Charlotte Islands, nor indeed of the commodious harbours to the east. That year the British Admiralty's Hydrographic Office cancelled its chart of this coastal area "as it was so inaccurate as to be positively dangerous to use for any navigation." As a result of inadequate surveys, the *British Columbia Pilot* for 1923 issued a warning:

> General coast charts should not . . . be looked upon as infallible, and a rocky shore should on no account be approached within the contour line of ten fathoms without taking every precaution to avoid a possible danger; and even with surveys of harbors on a scale of six inches to the mile, vessels should avoid if possible, passing over charted inequalities in the ground, as some isolated rocks are so sharp that the [sounding] lead will not rest on them.

Up and down the rugged coast, the names of rocks and shoals attest to the unsuspecting ships and mariners that "discovered" them. Thus, on 11 March 1900 the 1,950-ton British freighter *Ben Mohr* scraped over and "found" the unmarked Ben Mohr Rock in Trincomali Channel; and on 15 May 1901 the 1,884-ton Norwegian steamer *Horda* struck the then-unknown Horda Shoals in Captain Passage. Such incidents are legion. Nor were casualties limited to commercial shipping. Sky Pilot Rock and Pringle Rock in Homfray Channel suggest that the skipper–chaplains sometimes had their bad days too.

Long before *Columbia*'s launching on 4 April 1905, Antle had been lobbying the Hastings Mill Company to gain support for his planned hospital at its Rock Bay camp. This was a rough and ready settlement comprising some five hundred loggers, a store, saloon and hotel. As Antle recalled, the company's compliance was due less to its concern for the welfare of its workers, than to the missionary's brash manner. Whether the final confrontation with

Columbia *aground.*

Charles M. Beecher, senior partner of the firm, took place exactly as Antle described in his memoirs, we cannot be sure. But his account rings true to character and approach: "Mr Beecher, a hospital is going to be built on the coast, and the question for you to decide is whether or not your company, the largest operating on the coast, can afford to stand out of the movement."

Opening of Queen's Hospital, Rock Bay, on 9 July 1905. It was destroyed by fire on 3 September 1911. With Dr. Darrell Hanington (centre) are (l. to r.) nurses Kate Franklin and Jean Sutherland.

The bluntness of Antle's approach struck a responsive chord. A few days later, Beecher informed a church hospital committee that his company would not only build the hospital, but add one hundred dollars to the boat fund. "From that time until the firm's withdrawal from Rock Bay," Antle's journal reads, "Hastings Mill Company was an anchor to windward of the Mission." Furnished and equipped by the Victorian Order of Nurses, the Rock Bay Queen's Hospital opened on 9 July 1905. It was a joint venture; the Victorian Order of Nurses (VON) provided equipment and nurses, and the Mission supplied doctors and administrative services.

Cooperation between the logging companies and the Mission was crucial to success. Ultimately, the industry not only helped in financing the hospitals, it also collected the money from the loggers through Antle's "Dollar a Month" scheme, which the Workmen's Compensation Board later emulated in 1917. This was a type of hospital insurance whereby each logger paid a dollar a month to offset any medical costs incurred if he fell ill or met with an accident. It took time to convince a sufficient number of loggers that such foresight was necessary. In large camps companies actually made payroll deductions in order to keep the system operating, but individual loggers who worked on their own were often over-looked.

It was from Rock Bay that the first issue of Antle's monthly magazine, *The Log of the Columbia: The British Columbia Loggers' Journal*, appeared. *The Log*, as it was known throughout the coast, linked communities and served as a vehicle for their concerns. The first edition of March 1906 quite properly featured a photo story on the Mission:

> The Mission Ship *Columbia* visits the Camps in the Lumber District, from Cape Mudge North to Alert Bay, and is fitted up as a Marine Ambulance, with two hospital cots, dispensary, operating table and full outfit of splints, dressings and instruments. On board are a well stocked Library and a large quantity of periodical literature for distribution among the camps and settlements.

There was no hint of proselytizing or preaching, nor indeed of the traditional ministrations of the church. Social action was the key, and it depended on the three elements Antle had propounded on his first trip to Rock Bay: hospitals and medical aid, a circulating library and a monthly magazine. All three now seemed to be in place.

Advertisements from firms in Vancouver helped finance *The Log* and kept isolated people abreast of many of the allurements of "civilization." Johnston's Big Shoe House [on] Hastings Street featured "the best loggers' boots on earth," while Fletcher Brothers Talking Machine Headquarters offered the new Columbia Graphophone: "It plays and talks to you and is a sure cure for the blues." Victoria Cross Tea sold "Absolutely the Best 50c Tea today." Succeeding issues of *The Log* revealed more attractions. Thus A.E. Lees and Co., The Cash Clothiers, beckoned all coasters: "We'll be expecting you when you come to town—we never saw better Suits for $15.00, $16.00 . . ." Lees offered the discerning logger or homesteader "Good hats for $2.50. And better ones for $3.00," as well as "Good Underwear: When you want real good underwear that will keep you warm and stand the wash." For relaxation, Kurtz's Pioneer Cigar Factory touted its products as "the best in B.C"; while The British Columbia Book Company invited prospective customers to "Send to us for cheap reading." Precisely what kind of reading material was so inexpensively offered was never made clear. By 1907 competition in recording technology added new temptations with the announcement that "The Victor Talking Machine has attained the Height of Perfection . . . Buy a Victor and have a Concert in the Camp." Prices ranged from $12 to $120.

Advertising aside, *The Log* was attempting to do more than print local news about the work of the Mission, the hospital cases and jottings from the chaplain. It highlighted news of technological advances like internal combustion engines, steam engines, battleships and torpedoes. It featured epoch-making events like the naval armaments race in Europe and the technical advances made in building the new battleship HMS *Dreadnought*. Under the headline "Mauretania Starts on Her Record Run," *The Log* reproduced a brief story from New York about the huge passenger liner's steam turbine-driven crossing of the Atlantic.

On quite a different theme, the editor eventually introduced a Women's Page featuring notes, views and short articles of interest to the homemaker. These included tips on coping with isolation and locally-written stories and verse. Small as it was, this page must have helped to alleviate the sometimes desperate loneliness of women whose lives were shaped by the isolation of coastal pioneering. When *The Log: The Logger's Journal* folded after only three years of publication, it was perhaps the women who felt the loss most keenly. Following their men into a life of rugged individualism, the wives likely suffered the most from the beautiful yet terrible solitude of coastal wilderness. Many of them must have seen in *The Log* a tangible link with other members of their scattered community, and have drawn comfort from the realization that they shared common hardships, dreams and joys. Many men and women were likely saddened by the disappearance of *The Log*. For reasons that are not clear, it was not reactivated until 1930.

Yet as John Antle wrote in his first annual report of operations in 1905, the Mission had done more than prove it was meeting immediate needs; it had shown every promise for future successful ventures. Between the beginning of May and the end of December 1905, the medical mission had treated 1,250 cases both aboard the *Columbia* and at the Rock Bay hospital. During this time, the ship patrolled the waters bounded by Cape Mudge in the south and Alert Bay on Cormorant Island in the north. Antle himself served as captain, chaplain and superintendent; Hutton was the ubiquitous surgeon. A year of strenuous work had established the Mission and attracted a physician, Darrell Hanington, for the Rock Bay hospital. This left Hutton to devote himself to the shipboard medical mission which had become his home. "When I die I want to be buried at sea from the *Columbia*," he once told Antle. He would indeed be buried at sea, but not from the mission ship. Hutton's death came sooner than anyone had expected.

In June 1906, *Columbia* returned to Vancouver for refit and to have a more powerful engine installed. Hutton was long overdue for vacation and he set off on a trip from which he would not return. It began innocuously enough, but ended by triggering headlines in the *Vancouver Province*: "Tug Cut in Half Today by *Princess Victoria*." Fishermen interested in visiting Blunden Harbour to examine its potential for a commercial oyster farm had invited Hutton to go along as chemist. They had chartered the sixty-foot steam-driven tug *Chehalis*, built in 1897 for the Union Steamship charter and towboat trade. In the early afternoon of 21 July 1906, the little vessel set off from North Vancouver. At 2:00 p.m. the 2,000-ton CPR passenger ship *Princess Victoria* left her berth for the northern coastal run, working her way at fifteen knots around Brockton Point. A strong flood tide was swirling through First Narrows, holding the *Chehalis* back. Witnesses watched in horror and disbelief as the *Princess Victoria* attempted to overtake the tug too closely on the shoreward side. She sliced into the *Chehalis*'s port quarter, sinking her within seconds and trapping victims inside. Only five of the thirteen people aboard the tug survived; Hutton was not among them. The *Province* noted his passing as the loss of "an expert sent out by English capitalists to examine the oyster beds with a view to purchase." His close association with the Columbia Coast Mission was never mentioned. Nor does any trace remain of Antle's thoughts on the loss of his close and esteemed associate, except for the unfulfilled wish to name some new hospital-ship after him.

Antle never had any doubts that the Mission would become a permanent institution in a province sorely in need of social change. What he required most at this stage of development was a reliable cash flow and an organization that could tap into society's resources. Antle was influenced by the Grenfell Mission of Newfoundland and Labrador, founded in 1892 by the English Royal National Mission to Deep Sea Fishermen. While he envied Grenfell's organizational structure and financial base, he himself was not able to break out of the parochial and dependent mould in which the local church kept him. On 12 September 1907, the Columbia Coast Mission was incorporated with a board of directors and an executive committee, and with the Archbishop of the Ecclesiastical Province of British Columbia as president. Antle was answerable to him not only as priest to his bishop, but as superintendant of the Mission to the president of the board. Whereas the board of the Grenfell Mission existed primarily to raise funds, that of the Columbia Coast Mission governed policy. Where the Grenfell Mission had by 1912 incorporated itself as the nonsectarian International Grenfell Association, with almost entrepreneurial freedom to act and raise funds, Superintendent Antle of the Columbia Coast Mission found himself arguing with his bishop who, as archbishop of the ecclesiastical province, sometimes had a different agenda. This often meant squabbling over "Anglican" money.

Antle's primary sources of support lay with two Church of England organizations, the London-based British Columbia and Yukon Church Aid Society, and the Toronto-based Missionary Society of the Church in Canada. Both were captivated by the romance of missionary work among "lumberjacks, whites and Indians" on a remote rainforest coast. Founded in 1910, the British Columbia and Yukon Church Aid Society regarded itself, as its president, Jocelyn Perkins, explained to Antle in May 1918, as "the official agent for putting forward various claims of the Church in British Columbia to people living in the Old Country." Antle invariably got himself in hot water when he attempted to bypass its offices in order to approach wealthy potential donors in England on his own. Closer to home, the Missionary Society of the Church in Canada (MSCC) in Toronto operated a portfolio of strategic grants in support of evangelism: the seagoing Columbia Coast Mission, the land-based Prince Rupert Coast Mission and its vessel *Northern Cross*, and the Masset Inlet Mission with the *Western Hope*. The MSCC's mandate included clearly defined goals for reaching potential converts in Canada: "Mission among Orientals," "Work among Jews resident in Canada," "Mission to Japanese" and "Indian and Eskimo Missions." Yet it held fast to its principal focus as expressed in boldfaced type in its triennial report of 1924: "the primary and outstanding obligation is, and must remain, the work on behalf of white settlers."

Over time, however, the remoteness of these granting agencies from the Columbia Coast Mission's front line turned to disadvantage. Their great distance from the field of action made it difficult to maintain enthusiasm in eastern Canada and abroad for an essentially West Coast Canadian enterprise. In the early days of the Mission, grants from the Anglican Dioceses of New Westminster (headquartered in Vancouver) and British Columbia (based in Victoria) amounted to little more than $250–$500 per year. This imbalance between grassroots support and out-of-province subsidy constantly frustrated local initiatives, sometimes leading to bitterness. As one pioneer recalled much later, "what a lot of people never understood was that this was all paid for by funds collected in Great Britain and it was not until sometime during the Second World War when they [in Britain] found it almost impossible to keep the large number of Missions going [throughout the Empire] that they asked the Church of England in Canada to take over the reponsibility of the Columbia Coast Mission." In England, he wrote, one was ready to help out no matter how poor one was; "not so here in Canada." As late as 1937, Thomas Connold, a skipper–chaplain and physician resigning from the Mission, grew caustic about the problem:

> Although the Diocese of Columbia [on Vancouver Island] has done a fairer share in helping with the work, I regard it as a stigma upon the Diocese of New Westminster

Columbia Hospital, Vananda, Texada Island (1911), with VON nurses (l. to r.)
Hoolihan and Motherwell. Reverend Alan Greene is seated lower left, with the
cook (centre), known only as "Moon." Among the remaining unidentified people
is a Presbyterian missioner by the name of Walmsley.

which contains the great city of Vancouver, that it is so
unmindful of the coastal Lazarus lying at its gate full of
the sores of the most impossible religious notions, if
religious at all, and desiring to be fed with the crumbs
which fall from the rich ecclesiastical tables.

The first trial year nonetheless led into two years of expansion.
By the end of 1907, Queen's Hospital at Rock Bay had doubled
in size under the leadership of Hutton's successor, Dr. Darrell
Hanington, and the Tacoma Steel Company had donated a hospital
for its operations at Vananda on Texada Island. This second facility,
Columbia Hospital, served the company's miners at the copper
mine in Marble Bay. That same year, when the residents of Alert

Bay appealed to the Mission for hospital support, Antle was quick to report to the board that Alert Bay offered an excellent strategic location. Not only was it a centre for Indian life, but it was fast becoming a centre for the burgeoning logging industry. The appeal from Alert Bay catalyzed his thinking. "I shall not consider our equipment complete until this third hospital is built and we have a larger and faster boat making regular trips up and down the coast," he wrote in his 1907 annual report. These two items became his most pressing priorities for expansion.

Antle began his campaign for funds, not by approaching the local dioceses as might have seemed natural, but by heading east. His tours were arranged by the Missionary Society of the Church in Canada. This became the route that both he and his successor, the Reverend Alan Greene, followed when in need of money; local financial aid remained decidedly thin throughout the history of the Mission. The board of the MSCC approved the campaign when Antle petitioned it in October 1907. Thus when he met with representatives of the Alert Bay hospital project in January 1908, the required sum of $5,500 had virtually been raised. Antle recognized from experience that eastern Canada and England were prepared to fund new ventures; less promising, however, were the prospects for underwriting the maintenance and support of facilities already built. In short, he faced a major decision. Should he continue to build and expand with the money at hand, trusting to God's providence for the future? Or should he consolidate what had already been accomplished and set funds aside to ensure continuity of the existing service? He addressed these questions in an editorial in *The Log* in 1908:

> Experience [in fundraising] in the past has not been too encouraging; and while we are eager to meet this seemingly pressing need [of building in Alert Bay], we are forced to go careful lest we be found to have undertaken more than we are able to accomplish. Promise is one thing, performance is another; and in order to arrive at a fair estimate of the latter it is necessary, according to my experience, to discount the former very considerably.

St. George's Hospital, Alert Bay, just prior to its dedication on 15 June 1901.
Destroyed by fire in 1923, it was not officially re-opened until 1925.

Despite his own words of caution, "Rev. John," as Antle was affectionately known throughout his coastal ministry, was an aggressively optimistic man. He went ahead despite his misgivings. The new St. George's Hospital opened on 15 June 1909 with as much ecclasiastical and civic ceremony as could be mustered, the Right Reverend W.E. Perrin officiating. St. George's eventually became the most successful of the Columbia Coast Mission hospitals and continues its work today.

Antle had now established three small, modern hospitals situated about sixty miles from each other, each staffed by a doctor and nurses. He next faced a problem which he had already anticipated: the need for a larger and faster boat. The original *Columbia* was not sufficiently seaworthy for the open waters of Queen Charlotte Sound. These could be fearsome when high winds swept in from

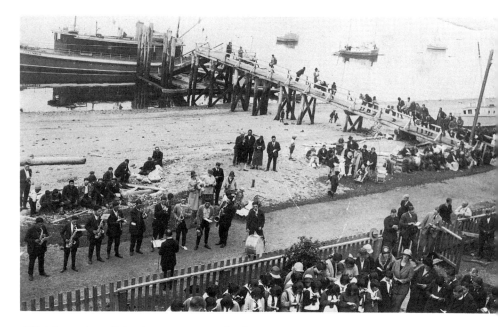

Official opening of St. George's Hospital, Alert Bay, 15 June 1909. Note, lower left, the Natives' ten-piece band of saxophones, clarinets and cornets.

the full fetch of the Pacific, piling up steep and often confused seas. Nor indeed was *Columbia* large enough to carry adequate medical equipment or patients with highly contagious diseases. Besides, her seven-knot speed was now too slow for the expanded patrol zone with its various medical and religious needs.

Thus, at the very time that Antle was trying to raise funds for the Alert Bay hospital, he was also striking out to obtain a new ship. So successful had he been in attracting money from eastern Canada and England, that in the autumn of 1908 he returned to Britain in search of a suitable vessel. He approached Lord Strathcona, the high commissioner for Canada in London. A strong supporter of the Grenfell Mission, to which he had given two ships, the wealthy benefactor seemed worth a hit. Antle's memoirs describe a rather cold reception:

> He insisted that he did not approve of persons coming from Canada to collect the pence of the poor for building their institutions . . . and giving the impression there

35

The second Columbia. Launched on 8 July 1910, the one-hundred-foot hospital ship served the Mission until 1958.

were no schools, no churches, no hospitals, "while we . . . spend thousands of pounds advertising Canada and assuring the people they will not lack them when they go to Canada."

Despite such an inauspicious beginning, Strathcona donated five hundred pounds to Antle's project.

It is typical of Antle's penchant for things English that he did not initially pursue the possibility of building a ship locally. This attitude reflected more than the prevalent mindset of the Canadian church, still known as the "Church of England in Canada." Antle was an inveterate colonial who gravitated toward British culture, whether it was flags, the Mother Church or shipyards. But his search abroad left him unsatisfied and he returned home to have

The original fluoroscopic X-ray machine aboard the second Columbia *in 1910. Books beneath the portable "wonder" include Davis's* Treatise on Obstetrics *and* Keating's Cyclopedia of the the Diseases of Children.

Columbia II built in New Westminster at the then extravagant cost of $24,000. This vessel remained the focal point of the Mission's work for forty-five years. She was launched on 8 July 1910, and dedicated on 8 August in Victoria by the Bishop of British Columbia.

With her one-hundred-foot length and seventeen-foot beam, the gasoline-driven vessel could cope with any of BC's coastal waters. *Columbia II*'s interior was equally impressive: a pilot house, galley and sleeping quarters, a main salon and a surgery with the most modern surgical equipment, including an X-ray machine.

In the summer of 1911, the same year Tom Barton commenced twenty-four years of paid service as secretary, the young man who would ultimately bring the Antle dream to its fullest expression joined the Mission. Not yet ordained, twenty-two-year-old Alan Greene came out from his hometown in Orillia, Ontario, for a challenging summer job. He did so at the invitation of the Reverend Cecil Caldbeck Owen, the Dean of Christ Church Cathedral, Vancouver, a close friend of Greene's father. According to rumour, Greene's father, the rector of St. James in Orillia, was the model for humourist Stephen Leacock's Dean Drone, in *Sunshine Sketches of a Little Town.* Greene recalled of himself and his five brothers: "We were brought up as country boys . . . All our outdoor life was so simple and wholesome." Yet even as a youngster he had learned the dangers of boating, for one of his brothers had drowned while boating on Lake Couchiching. His interest in wilderness and boats was deemed adequate nautical qualifications for the Mission job.

When first engaged as a student missionary with the Columbia Coast Mission in 1911, Greene was supported by the grand sum of $25 per month from Christ Church Cathedral. His apprenticeship was as direct as Antle could make it:

> I came out to take one of the little mission ships, the [thirty-foot] *Eirene,* in 1911, and John Antle broke me in. He took me up—we worked our way up [from Vancouver] to Vananda—and then he left me, and said "now Green, it's up to you." My heart went down into my boots, but it was the best thing he could have done. So he gave me my own ship, and left me absolutely free to work out my own salvation. And I went off with no knowledge whatever of tides or gas engines . . .

Nor had he any idea about navigation and the ways of the sea. In fact, young Alan had as little concept of the British Columbia coast as had his family in Ontario. Of the regions beyond the Rocky Mountains, he had but "a very vague, hazy idea that it must be pretty primitive." His parents had waved "their brave, devoted, missionary-minded" young son off from Union Station in Toronto as though he were heading for the remote Fiji Islands. Greene arrived on the BC coast with some trepidation. Quite obviously, Antle had his own reservations when he first met Greene. "I think he looked very doubtfully at me when I arrived, as anything from Ontario would hardly be a seaman. He thought the only seamen in the world were Newfoundlanders."

The main salon in the second Columbia, *arranged as a chapel.*

But Greene loved the work from the outset and had no fear of the sea. That first summer was largely exploratory. Based at the ten-bed hospital in Vananda near the northern tip of Texada Island, he patrolled from about the entrance to Jervis Inlet to the mouth of Bute Inlet in the north. His route took him to the growing town of Powell River, along the shore to Sliammon and Lund, and on up into Deep Bay and Malaspina Inlet. He ran to the Roman Catholic station at Church House and to Stuart Island at the southern approach to Yuculta Rapids. Church boundaries were not very important to practical missionaries. In Greene's words, "I called simply out of friendliness, and offered my ship for any services it might render." It was the people who were important to him, not their denomination.

In the summer of 1912 Greene took the launch *Eirene* into

Howe Sound where he explored the Squamish Valley and got acquainted with the Norton–McKinnon Logging Company. At the time, many hoped Squamish would become a major seaport, and he raised several hundred dollars for a new church. As he later recalled, land speculation was driving waterfront real estate as high as one hundred dollars a foot. Though he did not see his church completed, it eventually became the parish of his brother, Heber.

During the summer of 1913, his third tour of duty, Alan Greene worked aboard the *Columbia* at Campbell River, while his partner, Channel Hepburn, tended Quathiaski. For several months the *Columbia* served as Campbell River's first hospital, tied up at the International Timber Company's logging dump up the river. Recognizing there were too many parsons in the area—a Presbyterian was also based in the settlement—Greene headed for Whaletown on Cortes Island "in a small 14-foot open gas-boat" where he established himself in a shack. From there he worked a patrol through the Yuculta Rapids as far as Sayward:

> As I think of it now, I cannot picture myself risking this kind of work in a fourteen footer, now that I know more about Salmon River and the glorious tide-rips that make that area the bugbear of small craft in westerly winds. I ran this little boat till the snow fell, and eventually I decided that I had no business running here and there in her, when I had to sit for hours with about four layers of heavy clothing on, so stiff when the trips were over, that I could scarcely get out of the boat.

With the coming of winter, Greene took passage in commercial shipping: the CPR's *Queen City*, "a palatial old thing," and the Union Steamships' *Cassiar*. Then, in the fall of 1914, he accepted a curacy at St. Paul's, Toronto. He remained until 1916 when he went overseas as chaplain of the Tenth Royal Grenadiers Overseas Batallion. Yet, keeping in touch with Antle by mail, Greene came back to the Mission "and reported for action on the old and beloved battle front, June 1st 1919."

During Greene's absence, Antle had struggled along on his own. He had badgered for money at every opportunity, taken on theological students in the summer whenever he could, tried to attract doctors—and dreamed big. Greene's return must have eased some of his burden, since both men shared a common vision. Except for Native peoples, neither Antle nor Greene was particularly interested in winning members for the Church of England. They understood the "church" as a spiritual community for mutual nurturing and support, an ecclesia such as the early Christians had formed. During an interview many years later, Greene put it this way:

> [We were moved by] the desire to make them feel that the church as such, not the Anglican church, but the Church, was there deeply involved in their lives. We wanted them to feel that we were interested in their early pioneer struggles. The simplicity of their lives was very attractive. Friendship, I think, is as good a word as any. With a wise introduction of religion, if it suggested itself. You got it in, [though] not right off the bat. But it came inevitably, and perhaps pioneers that had been there for years, and out of touch with the Church, might say, well it's about time we had our children christened. And that might be the first entree into that family; and you would baptize the whole family, and make it a house gathering. The Church was the church of the house in those days, or the homes. We had no church buildings as such at all. The homes were the focal centres. In a little community you'd gather tiny groups in the nearby homes, and invariably the next time you'd have it somewhere else. The homes were the centre of religious and social fellowship. And it was all so informal and so natural that it was easy to do.

Homesteads like the one Ernest Halliday and his wife had been working in Kingcome since the 1890s offered few comforts. The Hallidays had begun homesteading with a piece of land, a rowboat, six head of cattle and fifty-five dollars worth of groceries. Stories are told of his rowing his expectant wife to Comox—a journey of three weeks—so their children could be born in a hospital. As

Greene said:

> He had a great deal more rowing to do before acquiring
> a gas engine and before a coastal steamer began to make
> trips up the inlet. For seventeen years, he made the
> four-day rowboat trip to and from Alert Bay to sell beef
> at ten cents a pound. For seventeen years, his beef and
> butter book showed no surplus at all. The Hallidays
> swapped and bartered with other homesteaders and the
> Indians of Kingcome Village.
>
> Then came that wonderful day when Ernest Halliday
> realized that he actually had a profit of twenty-eight
> dollars to spend as he pleased. It pleased him most to
> spend it on a six-foot kitchen cabinet for his wife. He
> loaded it into his rowboat and started for home, but a
> southeaster blew up and man and cabinet had to camp
> ashore for three days. Meanwhile, his wife imagined the
> boat sunk, her husband drowned and herself left penniless
> with the children. Neither of them will ever forget that
> moment when she, still watching the river with grim
> hope, saw her man tiredly rowing a piece of top-heavy
> furniture up to the home landing.

Rooted in this pioneering spirit, the Halliday homestead became
a focal point for Mission operations and a haven for sea-weary
missionaries.

Powell River was little more than a construction camp. The first
hospital was in a tent, as was the huge cookhouse which fed five
hundred men. There were no churches or any public buildings
in the town, and Greene's first church services were also held in
a tent. Camp authorities offered him the use of the cookhouse to
meet with any men who cared to come, along with any towns-
people who showed up. In all, it was a pioneering venture.

Greene was a man of strong religious convictions and he felt
he had a message. But he did not have any experience delivering
that message, especially not to the rough and ready loggers of the
province's remote camps. "It was tough going, and to fight your

way into these logging camps that had never been visited by a missionary or parson of any kind was pretty tough," said Greene. Yet he relished the work and managed to get a foothold in a few places that first summer:

> . . . if you did manage to get a hearing in a camp, you generally got the whole camp, something that was absolutely novel to me. Later on as the years advanced, this [sort of thing] disappeared; you got mighty few men forty years later. But at the beginning, if you made your entree into a little logging camp of twenty or thirty men, they'd come out of curiosity, and perhaps out of monotony, and readiness to listen to this youngster. I don't know what they thought of me and my message, but I know I was dead earnest about it, and believed what I was doing. And I felt that the . . . Columbia Coast Mission had a big job in the way of itinerant evangelism.

The record suggests that Greene was invaluable at this early stage, when John Antle was too preoccupied with fundraising and the building of hospitals and hospital ships to devote himself to front-line mission work.

Whenever Greene arrived at a new logging outpost, he immediately contacted the man in charge, introducing himself and asking permission to see the men. His first visit to the small operation at Grief Point north of Powell River was doubtless typical. "All right," the boss retorted when offering the use of the cookhouse tent, "but don't give any of the boys this darn sky dope." Fire-and-brimstone evangelists seemed to have preceded him. Greene was an unassuming, down-to-earth man, but no less direct. He announced at dinner that he would hold "a religious gathering" that evening and, perhaps more "out of curiosity than interest in the gospel," some of the men ambled in. Somewhat of a homespun musician, Greene packed along a portable Bilhorn organ nicknamed "Little Jimmy." Weighing thirty-two pounds, it spanned only three and a half octaves. Greene seems to have had a well-rounded repertoire of "those old sweet songs" that were popular at the time, and he entertained requests from his rough-cut audience:

> And a man would shout out, "give us something"; he'd name it, and I luckily knew these old, old songs, and then I'd say, well now, how about this for a hymn, and squeeze that in. And it worked. They liked your sort of wide range of music, and they listened very patiently.

Only on later visits did he ask for contributions to the Mission. One evening the men had been playing poker and a rather large amount of cash lay scattered on the table. Would they lend a hand towards the Mission's work? "Gas costs money," Greene enjoined, "and I've been visiting you for some time." As the hat went around, the men complained that they had nothing to spare. "'See the boss in the office, and he'll give you whatever you like.' And that's the way I got my collection finally, because there was nothing put in the hat at all." The boss in the office gave him a day's pay for a start.

It was during this first short summer that Greene learned his calling and established the style that would sustain and develop the Mission when he eventually succeeded Antle. But Antle was his mentor:

> "Greene, the only way is to get around amongst the people. You've got to get to know them to get any-where." I stuck to that, and made a vast host of very fine friends, both in the logging camps and in the com-munities. They were the pioneers, and I was working among the children of pioneers, the people that had moved in there say eighty years [earlier]. It was they and their children I was ministering to. And the result is that today [in 1969] I'm occasionally asked to minister to them, sixty years afterwards.

What was at work here was the Social Gospel, the nineteenth-century concept of Christian Socialism which some sectors of the

Church of England and others had espoused. As a means of reform, it aimed at social justice, among other things. It related all wealth and power to the question of stewardship: human beings held their wealth in trust for the purposes of furthering the Kingdom of God. The chaplain–skippers lived the social gospel—and occasionally preached it. At one point, *The Log* reprinted a sermon the Bishop of London had preached on the subject at Trinity Church, New York, and put the case succinctly to its readers:

> This is the Gospel. For the Gospel of Jesus Christ is the Gospel of the Kingdom of God, and the Kingdom of God is righteousness and peace and joy in holiness of spirit.
>
> This is Paul's definition of the Kingdom, and it tallies with Christ's teaching concerning the Kingdom. To preach to labor demagogues and millionaire tyrants that they are criminals against God and man because of their unrighteousness; to preach to both parties to a labor conflict that the way to social peace is arbitration, not war; to point out to all classes that the happiness of one cannot be obtained at the expense of the others, and that comes about through putting himself in one's neighbour's place, is preaching the Gospel.

For Antle, these words were "hopeful indications of the trend of thought in the Christian Church." It was a vision that allied with his aim of offering practical Christianity instead of preaching and religious gatherings—church Service rather than Church services.

World War One and its immediate aftermath created difficult times for the Mission. New money was scarce and potential medical staff were now either with the Imperial forces overseas or resettling once the armstice was declared in 1918. Antle had lost not only Greene to the army chaplaincy, but another priest whom the Mission had permanently engaged. To add to the difficulties, the provincial examinations set by the College of Physicians and Surgeons now prevented out-of-province doctors from joining the Mission. As a result, the medical facilities of the Mission had seen

The crew of the Columbia, with John Antle seated centre.

no major expansion for twenty years—merely a shifting and back-filling of resources. Antle found it increasingly difficult to recruit competent men to run the hospital ship *Columbia II*. This had forced him to leave her tied up for four months in 1917 while he went on a fundraising campaign in eastern Canada under the sponsorship of the Missionary Society of the Church in Canada. The ship was laid up again after striking Escape Reef in Johnstone Strait on 31 October 1917; pounded on the rocks for three hours, she incurred expensive damage. Morever, it was becoming clear that *Columbia II* and *Governor Musgrave*, which Lady Musgrave had donated in 1911 in memory of her husband, were proving inadequate for the expanded Mission area.

Wartime trade demands were impacting on logging, fishing and mining operations. Camps themselves were sometimes as itinerant as the workers they employed. The instability affected the work of the Mission. For example, decreased copper production on Texada Island led to the permanent closure of the Columbia Hospital at Vananda on 30 September 1920. The name did not die, it was taken by a small two-building floating facility the Mission had arranged the previous August for Carriden Bay, Wells Passage, northeast of Queen Charlotte Strait. Built by the local logging companies, the Carriden Bay hospital was founded to serve the northern sector of the Mission area. Yet throughout its brief eight-year history, it operated only intermittently due to the shifting work patterns and commercial fortunes of the logging industry. Thus when the Carriden Bay camps temporarily closed in 1921, the resident mission physician, Dr. R. Birdsall, who had been practising there only a few months, moved away to Rock Bay in Johnstone Strait.

Equally destabilizing were the effects of fire, always a threat in wooden constructions on the coast. Queen's Hospital in Rock Bay was destroyed by fire on 3 September 1911, but was rebuilt as St. Michael's within the year. Similarly, St. George's Hospital at Alert Bay burned to the ground in 1923. Here too, the Mission made a remarkable recovery by rebuilding it within the year. Not officially opened until May 1925, the hospital was actually ready for service the previous January. Provincial and private grants helped meet the cost of over $24,000 for reconstruction, and key coastal firms helped where they could. Two companies were especially noteworthy. BC Packers granted a 25 percent reduction in the price of lumber, while the Union Steamship Company wrote off 50 percent of the associated freight costs.

A shift in logging operations caused the floating Columbia Hospital at Carriden Bay to be towed to O'Brien Bay in 1924, the same year the Mission purchased the *Rendezvous* for spiritual ministrations in its southern sector. Fluctuations in the cedar market resulted in a further closure at the end of 1925. The floating hospital nonetheless remained an important facility, even though the Mission operated it at a loss. Antle kept it open as long as possible until closure of logging camps forced the decision to move the facility to Pender Harbour in January 1929. Working its way under tow from the sheltered waters of Havannah Channel into the more exposed waters of Broughton Strait, the vessel was struck by a sudden squall and foundered. As Antle wrote to a friend, it got "caught in the gale of last Thursday and is a total wreck, which on the face of things is a great catastrophe, but may turn out to be a blessing in disguise." Indeed, the floating hospital had

St. Michael's Hospital, Rock Bay (1911), the twenty-five-bed successor to Queen's Hospital.

been a temporary solution at best, and its loss triggered a campaign for the erection of a permanent hospital at Pender Harbour.

Built on land donated by Mr. R. Brynildsen of Garden Bay, St. Mary's Hospital became the focal point for widespread local initiatives and for the Mission's medical ministry. Resourceful local residents turned from their bread–winning labours to lend a hand. Mustered by Harry Dusenbury (who temporarily closed up his machine shop) and local boatman Captain Jackson (who tied up his boat), they set about clearing the land, blowing out stumps and blasting rock. Thanks to funds from government and private donors, the foundations were laid and the structure took shape. Located "on the wooded shores of one of the prettiest spots on British Columbia's coast," as Antle put it, St. Mary's was an ideally situated "haven of mercy" where he hoped to "form the nucleus of a group of cottages for convalescents from the city during the summer season." Eventually known as the Aged Folks' Guest Houses, the project evolved under Alan Greene's leadership. For the moment, Antle was content with St. Mary's as a haven for the injured and ill. "Protected at the back by a sloping hill and many trees, the building overlooks the Gulf of Georgia. Immediately in front is a natural lagoon, filled every tide through an opening wide enough for the entrance of a skiff. At low tide, three feet of crystal clear water covers its sandy bottom." The twelve-bed hospital comprised two small solariums with viat windows, a small operating theatre, a case room, x-ray room, maternity room and an "electrical therapy" room. Antle deemed it "the ultimate in modern hospitilization."

Everything seemed to be unfolding as Antle had planned, for as he had written to Harry Dusenbury, the chairman of the Pender Harbour citizens' committee, in January 1930:

> . . . I have been interviewing the Government, and stirring up interest in the Pender Harbour Hospital. My guess is that the Gov't will make a generous contribution . . . The first list of subscribers will appear in the *Sunday Province*. The flag is still floating high and I am full of confidence that we shall accomplish our object . . .

The provincial government granted one third of the $15,000 construction costs and the federal government built a wharf to provide direct access by boat. Church and missionary sources provided the rest. The new St. Mary's Hospital served a wide area well beyond Pender Harbour itself: Halfmoon Bay, Sechelt, Wilson Creek, Roberts Creek, Gibson's Landing and Egmont. The hospital was officially opened to considerable public acclaim on 16 August 1930 by Lieutenant Governor Randolph Bruce and Archdeacon Francis Heathcote. The mission ships *Columbia II* and *Rendezvous* attended. The Canadian Pacific Steamships' *Princess Patricia* brought two hundred visitors to join the flotilla of small vessels that had travelled up from Vancouver and crowded into Garden Bay. The opening of St. Mary's Hospital marked a full quarter century of medical success for the mission. It now had three well-equipped hospitals, two ships and a staff of over forty. John Antle's vision of outpost health care had become a reality.

CHAPTER 3

The Dirty Thirties

"THE DOMINION OF CANADA IS BOUNDED on the east by Wilfred Grenfell and on the west by John Antle. If it were bounded on every provincial and township line with apostles of similar purpose the world would stop praying 'Thy Kingdom come,' and rest its faith in an earthly democracy." In its unrestrained comparison of Antle's enterprise with the Grenfell Mission of Newfoundland and Labrador, *The American Magazine* paid homage to the idealistic and romantic vision that had breathed life into both of them. All the more reason to reprint the article when relaunching the magazine *The Log of the Columbia* in June 1930, after a silence of some twenty-three years. Yet, among all the many differences that distinguished one mission from the other, two were sufficiently important to affect the course of their respective histories. First, the articulate, entrepreneurial Grenfell understood public relations and knew how to solicit on-going support, whereas Antle did not. Second, whereas Grenfell was free to direct his mission according to his own lights, Antle lived under the thumb of the local bishop. These major distinctions were to shape the history of the two missions in different ways.

The relative weakness of the Columbia Coast Mission is found, for example, in the uneven history of its magazine, *The Log*. Designed to be the voice of both the Mission and those it served, the journal should have been central to the Mission's expansion, promoting its causes and linking its constituents. With *The Log* not publishing for many years, the Mission lost an opportunity to solicit the kind of ongoing support it so badly needed. Whether the hiatus was due to a lack of practical know-how or to an absence of diocesan support is open to conjecture. But the Mission lost its link with both its own community and the wider world of financial support, a major strategic and tactical flaw. The Columbia Coast Mission's business manager, Ben Drew, seemed to admit as much when he introduced the revived journal. Deftly filling in the missing years, Drew offered a tactful explanation:

> In its real sense, the "log" of the *Columbia* has never ceased to write itself. Year in and year out for the past three decades the mission boat has patrolled a route of over 10,000 miles, now proceeding in the face of tempestuous seas, now in sunshine and under kindlier skies, now antlike in the shadow of massive impending mountains, and often through waves that set the decks awash— but always forward with her message of comfort and relief. Vigilant, her wireless catches a cry of distress and, her bow pointed in a new direction and under full speed, the *Columbia* rushes to the scene of some fresh mountain, forest or marine mishap. Metamorphosized, she becomes the hospital ship, serving all men equally, irrespective of creed or nationality.

Featuring a photograph of the flag-bedecked *Columbia* captioned as "operating in conjunction with and in wireless communication with Alert Bay, Rock Bay and Pender Harbour Hospitals," the journal's first edition in the new series exuded confidence, efficiency and strength. Drew exerted a telling influence on the Mission until his death in 1943.

Antle was off on his annual fundraising campaign in June 1930. As usual, it had been organized in eastern Canada, by the Missionary Society of the Church in Canada. Despite his preoccupation in the east, Antle had met the deadline for the first issue by resorting to air mail. This exciting, innovative technology seemed to emphasize the journal's forward-looking purpose: "Its aim will be, as before, to further the interests of the Coast and the welfare of its people, not only materially, but intellectually and spiritually." This was a tall order for a modest magazine with slight resources. The first series, as its subtitle announced in 1906, had been designed as "The British Columbia Loggers' Journal," a tool to galvanize forestry workers into supporting a new social deal. The new series enlarged its mandate. It now wished to include others by inviting its readers to submit material for publication "if they have anything of interest to communicate to their fellow settlers." Settlements now seemed to characterize the emerging social order.

But the Mission had not kept pace with events and was facing a credibility gap. For instance, the logging camp run by the Merrill, Ring and Wilson Company at Rock Bay had undergone radical modernization since the days of its predecessor, the Hastings Mill Company. The familiar old store had been destroyed, a new wharf and rail track built, and the site, now "denuded of its verdant growth [was] crowned with oil-tanks." Expecting neither takeover nor new businesses after Hastings Mill left, the Mission had let St. Michael's Hospital fall into neglect. Caught off guard by the radical change, Antle belatedly recognized that the hospital "must now be brought to a state of efficiency both in staff and equipment, consonant with its position in an up-to-date camp." While the fate of St. Michael's hung in the balance, St. Mary's Hospital at Pender Harbour was preparing its ceremonial opening in July 1930.

Although the Depression had closed down many logging camps and curtailed the fishing industry, the Mission regarded 1930 as "a year of development and extension" for its work of mercy. This was despite the obvious fact that its hospitals would have to operate at a loss throughout the thirties. The closing of the Englewood mill and camps near Alert Bay, for example, sent seven hundred men from the district. In the face of radical shifts in population and the virtual disappearance of camps, medical care—with the hospital ship *Columbia* as key—remained the Mission's principal task. The CCM was running three hospitals—St. George's at Alert Bay, St. Michael's at Rock Bay, St. Mary's at Pender Harbour—and was operating three ships—*Columbia*, *Rendezvous* and the *Fredna*. The latter, which had joined the team nine months earlier, patrolled Jervis Inlet and the area south to Sechelt and Lasqueti Island. In all, the Mission supported 7,860 hospital days,

"A Haven of Mercy" in Pender Harbour. St. Mary's Hospital (r.) was opened by Lieutenant Governor Bruce on 16 August 1930. St. Mary's Chapel (l.) was added in 1940.

270 medical cases, 293 surgical cases and over 3,000 out-patients, 842 of whom were treated by the *Columbia*'s doctor. The Mission's 1930 annual report stressed that the work of the Alert Bay hospital's staff "had been of incalculable benefit to the Indians, who are depending more and more on the services of the Mission." The steadily increasing number of Native maternity cases meant improved health and child care.

In the tradition of seafarers everywhere, the maritime community joined forces to respond to emergency calls and aid the sick whenever possible. On one occasion Andy Johnson, the captain of the Union Steamship Company's passenger-freighter *Cardena*, saved the *Columbia* a 150-mile journey by calling at Rock Bay and taking a patient to Vancouver for special treatment. On another occasion, a towboat company responded to the CCM's request by redeploying two of its tugs on errands of mercy. Finding the body of a

The Venerable Archdeacon Sir Francis Heathcote addressing the crowd from a balcony of St. Mary's Hospital, opening day, 16 August 1930.

woman who had drowned near Quathiaski Cove while her husband was away working as a tugboat deckhand, Greene had placed the body aboard the Mission's *Makehewi* and informed the husband's employer, who immediately sent a tug to find him. Lacking radio, the tug eventually located the husband aboard a sister ship in Howe Sound and transported him back to Quathiaski to pick up his wife's body and deliver it to Vancouver. "Covered with a Union Jack in tribute to the woman's splendid services as a nurse in the Imperial Forces overseas," Greene wrote, "the coffin was borne home on the tug's stern." Greene liked to recount this tale as exemplifying the basic humanity of so-called "hard-boiled businessmen" prepared to ignore all costs when human need arose. It doubtless served as a parable when trying to raise funds for the Mission.

Death was a frequent companion on Mission patrols. It encroached on one's thoughts during seemingly endless watches en route through long stretches of uninhabited territory, and it lent shape to experiences, strangely etching them into the land. One of Greene's published soliloquies captures such moments:

> Often as I stand at the wheel of the *Rendezvous* my heart is touched with sweet, though sad, memories [which] some little bit of shoreline recalls . . . where hidden somewhat amid the trees and yet glimpsing a panorama of blue waters and snow-peaked mountains, a moss-grown grave may be found.
>
> A family of seven, where real want is experienced at times, living in a small dwelling built for the most part out of poles and cedar shakes, is suddenly stricken with . . . influenza. In spite of careful nursing day and night, one of the children dies, a lad about nine years old. Probably poverty had made the parents slow to send for the doctor, so many miles away, or again it may have been their hope that they might, by careful nursing, bring the children through. My arrival with the doctor, once they had sent word to me, at least meant that helpful direction could be given them with a view to saving the other children's lives, and allowed of my proceeding with the burial of the little chap.

The Mission's thirty-five-foot Makehewi. *Built in 1910 and acquired by the Mission in 1920, she served until replaced by the* Rendezvous *in 1924.*

The father made a small coffin out of cedar shakes, dressed with a smoothing plane till they looked like the finest product of a mill. He and his oldest boy dug the grave just beyond on a small point commanding a view their little son had always loved. We laid the coffin in a small dug-out canoe, and then the family, together with the doctor and myself, rowed over to the grave, towing the small craft with its precious burden behind. In the fast-gathering twilight we buried the boy. The trees, as they whispered quietly in the evening breeze, seemed to tell us that they would forever guard the little lad, and there, after the simplest of committals, we left him.

Curiously absent from his poignant, if somewhat sentimental, account is the mother. She is scarcely even implied in Greene's expression "the family, together with the doctor and myself" who

The United Church's Sky Pilot *(l.) and the Anglican* Rendezvous *ca. 1930.*

rowed over to the grave. Greene offers us no intimations of maternal grief. Here as elsewhere one senses his characteristically male cast of mind. Not untypical for his time, he tended to see women as the handmaidens of male enterprise. They were the Women's Auxiliary to the Church of England in Canada; the nurses, cooks, lay missionaries and teachers frequently listed without first names in early Mission records. They were the Ruths, Marthas and Dorcas of biblical lore—sewing and stitching and busying themselves about the house, and suffering exile in a strange land—and now re-emerging as the 'Mrs. John Does' and the 'Misses Smith' of mission endeavour. Workers in the Lord's vineyard to be sure, but only in support roles, never as leaders or aboard Mission ships.

The *Columbia*'s chaplain during this period, Gilbert Thompson, later remarked that "too often the wife and family are forgotten, but it is they who carry the heat and burden of the day." In 1938 another of *Columbia*'s chaplain's described in Dickensian tones a family whose "house was large, cheerless, pathetic in the little

A floating village and logging community, ca. 1935

usual things which were not there." Dependent upon the absent father who could send "only a meagre pittance, less than $20.00 per month, to feed eight hungry mouths and clothe eight needful bodies," a middle-aged woman struggled on in hopeless misery. "Obviously the isolation, the spiritual and physical starvation was breaking down the mental and moral structure of the hapless family." But like so many others cast back upon their scant and diminishing resources, she held on.

Yet on one occasion Greene did champion "our women folk" with vigour in public discourse. In February 1932, he reflected in *The Log* on the women to whom he ministered; women caught— perhaps even trapped—in coastal isolation:

> As one looks back over many years of ministering to a very scattered flock, perhaps the finest memory of all . . . is that of the heroic behaviour of the womenfolk, as year after year they have faced the prolonged monotony of the life on our so-called "stump ranches" . . . The present difficult times [of the Depression] are bitterly

exasperating to many a splendid capable working man, and they are chafing under the ordeal. I do not blame them. But I feel that they are experiencing something of the inner hunger and resentment that has for years bitten deep into the souls of their women-folk, a hunger for companionship with other women, and resentment at the awful limitations of their life as frontierwomen. On their faces little is revealed, as a rule, of the inner passion for an outlet to their mental and spiritual powers.

Ask any parson who has ministered to these folk, and I am sure that very rarely can we recall a word of complaint from these long-suffering women. The welcome given to the visiting clergyman has always been a cheery one, and out of meagre material resources, wonderful hospitality extended . . .

Sometimes men speak scornfully of our efforts among the womenfolk as though we hadn't the stuff to work among men. My retort is that in far too many cases, the only real MAN in the house is the woman. Were it not for them, many a home in these parts would go absolutely to pieces. In some cases, the virtues of courage, patience, honour, temperance and hard labour are found in the woman, and not in the man, and were it not for my longing to save the soul of the poor beggar, I'd have nothing to do with him. His wife and children would receive all my attention.

The effects of the Depression were being felt throughout the Mission territory. Returning from an orientation patrol in the *Fredna* in 1932, Antle reported that the logging industry had fallen quiet and that a great number of settlers had fallen on hard times. He wrote that, while both the provincial government and the Mission were doing what they could by supplying food and clothing, much hardship prevailed. Crushed by the collapse of international economics, "these people are showing a great deal of grit and fortitude" by holding on where they are and resisting the temptation to gravitate into the city. Throughout this period, the

Mission campaigned for funds, food and clothing while continuing its medical and pastoral patrols.

Antle's editorial in *The Log* for January 1932 portrayed a dismal scene in international politics and economics. "The nations are not by any means beating their swords into ploughshares . . . on the contrary, the keenest minds are bent on the invention of weapons which, if war comes, will make the last war look like a peace parade." He evoked desperate times and decried the "millions of men" suffering unemployment. Power politics, warmongering and skewed values seemed to him to lie at the root of it. As Antle expressed it in his headlong scramble of phrases, "we have forgotten our religion and all it stands for and as a consequence business and political morality is at a low ebb, and things cannot come back until men realize that material things cannot give happiness when they are acquired by sharp business practices which amount to theft."

Here again is the voice of the Social Gospel, the often acerbic reminder that wealth and power are ultimately matters of stewardship and sharing. To Antle's mind, the world needed a spiritual revolution to feed the hungry—not only with bread for the body, but also with the Bread of Life for the soul. Faced with this challenge, he wondered aloud whether the Church, "with its denominational differences, and its complicated system of theology, is [even] capable of getting down to the simple needs of men." And even if, by some prodigious shift of focus, people should finally turn to the Church, could the Church actually offer any credible leadership and a meaningful response? Such rhetorical questions reflect Antle's abiding skepticism about the apparent fortress mentality of the institutional church which, to his mind, refused to take risks outside its own walls. Mission alone seemed to him the vanguard of change.

Tension between the institutional church and a free-wheeling, nonsectarian mission runs as a major theme through Antle's life. For example, he had long been planning to build a new boat to supplement the work of the *Columbia*, "and to name her the *W.A. Hutton* as a memorial to one who had done so much to make a success of the work in its initial stages." Seeking funds for this project, Antle had written in 1931 to one of Hutton's former medical colleagues in Winnipeg, seeking help to establish a trust fund. The doctor's reply was "brief, cold and to the point." If we accept Antle's interpretation, the tone of the reply reflected the view that Hutton's alcoholism had made him unworthy of any memorial whatsoever. That, to Antle's mind, was a particularly self-righteous example of establishment thinking:

> [The Winnipeg doctor's] interests were very evidently with the ninety-and-nine in the safety of the fold, not with the lost one. Nevertheless I am told that the Winnipeg doctor is a good Churchman, and perhaps he is, but I reserve the right to say he is a very indifferent follower of the Good Shepherd, to whose judgement I am willing to leave W.A.B. Hutton with all his faults and his failings, and his strength.

Eventually, of course, new ships were added to the fleet. Ironically and perhaps self-servingly, they bore the names "John Antle" and "Alan Greene" while their namesakes were still living, not "Hutton" as a memorial to personal victory after a fall.

In the meantime, the *Columbia* and her sister ships maintained their patrols. These lent both substance and endearing myth to the phrase "The Columbia is coming!" which quickly embodied all Mission operations. Visitors were invariably impressed with her technology, particularly her diesels, which seemed to ride the wave of the technological future. Thus when a reporter for Victoria's *The Colonist* visited the ship early in 1932, he seemed more impressed with the vessel than with her purpose. Certainly he introduced the crew: Captain Ed Godfrey, the "genial skipper [who] knows the coast thoroughly," and "John Antle, JP," noted as a Justice of the Peace and Superintendent of the Mission. The reporter acknowledged the ship's nurse, Bessie Newbold, and the physician, Dr. F. Herschel Stringer, son of the Right Reverend I.O. Stringer, Archbishop of Rupertsland, whom he described as "a clever young doctor." And then there was the padre, the Reverend Gilbert Thompson, who "has had much experience along

the Coast [and] is always a welcome visitor to the small flock."
Indeed, "he has a way of 'dolling' up a sermon so that the loggers
and others very often do not quite realize that it is a sermon they
are hearing. And yet they have the benefit of it." (Thompson
soon resigned because he found the ship's schedule left little time
for preaching.) Highest praise is accorded the vivacious Cecil Fitz-
Gerald and "his big diesel of 140-horsepower, which is his pride."
One readily imagines FitzGerald's quick wit and ebullient good
humour when guiding the naive and rather inept reporter through
the ship:

> He explains in detail the workings of the intricate piece
> of machinery which drives the Columbia through the
> water at eleven knots. No one except those with a me-
> chanical turn of mind understands everything Mr. Fitz-
> Gerald says about his engine, but they all like to look
> at it and marvel at the spick and span shape in which
> it is kept.

As for the *Columbia* herself:

> She is a roomy ship and has fine accommodation. There
> is a good-sized lounge where social gatherings are held,
> and services . . . at the small ports where there is no
> church or town hall. There is a tiny organ and a col-
> lapsible altar . . . There have been fifty people in the
> lounge at times. There is much deck space . . . There
> is a nice space aft for deck chairs, while on the boat
> deck is a large area where parties are held during the
> summer months.

Lest the public gain false impressions about life in the seagoing
mission, Greene later pointed out what the ship was all about: "the
boat we use is not a 'private yacht,' but rather a public servant at
the beck and call of any living soul whom we may be able to serve.
And it is in this 'meandering ministry' that we find our great joy."
    Had the reporter looked a bit further, he could have also intro-
duced the *Columbia*'s cook of the past five years, whose reputation

for cheerfulness was legendary. Known as Tony to those he served, he had entered fully into the spirit of the ship's ministry, despite the broken English which betrayed his Japanese origins and made him the butt of well meaning though often tasteless anecdotes. Calling him "You likee tea please" was one of the least offensive, and calls to mind stories of another cook named Wong whose "Not understand—me have no blains" was apparently the source of much amusement within the CCM. Only with Tony's death on 16 July 1932 at St. George's Hospital in Alert Bay did readers of *The Log* learn the real stature—and full name—of the much-loved Tomekichi 'Tony' Katsumata: "Ask the ship's company and you will find that no one quite measures up to Tony, and his memory will linger long on board the *Columbia*. He was white clean through. He knew little of theology, but he was a good Christian." In an era when Antle and his culture regarded "China-men" and "Japs" as generally inferior human types, Tony had received the highest compliment. He was not only Christian, but "white clean through."

Cultural baggage was not the *Columbia*'s only burden. As a matter of course, mission boats delivered mail, parcels and small freight. This proved to be a particularly helpful public service when visiting out-of-the-way places normally inaccessible by sched-uled steamships and the occasional float planes, which were be-ginning to explore the coast. A special-issue postage stamp of 1932 depicted the *Columbia* plying her way through familiar waters. Above her, in blue lettering on white, stood "Columbia Coast Mission," while a line below the ship made an appeal to "Help Them in Their Hour of Need." Suitably franked letters addressed to any isolated posts were bundled by the post office and delivered to the Mission's headquarters in the Province Building, where the *Vancouver Province* newspaper had donated office space. Transferred to the *Columbia*, the mail was franked on the reverse side by a crew member, and a charge of one cent was levied for each letter delivered. These stamps—such as the one cancelled in Victoria 25 April 1932 and addressed to Elsie Miles, Surge Narrows, BC—are extremely rare today.

While seeking out and maintaining contact throughout its sprawling coastal parish, the Mission fostered both pastoral and ceremonial links with its constituents. High feast celebrations like Easter and Christmas quite naturally became important gatherings for coastal people. The events seemed to telescope the years into intense focal points, illuminating the resident's social and spiritual lives. No matter how modest, these festivals served as benchmarks for the Mission as a whole. Reunions of former Mission parishioners, as recently as August 1994 in Pender Harbour, thrive on memories of Alan Greene's Santa Claus escapades, when the gift-laden Mission boat pulled into lonely bays and inlets. As Greene recalled:

Christmas parties were fantastic as I went back and forth in my ship. I can remember crowding into these little schoolhouses stuffed to the roof with people and kids and dogs . . .

I had many adventures as Santa. Often gathering people as I went, I'd come to anchor, start rowing them ashore, and then pack these dear people on my back up over the mud flat. It was always low water, at night, of course, in the winter. And the number of fat women I've packed up on my rear end over mud flats, would fill a book! I began to know the dimensions and exact weight of every creature on the island as I packed them ashore, and it was really good fun! We'd have the most wonderful times.

These Christmas parties would start with a high tea or supper. Then they would tolerate me having a Christmas service, seeing that there were better things to come! I've seen men in those little services sharing in hymns that they hadn't sung since they were boys, and men that were digging memories out of the past. I was always the organist, playing on this tiny little "Jimmy" that I packed around. And the music that we got out of that, and out of the people, was thrilling. Showed 'em movies with my hand-cranked movie machine, lighted by six-volt storage batteries. Then my mysterious disappearance in search of Santy, telling the children I knew he was somewhere in the woods and I was going out to give him a hand.

I remember one occasion, having to adjourn to the little girls' outhouse as a dressing room. It was snowing heavily, I thought this was a safe spot, and started to robe, and I was in there getting robed by the light of a dirty lantern when two dear little girls arrived to do their stuff. Horrified to find a half-dressed Santy, they gazed at me in utter bewilderment at what St. Nick was doing there!

We had gifts for every child—I knew each one by name, and knew all the circumstances of all the families. Once that was all over and Santy went back to his reindeer . . . we'd have a dance, and by jove!, those dances in those tiny rooms with kids and little ones now asleep in heaps in the corners on piles of overcoats. Good old-fashioned stuff. There was nothing like it.

In 1932, *Columbia*'s Christmas cruise spanned twenty-seven ports of call in three weeks. Covering nine hundred miles in all weathers, it distributed presents to some 350 children, sharing Christmas carols, pageants, Holy Communion and fellowship with communities as small as four in Wells Pass and seven in Allison Harbour, to as large as seventy in Hardy Bay. By Antle's count, 640 people had celebrated Christmas *Columbia*-style that year. Operating in the southern area, Alan Greene's *Rendezvous* completed a similar voyage.

The success of these ventures entailed four months of preparation: gathering children's names and ages, obtaining and wrapping appropriate gifts, raising funds, purchasing and packing Christmas cheer, and identifying special needs. Typically, the Women's Auxiliary at St. Mary's Church, Kerrisdale, began in August so that the boats could count on starting their Santa Claus run by mid-December. Drawing people from all walks—the lonely, the dispossessed, the adventurers, the homesteaders, disbelievers and faithful alike—the Mission communicated the joy of community. No one wanted to be left out, and many made great efforts to attend. The journey of a woman known only as Mrs. Patterson of Maurelle Island was not untypical. Ill and frail, she could not make it on her own to meet the *Rendezvous*. Bedding her down in a straw-filled sledge hitched to the family horse, her two daughters drove three miles through bush to the water's edge. Placing her in a rowboat, the girls rowed "through the headwaters of the Surge Narrows to Billie Heinbuckle's place where she was obliged to walk a long boom-stick to get ashore." Here she rested before shuffling a half mile through the wooded trail to the school for the celebration. Heinbuckle's impromptu invitation to stay over prevented the family from having to push back home in the dead of night.

Billie Heinbuckle's became the focal point for quite a different kind of celebration on 10–11 November 1933. Alan Greene, a veteran of World War One, had established links with various branches of the Royal Canadian Legion. On this occasion, members of Branch 116 decided to gather at Maurelle Island to commemorate Armistice Day with their families. As with all social gatherings in the Mission district, weather, tides and powerful currents dictated the arrival and departure times. Skippering a variety of watercraft, the legionnaires straggled in from Valdes, Maurelle, Read, Stuart and Cortes Islands, feeling their way through thickening fog into the Heinbuckle landing at Surge Narrows. "The trail leads up through rather fine timber, across a surging torrent on great trees felled to make the bridge, and ends at the little school from which the light shone out and bade us welcome," Greene recalled. Then followed a festive dinner for fifty and lively dancing until 3 a.m.— precisely 11 a.m. Greenwich Mean Time in the Empire's capital. At that moment, the dancing stopped. Said Greene:

> . . . and everybody came to attention as we carried out a brief Service of Remembrance. We hope that our time coincided with that in London, England, where we could almost feel the presence of the great host there which was doing something in its essence exactly like ours, only with all the grandeur and dignity that marks the great ceremonies held in that centre of our Empire. [But] I think that just as sincere a tribute was paid to their memory, as rose from the Cenotaph in Whitehall, where the Empire had as its chief mourner, the son of our beloved King.

The first John Antle during trials in the Mediterranean in 1933 as the Greek Syrene. The seventy-foot vessel was sold in 1936 as she proved unsuitable for medical mission on the BC coast.

Such ceremonies with the Royal Canadian Legion became a regular feature of the Mission's ministry. In 1934, the veterans and their families convened in Whaletown, where Greene preached on the theme of peace, "sharing in a few moments of serious thought, holy memories, and earnest prayer, with thousands of fellow Britishers, an experience of oneness that made our little outpost of Empire seem vital to the unity of the Empire throughout the world." That Greene consider himself a "fellow Britisher" despite his birth in Orillia, Ontario, from an established Canadian family, and despite the fact that the Canadian Army in which he served overseas had not regarded itself as a colonial force, is striking, though perhaps not surprising. As a minister of the Anglican Church, Greene stood as much for the political order of the British

Stepping the mast of John Antle (ex-Syrene) at Lambeth Pier, London, in 1933. The Homburg-hatted Reverend Jocelyn Perkins, president of the BC and Yukon Church Aid Society, which financed the vessel, stands (second from right) beside captain John Antle.

Empire as he did for the spiritual order of the Kingdom of God. Ominous clouds were gathering in Europe; Hitler had seized power in 1933 and was mobilizing his nation while Chamberlain preached appeasement. Greene, for his part, "stressed the duty of our learning to live at peace with our neighbours before we presume to inveigh against those we call the warmongers of the world." Just how much he paid attention to political realities is never clear.

In the meantime, John Antle went to England seeking a new vessel for his fleet. With the full financial support of the London-based British Columbia and Yukon Church Aid Society, he acquired the seventy-five-foot yacht *Syrene* on 15 January 1933.

Built by Thorneycrofts in 1922 for a Greek millionaire, she was a beautiful, classic vessel: clipper bow, double teak planking and copper bottom, and an interior finished in birdseye maple and mahogany. Antle picked her up in the French Mediterranean port of Antibes, intending to return directly to London for refit. Suffering an engine breakdown en route, he put into the British naval base at Gibraltar where he had the old engines torn out and replaced with two new Winthrop diesels—at the donor's expense. While in Gibraltar Antle was feted at the first of two renaming ceremonies that turned the luxury yacht *Syrene* into the mission ship *John Antle*. Just who chose the name is not clear. One suspects, however, that while the BCYCAS endorsed the idea, Antle himself may not have been an entirely neutral player.

On 1 May 1933, in a ceremony in His Majesty's Dockyard attended by a bevy of VIPs—including the dean of the Anglican Cathedral, Gibralter's commanding admiral and numbers of his officers—numerous speeches extolled the achievements of Antle and his Columbia Coast Mission. In summarizing its history and proclaiming the missionary fleet's "great mission of help to the loggers, miners, white settlers and Indians of the vast British Columbia coast," the chaplain of the Missions to Seamen identified Antle's secret of success: it was "most obviously his ideals of service for the Master Pilot." In speaking thus, he expressed confidence that Antle would be "the skipper of this ship for a long time and that there will be ships named *John Antle II, III*, and *IV* to carry on the work in his name for generations to come." Other *John Antles* would indeed follow, but this one lasted barely three years.

Further refitting continued in London until the second official renaming accorded the *John Antle* her new status. Festivities began with Antle's delivering a sermon during evensong in Westminster Abbey, continued through to a public viewing of the vessel next day which thousands of Londoners reportedly attended, and finished with a garden party at Lambeth Palace. A service of dedication followed in Lambeth Parish Church during which, as the London *Guardian* of 23 June 1933 explained, "Bishop Perrin (formerly Bishop of British Columbia) gave a very inspiring address on Mr. Antle's wonderful work on the coast of British Columbia." The

Consecration of John Antle on 16 July 1933 at Lambeth Pier, London, by Right Reverend Arthur Foley, Bishop of London.

presence of VIPs—such as the high commissioner for Canada and the agent general for British Columbia—underscored the fact that this was viewed as much more than a strictly religious endeavour. Ceremonies culminated aboard the vessel at Lambeth Pier where the Lord Bishop of London, as chairman of the BCYCAS, blessed the vessel and her crew of eight. Mrs. Perrin then officially pronounced the change of name: "In the faith of Jesus Christ this motor-yacht is named *John Antle*. May it ever be used in promoting the welfare of His people and in the extension of His kingdom. Amen." An eyewitness reported that as the ceremony concluded, "the great gathering took up the words of the National Anthem [God Save the King] and sent them echoing across the river to the Houses of Parliament."

Her refit completed after many delays, the *John Antle* finally set sail on her nine-thousand-mile voyage to Vancouver, from

The first John Antle *in Vancouver, ca. 1933.*

Falmouth for Las Palmas on 4 August 1933, and thence to Trinidad and Panama, San Francisco, Victoria and Vancouver, where she was due to arrive by 6 October. The lateness of the season made her bypass St. John's, Newfoundland, where Antle had intended to call. By November 1934, the *John Antle* took up a patrol based in Pender Harbour. Her operational area embraced Lasqueti Island, Texada Island and Jervis Inlet, and ran through the Skookumchuck Narrows into Sechelt Inlet.

These ports of call were still virtually unknown to potential supporters of the Mission. For that reason, Antle invited reporters to experience a patrol as occasion permitted—and of course write a suitable story. "When in trouble—send for the parson," *Vancouver Province* reporter Derek Lukin Johnston had written in 1933 when summarizing the wisdom he had distilled from a patrol aboard the

Rendezvous. In a sensitive popular article entitled "A Sky Pilot Among the Enchanted Isles of B.C.," he evoked the reality of human suffering against the background of the romantic natural grandeur of the pastor's patrol. He noted that several missions were working on the coast: the Presbyterian mission of the Reverend John Pringle headquartered at Vananda on Texada Island, the Methodist mission ship *Thomas Crosby* in the Queen Charlotte Islands, and the Shantymen's hospital at Esperanza "along the storm-swept shores of the west coast of Vancouver Island." But the largest among these enterprises was the Columbia Coast Mission. "It is a great work these seagoing sky pilots of the B.C. coast are doing." But a major reason for their dwindling financial support during these Depression years, said the article, was the fact that they were largely unknown in centres like Vancouver, carrying out "unostentatious labor of which the outside world seldom hears." In describing the extent of the Mission's work—its emergency calls to remote shacks, its visits to handloggers and lighthouse keepers—Johnston sketched in a couple of the coast's eccentric characters: a recluse apparently suffering "weird delusions," and a "settler up Bute Inlet who just revels in old copies of the *Atlantic Monthly*." These scant cameos were meant to underscore the often abject isolation of coast dwellers. Whatever their religious persuasion or personal needs, all were the Mission's parishioners. In Johnston's view, this kind of ministry was unique:

> To begin with, the actual "preaching" is a minor matter. Services are held, of course, on Sundays at more or less regular intervals, but they are of the simplest character. Questions of doctrine do not worry these isolated settlers very much; over and again they found the sky pilot to be a "very present help in trouble" and they have come to look on him, not so much as a preacher, but rather as an exponent of eminently practical Christianity.

That grand process of social transformation was being carried out by a handful of dedicated workers with strained resources. In the case of the Columbia Coast Mission, this meant the *John Antle* based in Pender Harbour in support of St. Mary's Hospital (and

Funeral of Edward D. Tombleson, 1 May 1935, aboard Columbia. *Tombleson was a resident of Hardy Bay since 1910. His body was committed to the deep between Duval Point and Masterman Islands.*

being supported in turn by Harry Dusenbury's machine shop). It included *Rendezvous* at Quathiaski Cove and *Columbia* at Alert Bay. Committed workers made it possible for the Mission to carry on despite losing money in hospitals and medical aid. But if personnel came cheaply, ship maintenance did not. The 1935 annual report of the CCM revealed that the twenty-five-year-old *Columbia* was showing her age. Built of local materials, notably fir, she once again was suffering rot, although the Mission had already spent $3,000 to remove it.

It was clear that demand for mission services was outstripping the CCM's financial ability. To be sure, *Columbia* had run 17,724 miles, some 2,488 miles of which had been in response to twenty-nine radio-telephone calls. But "the area attended to by the ship has so increased that something will have to be done to limit it." Financial constraints prevented working the three ships any harder.

This was particularly worrisome in the case of the *Columbia*. As Antle and captain Ed Godfrey pointed out, "part of the boat's route, Queen Charlotte Sound, is a rough bit of water and the boat is subject to stresses and strains calculated to tax the strength of [even] new timber. It is not therefore good policy to keep her operating till an accident happens, perhaps a serious one for boat and crew." Yet she was kept running—until she struck bottom while transiting Greene Point Rapids in 1935 and was forced into drydock for the replacement of fifty feet of keel.

Another low point was reached that year when Tom Barton died after a brief illness. "T.F.," as he was affectionately known, had joined the Mission as secretary twenty-four years earlier. According to the Reverend Dr. T. Lane Connold of St. Mary's Hospital, "T.F." was "a small spare man of the gentlest manner and habit, shy and reserved, a lover of work, but, withal, the very typification of the twin virtues of 'Loyalty' and 'Honesty'." If Antle is the father of the CCM, he added, then Thomas Francis Barton is the foster father. Posthumously praised by Greene as "one of the most conscientious, scrupulously honest men that ever lived," Barton had developed an encyclopedic knowledge of the Mission and managed both its internal and external relations. He developed the contacts with Vancouver's business community which his successor and former assistant, Ben Drew, would try to exploit.

Greene's appeal for funds in 1934 was supported by the Vancouver Welfare Federation, which customarily made an annual grant of $15,000 to the Mission. Citing miles steamed, patients cared for and a series of anecdotal human interest stories of people in distress, the federation drew an exciting picture for potential donors to the cause: "Drama of death, love and life, romance and tragedy. The *Columbia* meets them all and plays her part as good neighbor irrespective of race or religion, winter or summer, fair weather or the foulest." The CCM spent between forty and fifty thousand dollars per year in Vancouver in support of its operations, the federation observed. Indeed, as most of the money was subscribed in England, the federation's own donation, by contrast, seemed "a pitifully small contribution to good-neighbourliness and to the medical and spiritual welfare of those thousands of our friends and fellow citizens who are scattered between here [Vancouver] and

Committing the ashes of Mission secretary T.F. "Tom" Barton from the afterdeck of John Antle, June 1935, off Pender Harbour. Barton had served continuously since 1911. Officiating are (l. to r.) Reverend B.H.L. Dance, Reverend T.A. Lane Connold, MD, and Reverend John Antle.

the Queen Charlottes." The Vancouver Welfare Federation raised its donation that year to $17,384 to include a special grant for overhauling the *Columbia*.

By 1936, the Mission comprised a staff of forty-three (clergy, medical and administrative personnel, cooks, engineers, captains); and its operational costs ran between $60,000 and $70,000 per annum. It depended upon a variety of revenue sources: the Toronto-based Missionary Society of the Church in Canada, the London-based British Columbia and Yukon Church Aid Society, the federal government's department of Indian Affairs, provincial government grants for medical services, the Workmen's Compensation Board, the Vancouver Welfare Federation, the Women's Auxiliary of the Church of England in Canada, and voluntary contributions.

In assessing its effectiveness, the superintendent's 1936 annual report divided the Mission's work into two major activities: "Hospital Work" and "Church Work." Clearly, hospital work formed the pillar of the Mission: 10,369 hospital days, 1,115 medical and surgical cases, 4,340 outpatient visits and 37 child clinics. In support of this the *Columbia* had patrolled a total of 14,661 miles, 3,467 of them in response to 49 emergency calls. By contrast, so-called church work seemed statistically less impressive, and caused both Greene and the Mission Board some concern: 265 church services, 137 celebrations of Holy Communion, 45 baptisms, 10 weddings and 12 funerals. This seemed to raise questions in some minds as to what the Mission was about: medical aid or spiritual welfare. One could credibly argue, of course, that the Mission's business was both. But with increasing governmental interest in social services in later years, and with increasing competition for funds in both the public and private sectors of the economy, the Mission had to decide where its priorities lay.

As so often in Mission affairs, calculations and planning were overtaken by events. The year 1936 saw the sale of the *John Antle* and the purchase of her replacement, the 55-foot former seine-boat *Florida V* from BC Packers, as well as John Antle's retirement in the spring, and Alan Greene's succession as superintendent.

Contrary to expectations, the *John Antle* (ex-*Syrene*) had not proven her worth. After less than three years in service she was

The Reverend John Antle (l.) and the Reverend B.H.L. Dance during a service aboard John Antle, *1935.*

The second John Antle (ex-Florida V) alongside Kingcome float in 1937. She was skippered by the Reverend T.A. Lane Connold, MD.

virtually laid up by June 1935, needing an expensive refit, including new engines. In October 1936, *The Log* diplomatically announced that, with the consent of the British Columbia and Yukon Church Aid Society, the *John Antle* had been sold and the proceeds put towards a new boat. Greene unveiled as her replacement the 55-foot diesel-powered *Florida V*, soon to be renamed the *John Antle* (precisely as her predecessor, without any numeral). He assured his readers she was "extraordinarily close to the requirements of a mission ship, in its evangelistic, medical and social work." She lacked only radio equipment and a set of binoculars, for both of which the Mission now appealed.

Behind the quiet announcement, however, lay bristling frustration and considerable friction between the Mission and the British Columbia and Yukon Church Aid Society. As Jocelyn Perkins of the BCYCAS put the matter, they had donated the original vessel three years previously under the express understanding that she was intended for spiritual ministrations only, not as a hospital ship. That was why the society had been convinced she was the right ship for the job and had been prepared to underwrite all her future operating costs. Faced now with the obvious need to sell the ship off, the society expressed itself "unhappy about all that has taken place and the appalling (and as it appears to us, needless) waste of money" their gift—and Antle's judgement—had incurred. More serious still:

> It would seem that Antle insisted on these particular engines [when in Gibraltar] against the better judgement of the firm who considered them unsuitable for that type of boat . . . It is grievous to think that Antle should have let us in for an expenditure on the engines something like twice the cost of the boat, if not more, culminating in what appears to be a collapse.

Except for his alleged retort that the complaint had used up "two perfectly good sheets of paper roasting" him for something he did not do, there is no record of Antle's reply to these charges of gross mismanagement. Comfortable with making radical decisions entirely on his own hook, he tended to take the most pragmatic approach. Requiring a new engine in Gibraltar, he would have found no need to dither about, for "if thine eye offend thee, pluck it out." Mere pencil pushers and office politicians could deal with the aftermath as they saw fit.

In 1936 as well, the Reverend Cyril Venables took over the six hundred-family patrol area that Greene had developed over the past seventeen years with the *Makehewi* and the *Rendezvous*. (Contrary to myth, the *Makehewi* had not been named after a Chinook princess abducted by cruel raiders, but after the first owner's children, Mary, Kenneth, Henry and Willie.) Calling upon his former parishioners to help the new pastor get established, Greene reminded them "it is not easy to become familiar with all the channels and anchorages or possibly the trails and roads that lead to your respective homes." Schooled neither in seamanship, navigation nor coastal lore, the new man "must become familiar with, and unafraid of, rapids such as the Seymours, the Greenpoint, the Ucultas, the Arran, the Hole-in-the-Wall, Surge Narrows and Okisollow." Greene's approach was essentially Antle's way of

Reverend Dr. and Mrs. T.A. Lane Connold with daughter Shirley Ann at Kingcome village, June 1937. Note details of CCM uniform: officer's cap and cap badge, blue blazer with pocket crest.

dealing with his new staff: "Here you are, get on with it!" Greene confessed that he himself had needed "a year to cover the territory fully, allowing for a decent time to visit each home." In fact, Venables would not last long; the lifestyle did not accord with his taste, nor perhaps with that of his family. Judging from his first contribution to the Mission's journal, however, he was zealous to a fault in proclaiming mission work as the vanguard of evangelism, and in denouncing "the apathy and indifference [which] many church people show to those agencies" such as the CCM which the church had commissioned "to take this Gospel and teach and exemplify it to all men." His primary concern was "the glaring fact that the Church has failed to make her voice heard in such as way as to be taken seriously by the great mass of people."

This was precisely the view of the skipper of the new *John Antle*, Reverend T. Lane Connold, MD. In his dual role of physician and priest, he had joined the medical staff of St. Mary's Hospital, Pender Harbour, two years earlier, in 1934. A devoted churchman and physician, he dedicated himself to both his professions while keeping quietly to himself his mounting doubts about the Mission's effectiveness. Frequently accompanied on patrol by his wife prior to the birth of their first child, Connold coaxed from Greene a warm acknowledgement of her contribution. Concealing perhaps a touch of chagrin, Greene confessed that she had become "a real friend to many an isolated woman." It would be some years before Greene would concede to women a seagoing pastoral role among the coastal communities.

Meanwhile the *John Antle* (ex-*Florida V*) patrolled its mission area out of Pender Harbour. Characteristically, it covered, during October and November 1936, a total of 1,277 miles, 206 of which were in response to emergency calls. A contemporary testimonial from Doug Dane, lightkeeper at Ballenas Island Light Station, described a typical scenario when a friend visiting the lighthouse fell seriously ill:

> Through my amateur radio station I contacted another amateur radio station at Savary Island, who sent the message by land line to Pender Harbour. This was at 5 p.m.; and at 6 p.m. I again contacted Savary Island, who had the reply "Florida leaving at 5:45." Words fail to express how comforting that brief and concise message was to us. At about 7:15 we saw a light in the distance, and knew it was the *Florida* on her way. They arrived at 8:15 and anchored in Maggie Bay, where I met them [in my boat] and brought Dr. Connold ashore to see the patient. It was decided to take him right away to

Pender Harbour Hospital, and at 10:15 the *Florida* was
on her way back . . . Here on this little island, so
isolated, it is indeed very comforting to know that a
doctor is within call and that he will come if humanly
possible.

The retirement of John Antle, the founder and grand mentor of
the Mission, lent sharp focus to the self-understanding and self-
image of the CCM. When Greene wrote his *Log* article in 1936,
he was perhaps not yet aware that he would be appointed Antle's
successor. In the article he extolled the work of the "Master Mind
of the Columbia Coast Mission," its "pilot" and "admiral [who]
after the fashion of British admirals 'strikes his colours'" after thirty-
two years in the venture he had founded. Greene tactfully admitted
that the Mission had experienced both successes and failures. Yet
in publishing the accolade, he challenged the logging fraternity
and the settlers whom Antle's mission had served so faithfully. In
assessing its value, they should "look at this Mission from the
standpoint of years and forget the few members of the staff who
were admittedly 'duds,' and think of the thousands of men, women
and children who have gone to the little hospitals and been relieved
of pains and illness that were making life unbearable and almost
made you throw up your homesteads." Service could only improve,
he implied, because the Mission would now be managed by a
board of clergy and laity, who were already assuming greater responsibility in order to free the new superintendent from some of
the details hampering his commitment to mission work. He linked
his valediction with a plea for funds.

Despite the many vicissitudes and disappointments, John Antle
could look back upon his remarkable achievements with pride and
satisfaction. In conferring upon him the honourary degree of Doctor of Divinity, the warden of St. John's College in Winnipeg
compared him to Grenfell of Labrador; in doing so he recognized
the singular achievements of both men: "a work so unique as to
render comparison with any other philanthropic efforts out of
place." Churchmen of international renown, both Newfoundlanders
had "brought medical skill, hospitals, nurses, schools, and all the
blessings and privileges of the Evangel in their ships." The warden

John Antle in his doctoral robes (1936) on receiving the honorary Doctor of Divinity from St. John's College, Winnipeg.

summarized Antle's achievement as "a vision of what the Columbia Coast Mission could accomplish for humanity, [and] he is here tonight with his vision a realized fact."

Public and private personae are necessarily two different things. Antle, for example, projected a stern authoritarian demeanor that masked his sparkling sense of humour. Robed in his doctoral gown for his official portrait, he struck an august figure seemingly lost in lofty contemplation of all that he had wrought. Yet behind the conventional mask of quiet dignity lay an impish boy delighting in having outmanoeuvred his bishop for academic honours. Unaware that his bishop had actually recommended him for the degree, he quipped to a former colleague in Vancouver's CCM office where the framed portrait was to be hung: "Once I arrive I shall take time off to call at the CCM offices and gaze and gaze on that resplendent picture." And then he added: "I'm sure the bishop when he sees it [will] put nature's favourite colour in the shade by flooding his countenance with a deeper hue of the same." Should the bishop suffer any "ill effect" from exposure to such glory, the CCM staff would doubtless be there "to assist his tottering steps downward to his office."

A more serious dichotomy in public and private persona found expression in the person of the priest-physician T.A. Lane Connold. On resigning from the Mission late in 1937 and returning to England, he left both a public valediction and a private report about his three years at St. Mary's Hospital and as skipper-chaplain of the second *John Antle*. As he wrote for *The Log* in September 1937, he would especially remember "the privilege of alleviating suffering, in helping in some economic distress, in comforting in sorrow and in death, in affording solace through our holy religion." He wrote a kindly farewell, remembering the friendships and the generous gifts in kind that had nourished the Mission and its parishioners in both body and spirit. "Let us not forget, too, the odd fisherman who meeting us would call 'Wanna fish, Doc?' and with a nonchalant air to disguise his shyness tosses on deck an enormous cod, or a fine spring salmon."

Writing to Alan Greene in private, however, Connold offered scathing criticism of the Mission, despite being "greatly impressed with the necessity for and value of such work as we are doing along the Coast." He disapproved of "the waste of time and money spent in rushing about from place to place merely to inquire if all was well," instead of planning a regular schedule of medical and pastoral visits. Mileage statistics may look impressive, he pointed out, but they mask a squandering of resources. He harped against the Mission's levying fees in the hospitals instead of dispensing medical care as charity, and against working chaplains at sea where they never have time to take services and where, again, "mileage counted more than instruction." Indeed, he was fundamentally disturbed by the Mission's lack of solid evangelism. "The characterless, sentimental type of religion will not do." More substantive fare was urgently needed: "some definite strong faith with full Sacramental teaching should be aimed at with the privileges of Grace strengthened by healthy discipline." Finally, he viewed "with apprehension the difficulty in maintaining Mission work financially in view of the poor support afforded by the Dioceses in which the work is carried on." By Connold's largely correct financial analysis, most of the Mission's money came either from abroad or from eastern Canada. Greene took much of Connold's critique to heart. As the emphasis on medical mission waned, the pastoral mission became the sole reason for the Mission's continued existence.

Greene's 1936 appointment as superintendent signified in many respects a sea-change, though he always felt himself fondly indebted to his mentor. Antle had encouraged Greene, the former deckhand of the early pioneering days, and had enjoyed his company. Between them, earnestness had shifted with jocularity and whimsy— and an occasional good "cuss"—whenever Antle wanted his trainee to get something done. Their change of command was no different. "When he left, that old devil, he said to me, 'well Greene, you're now in charge of this bloody mission,'. . . 'I built it, and you can destroy it!' In the event, Greene would rebuild it, renew it and, years later in his retirement, watch its demise.

CHAPTER 4

The Greening of Columbia

The BEGINNINGS OF GREENE'S LEADERSHIP were fraught with grave challenges. The Mission was strapped for human and financial resources in 1936, and the effects of the Depression were still reaching into the remote regions of his territory, where a great many people suffered in quiet desperation. Demand for social assistance was running high. A major change in mission style was marked by Greene's recognition of demographic shifts along the coast. Transient camps were being replaced by more settled communities, no matter how primitive and small. The "meandering ministry," as Greene once called the itinerant mission boat life, now needed the more permanent type of support which could only be gained by establishing parishes.

In 1938 Greene announced three innovative projects. He would build St. Mary's Church in Pender Harbour as "the centre of the corporate religious life of the community of Pender Harbour, as well as the place of worship for our staff and patients" at St. Mary's Hospital; and he would establish two new parishes, one on Lasqueti Island, and the other at Sayward. "I want to build chapels and churches that are worthy of the work, and which will be simple but beautiful in design, with due care being given to the building's fitting into the particularly beautiful surroundings on the seashore and in the forest." The consecration of St. Mary's Chapel, Pender Harbour, on 31 March 1940 marked the first step. Greene used the occasion to reflect on his dependence on external funds: "and so it is whenever a frontier church is built. It invariably owes its existence very largely to those who many never see it, or worship in it, but who by their gifts and sustaining prayers and sympathy are one with the actual week-by-week users of this small but beautiful House of God." Aware that he was breaking new ground, if not actually running counter to Antle's concept of mission, Greene was launching himself into long-term modernization which would include the building of new ships. Ships, parishes and homes for senior citizens would command his attention in the following years. At the same time, the work of the mission at sea continued.

The navigational record of the mission boats provides little insight into the human condition with which the Mission dealt. Greene admitted as much in 1936, but allowed that logs do "recall to the skipper, journeyings sometimes full of romance, tragedy, [and] hard struggle." And yet, he wrote two years later, "perhaps behind one of these perfectly commonplace jottings [on weather, courses steered and departure times] there's a story that meant much to a family here, a child there . . ." Greene himself has left us the record of one such case:

> Away up Jervis Inlet in a little bay on the left hand shore, a man and wife by the name of Groven have lived for many years. They have struggled along with the prospects of a mine as an almost forlorn hope, but there was courage and optimism . . . that at some distant date the tide might turn in their favor.
>
> A simple cottage was their home, and their only neighbor lived across the bay. Both families were very dependent upon each other and the men folk would alternate . . . collecting weekly supplies and mail, taking their small craft to Vancouver Bay, further down the inlet. The main traffic of the inlet went past their doors, as steamers and tugs travelled to the head of the inlet, little realizing the struggle that was going on.

Lean in detail and tinged with private sentiment, this account nonetheless evokes the pervasive reality Greene had known since joining the Mission in 1911. When the *Rendezvous* chanced upon

"Home, Sweet Home" pioneer style in the 1930s and 1940s. Note outdoor plumbing (l.) and the typical "Japanese" live-tank cod boat (r.) also used in gill-netting and crabbing.

this scene, she was commanded by lay missionary Wally Smith, who had previously served as engineer to the Reverend Cyril Venables. What first caught Smith's eye was "a little white flag fluttering on a mast" at the Grovens' shack, "indicating that they wanted someone to come to them at once." Learning from Mrs. Groven that her husband had rowed off at 6:30 that morning to intercept the passing Union Steamships for mail and had neither returned nor been seen over four hours later, Smith set off in search—only to find the boat washed ashore some three miles off, the husband lying dead inside. Records give no hint of the cause of death. Instead, they reflect the austerity of the discovery, and

The second John Antle's engineer Wally Smith with skipper Connold's daughter, August 193?

the pastoral care and comfort which apparently random circumstances had summoned the Mission to perform. In Greene's words, "there are many isolated couples like this who are living in very reduced circumstances, probably hanging on . . . to some precious hope in the form of a mining claim, or a little bit of timber, but feeling that they may realize enough to give them just a little ready cash to tide them through their declining years." As with so many pioneer stories, we never again hear of Mrs. Groven. Coming briefly into focus in a quickly jotted note, she lived and died in obscurity.

That was the sombre light in which many pioneers of the thirties suffered deprivation. Sleuthing among the Mission's records, however, one is struck by the quiet dignity and deference with which people sometimes sought aid when they could no longer go it alone. Pencilled notes and penned petitions frequently reached the Mission:

> Could it be in your possibility to get me and my wife some second hand clothing, women's dresses, and underwear for both of us? We are both getting old and

have not much money to buy anything. Anything will
be appreciated. Thank You.

Not only the elderly found themselves in need. Young families
also faced poverty and disease, and feared an uncertain future:

> I have been in [the Mission's] Hospital for the last month.
> I had to have another major operation and am only just
> home. With me being sick so long, I haven't been able
> to use the sewing machine and make over the clothing
> as I used to do, and we are getting so short of clothing.
> I wondered if we could get some through the Mission
> . . . we are really up against it for clothes and the cold
> is coming on. I don't like to have to ask, but I can't
> see the children going without and I know you will
> understand.

Despite such hardships and the inactivity of many logging camps
well into the summer of 1938—a slump Greene attributed to the
"slack log market"—settlers did not lose heart. Greene was impressed by "the prevailing spirit of cheerfulness and optimism"
which seemed to characterize the pioneer cast of mind. Optimism
seemed in order for the Mission too, due in part to three recent
developments. By this time, Greene had recruited students from
the Anglican Theological College in Vancouver to spend their
summers as student missionaries; the *Columbia* had returned to the
northern patrol after further refit; and Alert Bay seemed once more
under firm church leadership since the arrival of Cyril Venables.
For Greene in 1938, Alert Bay stood as "a strategic centre for the
Church's work among the Indians." Its now well-established hospital would celebrate its thirtieth anniversary on 15 June 1939. Yet
Alert Bay still remained an outpost, "that amazing little place with
its couple of miles of diversified road—diversified as far as the
number and depth and size of the holes in its surface are concerned—its sixteen automobiles, one motor-bicycle, and its strings
of fresh washing flapping in the front yards."

Outsiders shipping aboard *Columbia* for an orientation tour invariably marvelled at the wonders of the BC coast and grasped

The new St. George's Hospital, Alert Bay, in 1937. Staff at the time: Dr. David B. Ryall, nurses I. Wilson, M. Parkes, G. Williams, with G. Trent as orderly and B. Gulliver, cook.

the meaning of the ship's mission. For landlubbers who had never experienced frontier life, as a woman visitor explained in *The Log* in September 1939, the impressions could be overwhelming:

> In this whirling maelstrom of thoughts, I catch glimpses of fish boats and gill nets, booms of logs, and salmon, cool dark pools in which mountains are mirrored, totems and picturesque villages, a moonlit pathway which searches out the narrow reaches beyond Hardy Bay, where the stillness is broken only by the sound of the salmon jumping. I see a long hard road which leads on and on through the woods and back again to the little settlement where friendly lights bespeak fireside evenings and the *Columbia* lying alongside the wharf.
>
> Time after time I heard it said, "when we saw the

The Governor General visits Columbia (1939) where he heard a "British broadcast from the Old Land" in which Britain's prime minister, Neville Chamberlain, spoke on "the European situation." Favouring appeasement, he failed to recognize the threat of Nazism. (l. to r.) Captain George MacDonald, Lord Tweedsmuir, Col. W.F. Kemp, Reverend Alan Greene, and Mr. G.V. Pearce. Kemp and Pearce were members of the Mission Board.

Columbia come round the point we knew all was well." They will tell you of anxious hours spent waiting in the chill wind on a float, watching and waiting for the ship to come round the bend, while perhaps a life is hanging in the balance, the result of illness or accident. It is not only at times like these that the people seem glad to see the *Columbia*. To them the ship has real personality and with the crew they also share their joy.

The outbreak of war left Alan Greene virtually on his own to run the Mission. "I am left as the sole Missionary Priest on the

The forty-eight-foot ketch Reverie, skippered by eighty-one-year-old John Antle, leaves BC for the West Indies in 1946. He brought her from England in 1939.

staff, let alone the absence of lay missionaries. It is a serious situation for the spiritual undertakings of our Mission, but until men and money are forthcoming, I hope to carry on over the entire territory, using the *John Antle* and the *Columbia*, and the coastal steamers in my efforts to keep all the established work going that I can possibly manage." For some time now, doctors were being attracted to better paying positions elsewhere, and pastors were being drawn to established parishes that offered more financial and social stability for family life. War mobilization attracted others to the Army Medical Corps and the Chaplaincy Service. Military service and jobs in larger centres siphoned off the remaining lay workers into a burgeoning economy that was radically changing Canadian life. Thus while "the old ship *Columbia* plugs along, over and over the same route," as Greene observed in September 1939, the winds of change cast him back upon his own resources. Undaunted, he remained more convinced than ever of the vital link between health care and pastoral care, for "sick bodies make difficult temples for the Spirit of God."

Throughout this period, Greene maintained contact with his

former mentor John Antle, that "adventurer and seaman of the first order," as he once called him. Not that Greene needed advice so much as an understanding friend. Antle had left Vancouver for Dartmouth, England, on 26 July 1938 to pick up his forty-eight foot yawl *Reverie*, which he had traded sight unseen for his small piece of property in Maple Bay. Built in 1934 on a tea plantation in Assam, in the hill country of India, the *Reverie's* history alone must have fascinated Antle. It had been taken eight hundred miles by rail to the Indian coast, thence by freighter to England to be launched in the Thames. Entrancing in both name and line, she was Antle's retirement retreat. He took two years to repeat the 1933 voyage of his namesake *John Antle* (ex-*Syrene*). As *Reverie* lay alongside the Royal Jamaica Yacht Club in Kingston on 18 March 1940, Antle shared his reflections in a letter to Greene:

> You are up against a tough job in taking the mission through this war. It was a struggle last war, but I fancy this one will last longer and its effects be more far-reaching. The business men of Van[couver] saved the day for us then. Many of them increased their subs[idies] rather than see us go under. The mission is better equipped to stand a siege now, and if the war is not too prolonged it ought to come through. The logging camps ought to wake up to the fact that were the mission to close down it would leave them awkwardly situated.

Driven by zeal, Greene had to keep going. His principal hope lay in promoting the Mission in the old stomping ground of eastern Canada, as well as locally throughout the dioceses of New Westminster and British Columbia. This often meant arguing for funds not merely to sustain the Mission, but to renew it. Of course, he could attract new funds only by demonstrating the Mission's "success" and relevance. As so often in the past, success had to be sold to the Mission's supporters—including the board and the bishops—by marshalling convincing statistics on health care, miles steamed, and patient-days underwritten. These were precisely what Connold had decried in 1937; that empirical data missed the purpose of mission altogether. Nonetheless, the old tensions between maintenance versus expansion, and between quantity versus quality continued to be a source of discord between missionaries and administrators.

Not surprisingly, a special issue of *The Log* marketed the enterprise in terms of demonstrable growth and productivity when celebrating the Mission's thirty-fifth anniversary in June 1940. Between the twin portraits of *The Log*'s cover page—Antle in his doctoral gown at St. John's College, and Greene in blue skipper's uniform aboard ship—stood comparative statistics indicating the Mission's growth. 1905: one hospital, one hospital ship, one doctor, two nurses, one clergyman and one secretary-treasurer, making for a total staff of five. 1940: three hospitals, two hospital ships, one mission ship, five doctors, thirteen nurses, two clergymen, two school teachers, four office staff and twenty-two employed in hospitals and on ships, for a total staff of forty-six.

This largely pictorial survey of the Mission's history included greetings from constituents as a means of illustrating broadbased popular support. The Lieutenant Governor of BC, the Honourable Eric Hamber, recalled "the most excellent work carried on by the Columbia Coast Mission a great many years ago when I was connected with the Hastings Saw Mill's Lumber Operations at Rock Bay"; and the BC Loggers' Association expressed gratitude for "35 years of work of such sterling and humanitarian benefit," particularly as "the people employed in the camps and communities in the Coast logging industries have probably received more from the work of the Mission than the rest of the inhabitants" in the province. Representing the old timers, Ernest Halliday of Kingcome Inlet spoke of the lives saved by the Mission's hospital service, of the sense of community it engendered and of its "spirit of good fellowship and willingness to assist in every way." Former staff members and patients added their mite, and Greene reported on "the generous response of many friends" to a recent appeal for funds. In all, the anniversary edition was designed to show that the Mission had met its commitments in fundamental humanitarian aid, and was deserving of further support.

Having mailed copies to potential supporters across the country and abroad, Greene headed east in September 1940 for his fundraising lecture tour of Ontario. St. George's Hospital needed extensive refurbishing and upgrading, and operational expenses were not being met. Greene's departure virtually coincided with the arrival in Vancouver of the seventy-four-year-old Antle aboard his yawl *Reverie*. Dubbed "the West-Coast Grenfell" by the editor of an American magazine, Antle looked "as young as ever despite the trials and tribulations of such a long voyage." He recounted his exploits before service clubs and business organizations to gain support for the Mission. Marking the Mission's thirty-fifth anniversary and Antle's return to the coast, Dr. Darrell P. Hanington, one of his earliest physicians, underscored the Mission's vital role:

> To my mind, the Columbia Coast Mission is one of the best examples of a real Social Service. Combining as it does Medical aid with sympathy, personal contact and a religion which is always at hand, and yet unobtrusive, it has become an institution recognised throughout Canada as outstanding in its unique usefulness. It has been said that every great achievement is but the lengthened shadow of one man, and it must be a deep satisfaction to the "Skipper", who, in this, his latest jaunt, has literally steered between Scylla and Charybdis, to be "home from the Sea" in the waters which to him, are as familiar as the City Streets.

If statistics and personal testimonies formed one arm of public relations and fundraising, then what Greene invoked as "the truly picturesque" aspect of missionary work—"the pure colour and old-time romance" of encounters with exotic foreign cultures—formed another. Significantly, the appeal of neither one could compete successfully in the media with the cataclysmic events unfolding on the international stage.

The outbreak of the Second World War and the expanding national war effort now proved far more momentous than stories about a medical mission on the BC coast. War bonds, war savings stamps, and aluminum and clothing drives provided opportunities for citizens to involve themselves in the great moral and patriotic cause of defeating Germany. Indeed, parish fundraising itself was

The Long House at
Gwayasdums, Gilford
Island, 1940.

also challenged by demands to help England, the Mother Country,
in her time of need. Perhaps in an attempt to recapture public
attention, the Mission highlighted the exotic. Doubtless with this
in mind, Greene recounted "an unforgettable scene" from its ministry to the Native peoples at Christmas 1940:

> The *Columbia* came to anchor in the small harbour that
> circles around the Indian village of Gwayasdums, up on
> Gilford Island. All around us lay small gas boats at anchor
> and alongside a float that led to the shore, many more.

Indian dugout canoes, some of them quite recently carved out of great cedar logs, lay on the beach. A huge scow, with its store and clam-buying Indian manager, was anchored fore-and-aft off shore, and to it there came from time to time all kinds of Indian craft. The shore of the village had many small shacks scattered here and there, and then up above on a higher level there stood a medley of unkempt buildings, housing a number of families . . .

There was one huge old potlatch house, encased in split cedar shakes, with a great hole in the roof from which there poured smoke as it rose from a log fire built on the earthen floor in the centre . . .

Just one great gloomy interior with no windows. A platform runs round three sides of it . . . about a foot above the level of the earthen floor; families, with all their possessions gathered closely around them, sleep in groups . . . Almost filling the wall space at each end are enormous winged totems that seem to hover over the gaunt interior or its occupants. The enormous beams that support the roof and have been placed there by hand . . . run the full length of the building.

Here on a recent Sunday evening there gathered 150 Indians of both sexes and all ages. They squatted in one great enveloping square of blanketed humanity, ready to take part in a religious service. A quiet conversation goes on until the missionary begins, and then they pay serious attention. The older folk do not know English, but the younger do. So they sing the hymns in both English and Quaquala, and it makes a weird mumble of music and words. They stand for the prayers, and are very reverent. As the preacher . . . who led the worship, I stood behind a table covered with a white cloth, the smoke from the great fire occasionally drifting my way and cutting [my congregation] off from view . . . The singing rose to heaven in surges as they caught the strain of a more familiar hymn. A girls' choir of some eleven voices sang "Hark the Herald Angels Sing," and their sweet voices rose to the great roof overhead.

At the close of the service I asked them all to gather in a great circle around the fire as I led them in prayers. They are inherently loyal people, and followed earnestly the prayers for the King and all His Majesty's forces throughout the world.

Such scenes lent substance to the fascinating impression of what *The Canadian Churchman* in 1940 called "Thirty-five Years of Romantic Christian Service on the Pacific Coast." Greene and his supporters seem to have regarded faith and patriotism as the abiding qualities of the Native settlements they visited; at least, those were the twin pillars he wanted to establish within these communities. As would be seen later, his paternalistic and sometimes self-serving views diverged from that of his mentor Antle.

Some measure of the Mission's success in acculturation may be seen in the wedding of Charlie Dawson of Kingcome and Annie Flanders of Village Island on 24 March 1941, which was featured with text and photograph both in *The Log* and in the society's annual report. Timed to coincide with a dramatic event in the fishing season—the eulachon run in Kingcome Inlet—the wedding combined the practicalities of Native life with cultural adaptation to British custom. The eulachon, eight to ten-inch-long salt-water fish sometimes called candle-fish because of their high oil content, were a staple of the northwest Native fisheries. Teeming on the scene each spring to spawn in coastal rivers, the fish were caught by various methods and rendered down in vats. As the wedding feast—and the eulachon frenzy—approached, fishing boats and canoes began gathering in the estuary in ever-increasing numbers. Bringing members of the wedding party two days ahead of time, the *Columbia* itself arrived—with Alan Greene as officiating priest. Leaving the mission boat anchored at the head of the inlet on a brisk Sunday morning, the Mission's physician, Dr. Harvey Hamilton, headed upriver by outboard skiff. He recorded the extraordinary scene:

As we ascended the river, great flocks of sea gulls, attracted by the abundant food supply, wheeled and screeched overhead. Uncounted thousands of others

Mission house and totem pole at Kingcome, September 1936. Later named the "King George V Memorial Totem Pole," it was dedicated in 1938.

spread over the flats like fields of white tulips. Seals, sealions, eagles and other forms of bird and animal life had also gathered for the feast. Pity the poor eulachon; he gets caught no matter which way he turns.

Threading our way between numerous gas boats, dugout canoes, skiffs and row boats anchored in the river opposite the village, the Mission was reached and a hearty welcome, accompanied by hot tea and cakes, awaited us from Mrs. Massey and Miss Kirby, the resident missionaries.

Two services were held that day, the traditional Anglican 'elevenses'—matins at 11 a.m.—and a special afternoon service "in conformation with the proclamation by the King for a day of intercession for the guidance of the British Empire in the present crisis." Medical rounds with an interpreter, and pastoral visits, filled the afternoon.

The wedding the next day revealed little trace of the Native couple's cultural origins. Stepping from the Indian village into St. George's, packed with 250 guests, the bridal party reflected the

St. George's Church, Kingcome Inlet, built in 1938.

conventional white wedding of English tradition, even to the processional march from Wagner's *Lohengrin*. The reception in the mission hall featured a sit-down meal consisting of "a generous helping of vegetable and meat stew," a four-tiered wedding cake, and only then the traditional orations by Native leaders on the duties and responsibilities of marriage.

Greene frequently reflected on the changes wrought by both Mission work and the passage of time. In the summer of 1941, he especially pondered the passing of the old generation of pioneers who had come "into these parts forty, fifty and sixty years ago and formed the very backbone of the country." They included such colourful characters as Mike Manson, Fred and Charles Thulin, C.H. FitzGerald senior, known as "Pop-pop," and an unnamed character known only as "The White Frenchman." A new generation, one "far different in things material" had succeeded them with all the new necessities of modern technology: "radios, telephones, gasoline and diesel launches, motor cars"—even radar.

Ever the storyteller even in retirement years, Greene regaled his listeners with tales of the manly world before technology took over:

> You had to be a boatman and love it. I loved it! To me it wasn't any virtue in going to sea. I was thrilled that I had that kind of a job. I thought I was the luckiest man in the whole Anglican church. There wasn't anything like it! With my daily duties, there was an element of sport every day that I went to sea. Fighting the elements, fighting the tidal rapids, facing adventures with fog occasionally, bad weather. Occasionally piling up on reefs and rocks, never with any fatal results, but you never knew from one day to another what the adventures might be. And I was just hilariously happy in the job from beginning to end. And the tremendous contact with humanity, and the rugged types that one confronted and was confronted with, the logging fraternity, they're pretty forthright people. That was part of the ruggedness of the whole thing. You loved the directness of approach

and attack. If I got into a tough situation amongst men, it was just like a tough day at sea; it was good sport to see how you came out. And you left very humbly; you may have won a bit of ground, you may have lost. I never worried about it very much.

Yes, I'd study the chart right from beginning to end. I studied the charts every trip that I made. I never pretended that I knew those waters. We didn't have any radar and were all the better without it, because we had to develop an acute sense of distance and objects and echoes and whatnot. You were the radar yourself. In fog, you'd have a sharp, penetrating air whistle, and guess your distance from shore by the time taken to get an echo off the shore. If you were close to shore, it was very sharp and very quick, and you took the necessary precautions. We didn't do more navigation in fog than was necessary. There was nothing compelling you to go. It wasn't like the Union Steamship men who had to go under all conditions 'cause they had a schedule to carry out. Well, I could back away from a job if it wasn't too important, and say, "not today, thank you; wait till this fog lifts". But I've often been caught in heavy fog.

Greene seemed to nurture a nostalgia for the old lifestyle: "it is a treat to go far back into an inlet and find a man of the old school, living in his rather bare cabin on mighty little, and yet welcoming you as though he had everything to offer you that true hospitality calls for." Not that the new generation was less kindly, he hastened to add. Just the sense of loss that one's own lifestyle has had its day, and must give way to "a keener, younger crowd."

As much as anything else, it was perhaps the harsh realities of the present that moved Greene to look so nostalgically upon times past. Certainly, it must have been disheartening to maintain a medical service when a great many of the users refused to pay a cent—even when they could well afford to do so. Medical work at St. Michael's Hospital, Rock Bay, had increased, for example, and many logging camps—Ellingsen's, Flesher & Richardson, Miller

& Crawford, Smith & Osberg, and the Esperanza Logging Company among them—were signatories to the Mission's Hospital Contract Plan which solicited contributions of $1.25 a month as an early form of medical insurance. Despite this voluntary payroll-deduction plan, the hospital in 1940 ran at a loss of $3,500. It faced another deficit in 1941 if all eligible loggers did not join the scheme.

Greene put the case squarely in *The Log* of December 1941: "If the loggers and the operators are not prepared to support this hospital, it will have to be closed." Signs that the hospital might be superseded even sooner than expected appeared in the summer of 1941, when one of the logging companies chartered a float plane for an emergency medical run to Vancouver. Only eleven hours elapsed from the time of the accident on a mountain slope in Loughborough Inlet until the patient's arrival at Vancouver General Hospital. How different from the previous year, Greene remarked, "when a logger with similar injuries lay waiting for days on end in a rowboat in Johnstone Straits in the hope of intercepting a passing steamer." In a sense, the Mission's hospitals were too dependent on the sawmills' fortunes. For example, the Merrill, Ring & Wilson Company of Rock Bay had been the principal supporter of St. Michael's Hospital. When the company closed in the early summer of 1942, the demise of St. Michael's seemed certain. Yet the hospital remained open.

The Hospital Contract Plan is but one example of the ventures that gradually moved the Mission into a special kind of obsolescence. By integrating itself into the social processes of the secular world, the Mission necessarily subordinated its distinctive identity to the pastoral goals it had set for itself: church Service, rather than Church services; Social Gospel, rather than Christian doctrine. By openly engaging in the process of secularization, the Mission was nurturing the seeds of its own demise. Antle would have regarded it as the sound Biblical doctrine of becoming the leaven in the bread of pioneer life: the form of the Gospel's delivery would change, while its substance would remain. As Greene once put it, "it is this constant crossing of the sacred and secular that gives charm and interest to our work. In fact, so interwoven are the two, that one feels that everything is sacred, so closely linked is it with the spiritual motive underlying our work."

Meanwhile, staff was constantly changing. Dr. W.A. McTavish died suddenly on 8 January 1942, leaving the *Rendezvous* without a doctor. The skipper of the *John Antle*, Wally Smith, who had joined the ship as engineer in 1936, resigned to cast his lot with the war effort. Dr. T.R. Blades of St. Michael's Hospital, Rock Bay, and Dr. D.B. Ryall of St. George's Hospital, Alert Bay, took commissions in the Royal Canadian Air Force. Returned from specialist internship in the United States, Dr. Harvey Hamilton opted for service in the RCAF as well. Dr. Keith Wray-Johnston, for several years the resident doctor successively at St. Michael's, and at St. Mary's at Pender Harbour, was serving with the Royal Canadian Army Medical Corps. These staff losses strained the operations of the Mission and tied up mission boats for weeks on end, sometimes months.

The Log frequently published human interest stories about mission people in military service. Some accounts, like that of Derek Lukin Johnston, a young lieutenant in the Royal Canadian Navy Volunteer Reserve who had served the mission as a summer student, were success stories. In a narrative entitled "From Mission Ship to Mine-Sweeper" Greene described Johnston's sea-change and assured readers that his former protege "will maintain to the full the ideal of fine British service that his father and mother instilled into him." This seemed a self-fulfilling prophecy when a subsequent story recounted how Johnston's ship, HMS *Harvester*, rammed a German submarine and picked up German survivors. But it too was soon sunk by another U-boat, which in turn was rammed by the merchant vessel *Aconite* which the *Harvester* had been helping to convoy. Such a string of seemingly fortuitous events portrayed war as something of an adventure.

Other stories, by contrast, cast combat in a more somber light. When Flying Officer "Hobb" Marlatt, the son of Dr. and Mrs. Marlatt formerly on staff at the Vananda hospital, was lost in action over Germany, *The Log's* lean announcement scarcely intimated the pain felt throughout the Mission community. For Greene, the sorrow must have been acute. He had christened the young man when a babe in arms, and had presided at his wedding just two years earlier. A distant war was casting its shadow on the peaceful Mission community. At the same time, it was also strengthening existing bonds. *The Log*'s announcement of the death of Flying Officer Robert Pringle in action overseas reminded readers that the Mission's community and purpose surpassed sectarian boundaries. His parents, the Reverend George and Mrs. Pringle—"associates of ours in the United Church Marine Mission," as Greene expressed it—had for years dedicated their lives to mission work. Greene's tribute to the son occasioned an accolade to his parents from "many old friends up-coast who have everywhere expressed to us their real sorrow in the loss of this young man, both because of his great promise as an ordained minister of the United Church and of his being the son of parents who made a rich contribution to up-coast life for some number of years." Other signs of the times suggested that war could come even closer to home. Readers of *The Log* must have suspected as much when reading in the spring of 1943 that gas masks and other equipment of the civilian Air Raid Patrol had been issued to the Native settlement of Kingcome.

The Mission reached a major turning point in January 1943 with the arrival of Alan Greene's older brother, Heber, as the new chaplain of the *Columbia*. He would not retire until 1958. In his own inimitable way, the Reverend Heber Greene, or "Landlubber" as he called himself in articles written for *The Log*, became a legend along the coast. As a fellow missionary, the Reverend Eric Powell, recalled over forty-five years later:

> . . . he was a great man. Out of the three "rocks" of the CCM . . . Heber was probably the most gentle and beloved . . . Alan and Antle were both rogues in their own style. They had to fund the Mission; they had to cajole the people [into giving money]; they had to keep the mission financially afloat, so it meant a great deal of travelling [outside the mission area and BC]. Heber on the other hand, was the one star of the Mission which was always in the shadow of his brother, who was the superintendent . . . Heber was loved by everyone on

Visit to Columbia of Earl and Countess of Athlone on 2 May 1943. (l. to r.)
Governor General, captain George MacDonald, Harold Auchinleck (shaking
hands) and Reverend Alan Greene. "Auchie" Auchinleck was ship's cook and a
long-time servant of the CCM. He was the cousin of Lt. Gen. Sir Claude
Auchinleck, commander of British troops in the Near East until late 1942.

the coast. He was probably the most untidy priest I have
ever met—although I've met many in my travels around
the world. There was no real protocol.

Heber was quite the antithesis of John Antle and Alan Greene.
Eccentric and ingenuous to a fault, he was a trusting lamb in the
service of his great Shepherd. For him, the hospital ship was
everybody's parish church; her commodious cabin had on occasion
housed congregations of forty-five people. Yet he was never averse
to leaving the *Columbia* to her medical rounds and taking Union
Steamships—the *Cardena* or *Catala*—to some settlement for Sunday
School and services. A rambler at heart, he thought nothing of
hopping a converted landing barge in order to reach a distant

camp, or paddling for hours without plan up an inlet in the hope of finding someone in need of human contact. As his military metaphor explained, doing a "recce"—checking out the territory—remained a primary task. Stories abound of his simply disappearing into the bush for weeks at a time on his pastoral calls, only to reappear with a gentle smile as though he had been gone only a couple of hours. Put ashore by the mission boat with a promise to await pickup at a specific location, he might end up somewhere else altogether, either by hitching a ride or by boarding a regular Union Steamships run. He shifted as he believed the Spirit moved him. Had he chosen a motto for his ministry, it might well have been Jesus' words to his parents when they lost him in a crowd and found him teaching in a temple: "Know ye not that I must be about my father's business?"

Despite his unworldliness—even other-worldliness, as a family member recently recalled—Heber Greene had not lived a cloistered life prior to joining the Mission. Ordained among the Haidas in Masset he served as army chaplain in France during the Great War (while his wife worked in a munitions plant in England), then variously as missionary priest in the Queen Charlottes, at Stewart, Smithers and Squamish, as well as in the parishes of Mission and Agassiz. Now, under his younger brother's direction, he was made responsible for the northern section of the Mission's patrol zone, while Alan made himself personally responsible for the southern section, based in Pender Harbour.

Writing in *The Log* in the spring of 1943, Heber reflected a wondrous delight in all he experienced aboard ship. Though historically imprecise, he saw himself as launching a "voyage of discovery, pretty much along the course of the great navigator and explorer Captain Vancouver in his search of the much sought northwest passage." Fascinated by BC place names on nautical charts—"haunted by the ghosts of admirals great, captains famous, and lieutenants faithful in the naval battles of Britain in the days of yore"—Heber saw himself on a romantic foray into untamed territory. As a priest in what he called the Church Militant—a preaching, converting church—he made no excuse for resorting to "military metaphor" when describing his plan of attack: reconnoiter, forage, make contact and (though he never used the term) project power. Calling himself variously a "landlubber afloat," and a "chameleon" who merges into his background, Heber saw the operative principle of his ministry as networking: "this pet idea of mine, that all our church work is like a network system—one thing leads to another in surprising ways at times." Always stressing in his plan of action "individual contacts rather than [church] services," he visited 175 different families between Rock Bay and Alert Bay in the month of January 1943 alone. "It all proves that the law of the physical universe, the Conservation of Energy, is equally applicable in the moral and spiritual world," Heber wrote in the spring of 1944. "No good effort is ever lost in the long run." Having thus set the pace for his roving commission, he journeyed by whatever means available: backpacking on foot, island-hopping by RCAF crashboat, snatching a lift with fishermen or coastal passenger-freighter or even, when they could find him, by mission boat. Occasionally he travelled ecumenically by hopping rides on the United Church's ship *Thomas Crosby*.

Within a year, however, his work was severely curtailed by financial shortfalls and lack of manpower. "The exigencies of war," as Heber expressed it, had forced him ashore and the *Columbia* alongside as stand-by for emergencies only. Cast back upon the Union Steamships and the goodwill of passing seafarers, Heber found Canada's war effort was simply drawing too much talent away. "Well do I recall the summer and fall of 1917 at a base hospital in France. There we had 25 doctors and 125 nurses for a 2,000-bed hospital which was hardly ever full up." Now based in Alert Bay and serving "roughly 1,000 loggers and some 500 Indians with only one doctor," he had to accept the Armed Forces' priorities, though he found them "disproportionate in the matter of doctors." So strapped was the Mission for medical support that it found itself occasionally calling on the assistance of the medical officer stationed with the Canadian Army Medical Corps on the tiny outpost of Yorke Island. Located about three miles north-northwest of Kelsey Bay at the junction of Johnstone Strait and Sunderland Channel, the island's gun battery—with two 4.7-inch guns and medical staff—was supposed to defend the approaches to Discovery Passage against southbound Japanese surface forces.

Working sporadically throughout the war years, mission boats carried on the countless tasks of spiritual mission. Their navigation logs provide little insight into their accomplishments. The log of the *Rendezvous* for the period November 1941 to August 1944, for example, is a scrawly, sketchy book with huge gaps in chronology. Spotty at best, it permits scarcely a glimmer of mission work: "Body of Landers aboard. Funeral—Whaletown" (November 1941); "SE Gale and How!" (December 1941); "Sunday School picnic, 14 children, 4 adults" (28 August 1942); "Stopped five minutes for committal of ashes of the late Ada Mary Power of the Japanese Mission—Vancouver" (14 Feb 1944). It is not clear precisely where *Rendezvous* had stopped for the brief ceremony; the log's notations suggest it could have been anywhere between White Islets (west of Roberts Creek) and Lion's Gate Bridge.

Occasionally, however, one can at least detect attitudes in the skimpy log entries. Thus Alan Greene noted on 22 October 1942, "took Jap woman and baby to their camp next bay up coast"; and later that day, not knowing precisely where he had let them off, "?camp: put Jap ashore." Though he always mentioned Caucasians by name—deferentially with the honorific "Mrs." in the case of married women—he mentioned "Japs," "Chinamen" and "Indians" only by race. He only gave Indians' names if they were chiefs. This was common practice outside the Mission as well, where cultural and racial assumptions about British superiority prevailed. It was no different, for example, in Allied war records of the day covering ships sunk at sea, where reporting officers were content to list white survivors by name and rank, but other, presumably lesser, mortals by number according to race: Captain John Smith and five Chinese. This racial bias was not considered something that had to be kept under wraps; it was simply the way the dominant culture thought. Even when publishing in *The Log*, Greene resorted to racial stereotypes in a matter-of-fact and unself-conscious way. Once, for example, he recounted the story of "a Chinaman" who had drowned and whose body someone had left in a freight shed pending the arrival of the police, who found $700 in the deceased's pocket. The whole point of the anecdote was whimsical speculation on what a haul the first finder would have made if only he had checked the dead man's pockets before the police arrived. *The Log* offers us no sense of the tragedy of this man, no reflection on his hopes and dreams and no interest whatsoever in his identity as a person.

Meanwhile, Alan Greene had been developing plans for retirement homes for senior citizens as John Antle had once envisioned. These were the Aged Folks' Guest Houses at Pender Harbour. His "adventure in Christian Social Service," as he called it, was intended to provide housing for otherwise indigent elderly pioneers who found themselves without resources of their own. By the spring of 1944, Greene had managed to solicit $1,000 for his project from the Missionary Society of the Church of England in Canada, and a further $5,000 from private sources. With another $6,000, according to an announcement in *The Log*, he hoped to begin to lay the foundations. The idea appealed to supporters across the country. One couple financed a complete cottage as a memorial to their son killed in action overseas. By early summer, Greene had bought waterfront property with two cabins on it in Garden Bay, near St. Mary's Hospital, and had begun renovating. This new enterprise offered the elderly independence from institutional care as well as views over Pender Harbour toward Texada Island. For Greene, it represented a departure from the conventional pattern of accommodating the aged:

> A home, not an institution crowded with those to whom no shelter is possible save that they must perforce share with a great crowd of elderly folk. A little cottage, beautiful in its setting, and adequate in its interior and layout for all their needs. $250 to $300 should build these little single-roomed cottages with a simple plan which gives an aged person everything they need within the compass of a room fourteen by twenty feet.

Greene offered one of the homes to John Antle. Antle replied in September 1944 that for the past year he had "been looking for a place where I could build a small shack where I could hole up in the winter time as I am finding the winters rather damp onboard

Dr. W.R.
Simpson sutures
a logger's head
on board John
Antle, 1942.

a boat . . . and money is a bit scarce for shack-building." In the event, Antle continued to enjoy his live-aboard.

Greene's achievement in raising funds for an entirely new project is all the more impressive in the light of his annual report for 1944, which showed revenues of some $87,000 and expenditures of some $97,000. By year's end, the board had managed to make up the deficit by securing a special $5,000 grant from the provincial government, and an equal amount from the Missionary Society of the Church of England in Canada. Provincial government interest was contingent upon the Mission's providing medical services as a public benefit. Yet the records were already beginning to indicated diminished needs, or at least diminished ability to meet those needs. Difficulty in obtaining sufficient medical personnel in these years may have been a cause rather than a symptom of a smaller

Open air service at Doriston, Sechelt Inlet, in 1941, with Reverend Alan Greene and student missionary Roland Hill officiating. John Antle at anchor in background.

case load. The hospital ship *Columbia* reported an increase in patients: from 637 in 1943 to 921 in 1944. But these patient counts included those who had attended for little more than public health vaccinations. In purely church terms, the three ships—*Columbia, John Antle,* and *Rendezvous*—reported combined totals of fifteen baptisms, five burials, four marriages and three confirmations. On the basis of statistical arguments alone, Greene would have found it difficult to justify his operations.

By this time, too, the airplane was beginning to exert pressure on the Mission. Throughout the 1940s, Alan Greene observed the readiness of logging companies to charter float planes to rush serious medical cases to Vancouver, or even to bring in a Vancouver medical specialist to operate in the hospital at Rock Bay. Yet Greene regarded it as "no reflection [on the Mission's medical skills] whatever to send these men to hospital." Far more important was the fact that the Mission had tended them "through the first period of shock, and those hours where life hangs in the balance." Where outsiders might have regarded the Mission's hospitals as merely staging posts or first-aid holding stations for medical evacuation of critical cases, insiders saw them differently. The established mission hospitals at Alert Bay and Rock Bay responded to a deeper need of on-site community care and long-term ministration. Certainly, that was Alan Greene's position. By 1944, he was actually contemplating turning the building at Rock Bay into a home for "aged folk who will be sent to us through Government channels and for whom a reasonable cash payment will be made." This, however, would merely have been a stop-gap. "We know our limitations in any of our up-coast hospitals, and again and again have sent these [injured] men through on seaplanes to Vancouver where the city hospitals have everything that modern medical science can offer in the fight for a man's life." Yet the role of medical mission involved continued presence, first aid and evaluation. Mission hospitals alone offered the means for that special kind of pastoral care, as proclaimed by John Antle's Biblical motto: "Heal the sick and say unto them, the Kingdom of God is come nigh unto you."

It must have become clear to Alan Greene that new technology and communications were threatening the form in which the Columbia Coast Mission was delivering pastoral and medical care. As though to fend off complaints of the Mission's perceived inadequacies, he wrote in *The Log*, "the loggers should be mighty grateful that there are hospitals such as ours nearby where the essential first treatments are available." Whether such potential contributors were grateful or not, there were certainly skeptics among them when it came to actual financial support. Despite Greene's earnest appeals for help, St. Michael's Hospital at Rock Bay closed permanently on 4 December 1945. Closure was caused by the diminishing amount of its medical and surgical work, and by a decision of the budget committee of the Community Chest of Greater Vancouver (a forerunner of United Way) to withdraw financial support. This left the Mission with an annual loss of $6,000 for which there was no provision. Despite petitions circulated among the population of over 1,000 souls living in the

Mission district affected by the closure, forty years of medical work on the site came to a quiet end.

Working behind the scenes, and leaving scarcely any paper trail of his enterprise, Greene was experiencing serious problems with the board about finances by the spring and summer of 1944. Judging by what little remains of his exchange with John Antle on the subject, it appears the stumbling block to the Mission's success lay in the vested authorities of the church establishment. They apparently preferred investing in mortar than in mission. Never fond of the titles and higher stations that others might hold, Antle was quick to target the institutional church as the chief obstacle to Christian mission and outreach. He had always seen things that way. Writing from Maple Bay on 4 September 1944, he cautioned Greene on his old theme:

> Regarding Bishops, you must not expect too much of them as they usually get to their elevated position by a judicious use of what is vulgarly known as the "bean" [self-interested cunning], and by the time that end is accomplished, they have acquired certain habits of mind that their approach to any question is bound to be devious. One would imagine that such action from the chief shepherds of the flock would wreck the fold that we call the church. But we musn't forget that the Lord is interested in that institution, and as long as it is of some use in His plan of world development the church will live in spite of the incompetence of the Chief Shepherds. True, the Lord has scrapped a church before and may do again when it ceases to be useful.

Yet even as the Mission struggled in some areas against growing indifference, other ventures gave cause for hope. In 1944 Alan Greene had recruited the Reverend Rollo Boas while on a fundraising trip to Montreal. On reaching the coast, Boas had been assigned to the *Rendezvous* based in Whaletown on Cortes Island. Encouraged by having added two ordained missionaries to his staff within the last year and half—his brother Heber and Boas—Greene anticipated expansion of the Mission with greater equanimity.

Embracing modernity in early summer 1944, he commissioned the Vancouver firm of Spilsbury and Hepburn to install a radio- telephone in the *Columbia*. The ship had previously been limited to radio contact with government stations; now, as Greene wrote, the new technology enabled her to communicate directly "with logging camps, canneries and other vessels, and our head office in Vancouver, at all hours of the day or night." In a period of tight finances with no substantial capital reserve, he rationalized "the heavy expense" as a means for saving life and easing "prolonged suffering in far-away places." As expensive as the new technology was, such upgrading had to be undertaken if the organization was to remain in the mission business. Perhaps as much to meet the exigencies of wartime communications as those of logging and commerce, a new road had been pushed through on Vancouver Island, linking Campbell River and Sayward with twice-weekly bus connections. As "Landlubber" Heber Greene observed in *The Log*, "you can now leave Sayward at 5:30 a.m. and be in Vancouver via Nanaimo by 6 p.m. the same day." It was clear that times were changing and that the Mission had to adapt to the new world on which it hoped to exert influence.

The closing months of the war saw Greene raising funds to replace the *John Antle* (ex-*Florida V*). Refits and upgradings had only temporarily cured what Greene had whimsically called her "rheumatoid arthritis condition in the main bearings." She was getting far too expensive to maintain. Laid up in the spring of 1944 for lack of crew, she may in any event have been unable to continue "functioning with a cheerful grace." Greene appealed to local yachtsmen for the loan of a small replacement launch if he could not man the *Antle* by winter. In August 1945, he announced the acquisition of a thirty-six-foot former RCAF boat as the third *John Antle*. Three benefactors made the new ship possible: the British Columbia and Yukon Church Aid Society in England, the source of the major donation for the original vessel; BC Packers, who cancelled an outstanding $1,500 mortgage on her; and an anonymous donor who responded to Greene's appeal in the *The Log* by sending a draft for $3,000. Altogether, Greene scrounged $8,000 for his new ship, which underwent sea trials on 6 October 1945. Such generosity encouraged his view that statistics alone were not the decisive argument in supporting the role of the Mission. Something far more profound was at work. All his ships, "from the *Columbia* down to the *Gwa-yee*," had integrated themselves into coastal life and been part of personal rites of passage as diverse as baptism, marriage and death. They were the medium for a message such "as the Church with all her understanding of such moments gives of her rich store of comfort and hope." The words were Alan Greene's but the concept was Heber's networking at its best. If the previous forty years revealed "fellowship with thousands in their joys and sorrows," the future promised "endless duties confronting all of us in the days to come."

CHAPTER 5

Rendezvous Patrols

"I F YOU CAN ASSURE ME YOU CAN get along with the gas engine, [then] you can soon learn about the sea, about boating, and the coast." With these words Alan Greene ended the interview with his most recent recruit, the Reverend Rollo Boas, and began a mission based in Whaletown, Cortes Island, which lasted from 1944 to 1954. As skipper of the *Rendezvous*, Boas covered a patrol area of thirty settlements, in time establishing a medical and dental clinic, and building a church. It was an entirely new life in which he and his wife Kay, a registered nurse, with their two daughters Louise and Yvonne, ventured across unexplored frontiers of faith. After a short briefing in the Mission office in the old Vancouver Province Building in June 1944, the Boas family departed by ship for Whaletown where they landed at 6 a.m. and were met by Alan Greene in the *Rendezvous*. Greene initiated Boas to his captaincy just as Antle had done to Greene in 1911: he admonished him to become a good seaman, set him loose onto unknown seas with scarcely a blessing and urged him to "read your tide book as often as your Bible."

Boas's published sketches in *The Log* reveal his first impressions. Having entered this unfamiliar nautical world with its own language and lore, he had to learn the ways of the fishermen with their "humps," "live-boxes," "gurdies," and "springs," and those of the loggers with their "whistlers," "widow-makers," "pike-poles," and "cats." He scarcely could have anticipated a more challenging

The Reverend Rollo and Mrs. Kay Boas with daughters Louise and Yvonne and friends, ca. 1950.

world. Like Greene and others before him, he learned what a boat actually meant, particularly when it needed serious attention:

> I am more than surprised at the way in which this boat has crept into my affections. She is in my thoughts day and night. "Is she safe?" "Will this make her more presentable?" "Is she ready for any emergency?" "What about gas, oil, water?" "Is the bilge pumped out?" And scores of other thoughts continually ply my mind. And, somehow, along with all these thoughts has come a man's love for his boat. It is not only a matter of possession and worth, but it has become a precious means at my disposal with which to carry on the mission Christ has given me . . . Only today do I realize my helplessness without my boat, because I am tied up to the float . . . waiting for repairs.

The *Rendezvous* patrol turned out to be a family affair. Kay and the children accompanied Rollo as often as they could. Greene never liked the idea of having women aboard and tried to dissuade Kay from going along. His attitude endured even later, when female physicians joined the Mission. Only when Boas insisted that either his wife accompany him, or he himself would not go, did Greene accede. The Boas family travelled together for five years, with the children continuing their schooling by correspondence. This arrangement proved to be a wise decision. A family ministry offered special opportunities among coastal communities.

As the Boas family settled into their work of pastoral and medical calls, a rough pattern emerged that enabled them to visit each district approximately once a month. Each week the *Rendezvous* took a different route. Week one: east side of Cortes Island, up toward Desolation Sound, Bliss Landing, Squirrel Cove, Refuge Cove, Teakerne Arm and Toba Inlet. Week two: Whaletown, Mansons Landing and Read Island. Week three: Surge Narrows, Owen Bay, Granite Bay and Rock Bay. Week four: Yuculta Rapids, Bute Inlet, Redonda Bay and Stuart Island. Consistent with Mission practice, Boas was left on his own, with no real accountability to head office except for the irksome requirement to render statistical reports on such matters as baptisms, marriages and religious services performed. To Boas's mind, such bookkeeping was not what the Mission was about. "I might be in a bay all day and only see two persons," he once recalled with amused irritation at anyone who would presume to quantify the value of such a visit.

As with other mission ships, the logbooks for the Boas period offer no narratives of his journeys. Jottings form the bare-bones substance: points of navigation, persons carried, arrival and departure times, ports of call, mechanical breakdowns and repairs, patients carried and their ailments. While often interspersed with notations about pastoral visits and discussion groups, about ferrying school children and ladies from the Women's Auxiliary, or the Legion picnic, the record remains decidedly thin. The log entries reveal virtually nothing of the life, or reflections, experienced throughout the often arduous journeys. These must be read between the lines of cryptic comments on wind, weather and currents, from running times between points, or the comments about sick patients. The entry "Beginning of clinic Mar 8/46" affords no insight into the

Rectory and clinic at Whaletown, Cortes Island. The expanded clinic, shown here, was officially opened on 8 November 1951.

importance of the clinic for the communities; nor does it offer any glimpse into how Boas recruited specialist help when needed. In the event, he had met Dr. Bathurst Hall during a stopover in Campbell River. Hall was a churchman and former *Columbia* surgeon with a medical practice in the town. Invited to help set up a clinic in Whaletown, Hall agreed to travel via Quathiaski Cove on the second Friday of each month. As Boas later recalled, "we set up a consulting room and an examining room in two bedrooms in the mission house, and then three months after that the first dentist, Dr. Oscar Rose, set up shop in the third bedroom" with his portable chair and treadle-operated drill.

Boas revealed a strong feeling for history and tradition. His logs record in pencil the dates of state occasions (King's Birthday, Armistice Day) and church feasts. These were reminders of cultural associations from whose pomp and pageantry he must have felt isolated in the extreme. Similar sporadic entries buoyed the channels of the Mission's own history: "Oct 25/45, Skipper Antle's 80th Birthday, 40th anniversary of opening of Rock Bay Hospital"; "Feb 11, 47, 20th Anniversary of St James Manson's [Landing]—53 [at church], 75 [at reception in] hall." Cryptic entries barely hint at the significance of human encounters. The pencilled comment "1 Sept 48 Skipper Antle and the *Reverie*" virtually masks his chance meeting with the Mission's founder while on patrol. (Antle had just completed another major voyage, through the Panama Canal to the West Indies and back.) Mission history is the poorer for having no record of the conversations of these two men of faith and action. Other entries raise more questions than answers. One wonders what lay behind the entry "Public Health Nurse arrives at Heriot Bay," with the implication that government services were now moving into Mission territory. And what story might lie behind the entry: "3 Nov 48 Mrs Boas emergency call, logger hurt"? Like so much Mission history, tantalizing sparks of evidence die just as soon as they are struck. Sometimes, however, log entries do reveal the sort of pioneering missionaries Rollo and Kay Boas actually were. Their preparations to build a proper medical clinic at the mission house in June 1949 are a case in point. Returning from the Klahoose Timber Company in Bute Inlet under "heavy westerly [with] 10 cedar logs in tow for clinic," they eventually sought shelter. "Storm bound," the entry reads. Once arrived in Whaletown—"The outboard brought me back!"— they began another phase: "sawed lumber," "loaded lumber," "dig clinic well." That month Boas summarized in the log the "work" he had done: "1021 miles run, 83 calls made, two child baptisms, evensong and matins said once each, Holy Communion." Skeletal details indeed for a couple physically involved in building their own vision of mission.

Central to the ministry of Rollo and Kay Boas was the ability to take advantage of situations as they arose. In November 1948, for example, they encountered a naval flotilla consisting of the American submarine USS *Baya*, the minesweeper HMCS *Rockcliffe*, the hydrographic ship *Ehkolip* and the survey vessel *Cedarwood*. At first glance, the event seems no more noteworthy than the occasional deadhead Boas would note in his log. Yet external evidence suggests he saw here an opportunity for evangelism. Indeed, the entry written a few days later at anchor in Nodales Channel reveals a Sunday morning "Service aboard HMCS *Rockcliffe*, 45 present." One searches in vain for some record to indicate how the service came to take place and what human contact was established. Ashore too, Boas would cobble together a church atmosphere, shaping a liturgy according to the inspiration of the moment for people who did not necessarily have any Anglican background, but who had expressed to him a need for some spiritual focal point in their lives:

> And you'd go up there early . . . and clean up the school or the hall . . . try to set up an altar . . . I always felt that the semblance of an altar—with a fair linen cloth on it, and a cross that I carried around with me on the boat and a couple of candlesticks and flowers—enabled people to feel . . . part of a congregation, part of a family. [These were] the outward and visible signs. Then I always wore a cassock and surplice . . . No organist, no piano, so [we'd] sing what people knew—numerous times the music consisted of "Onward, Christian Soldiers," or "Abide With Me" simply because people knew them, if only in fragmented form.

Like other padre-skippers, Boas was adept at impromptu civic ceremonies as well. Catching sight of people hanging about on the wharf of Refuge Cove, Desolation Sound, on the Remembrance Day holiday, he called out:

> Isn't there anybody going to say "let us sing 'O God our Help in Ages Past' or 'God Save the King'?" . . . So we stood there and I put my wooden cross on the top of a gas barrel and we sang [those songs]; of course I carried around little hymn books with me . . . [and] I gave a talk and a prayer. Alan Greene and his brother Heber were very apt at that.

The only time in the Boases' ten-year ministry that Rendezvous *"discovered" a rock. She lies here in Coulter Bay, 1953.*

Such small, spontaneous gatherings were common to the missionaries' cause. Yet, within the broader context of the Mission, services of whatever kind were generally very low on the list of priorities. John Antle's guiding principle of "service before services" continued to inform the essence of CCM ministry.

By spring of 1947 the Aged Folks' Guest Houses in Pender Harbour were housing ten retirees, and Alan Greene was trying to raise $10,000 to purchase more waterfront property next to his present holdings. He planned on building more cottages and a central apartment with common dining room and lounge. He saw the guest homes as playing a unique role. On the death of one of the residents, eighty-two-year-old Edwin Goodall, Greene used the occasion to promote his concept and to highlight the pioneer spirit which continued to animate the community. Goodall and his wife had spent twenty-seven years in northern British Columbia. Despite his years, the old man had taken over the daily chores that other retirees could no longer handle: splitting wood, filling wood boxes and oil tanks, even investing in a small boat to fetch the community's supplies. His was an example of the fortitude and service the Mission always revered.

If the Aged Folks' Guest Houses projected stability, other factors hinted at radical change. In presenting the 42nd Annual Report of the Columbia Coast Mission covering the year 1947, Greene took stock of two trends in mission operations: reduction in medical services and demographic shifts. St. Michael's Hospital had served the Rock Bay area from 1905 until it closed for lack of business in 1945; St. George's Hospital had operated in the Alert Bay area from 1909 until 1946, when the building was leased to the St. George's Hospital Society with a mandate to serve the same constituents. Greene's report admitted that St. George's was now "giving bigger and better service today than it did under our regime, because of stronger financial backing and the presence of additional doctors in Alert Bay." Whaletown's monthly medical clinic was still operating out of the vicarage, but it too was drawing on secular help: the provincial government recently had contributed $1,000 towards erecting an outpatient clinic, and had expressed interest in engaging a full-time nurse. This left but one hospital as the Mission's sole institutional base, St. Mary's at Pender Harbour, located within fifty miles of Vancouver.

If St. Mary's Hospital was going to survive, it needed upgrading to include a new staff residence and the acquisition of new equipment. Local initiatives raised the money: $5,000 from the provincial government, $3,000 from the Mission, $2,000 from BC Forest Products, which had two large logging camps in Jervis Inlet, and $8,000 from the local hospital society. Although the new residence officially opened in August 1948, it was already too late. Greene did not confess as much, but the Mission's medical services were being backed against a wall, as much by the war years, as by a function of the changing economy and expansion of government services.

While noting in his report "a very definite reduction in medical work" because of mission hospital closures, Greene highlighted "the development of our work along the lines of Social Service and Evangelism." He appended a statistical summary—omitting entirely any reference to medical issues like numbers of patients treated or surgical interventions. In 1947, mission ships had steamed over 23,000 miles: *Columbia* (11,979), *Rendezvous* (5,361), *John Antle* (4,696), and *Gwa-yee* (1,000). Serving a population of 8,200, the missionaries had performed eighty baptisms (attended by 452 people), nine marriages (attended by 235 people), eleven burials (attended by 716 people), and 191 services of Morning and Evening Prayer (attended by 3,246). Seventy-seven services of Holy Communion had received 440 communicants. Significantly, this church activity had attracted only $1,700.14 to the collection plate. Without the support of the provincial government, the Missionary Society of the Church of England in Canada, and medical earnings through patient fees (which accounted for the major portion of income), the Mission could not have survived as a viable business proposition.

Although Alan Greene claimed in the 1947 annual report that both he and his brother Heber were finding the work of evangelism "most challenging and distinctly interesting," he left little doubt that its character had radically changed. To be sure, he reported there had been an increase in church services, and that home visiting remained "worth while." But the changing social context of logging operations had, in large measure, supplanted the socializing features of mission ship visits. Big logging camps, for example, were supporting community living and family life by providing "substantial attractive dwellings, recreation halls and playgrounds." He might also have added that they were also prepared to use aircraft for medical evacuation. Greene's signal to the board recorded the changes and tried to reconcile them to Mission outreach:

> The days of the old bunk-house with its double-decker bunks and the huge stove over which there hung heavy masses of sweaty clothing to dry, are gone forever. We admit that we find it impossible to really touch the hearts and minds of most of the logging fraternity as they are constantly moving from camp to camp, but we do feel that the Church is slowly regaining a footing among the key men in the logging camps, and in the family life . . . And there is a great field for personal evangelism with the isolated men who eventually respond to the friendly visits of the itinerant parson.

Columbia *aground in Warner Bay, Seymour Inlet, 4 March 1948, with an amphibious Grumman Goose supplying aid.*

One senses here a certain ambivalence. On the one hand, Greene argued that evangelism was difficult because of shifting populations of loggers; on the other hand he insisted that it was no less difficult among large stable populations in major camps with community facilities. Greene still maintained that the Mission must continue to serve human needs. Yet, if the church were indeed "slowly regaining a footing among key men," as he claimed, he nowhere explained what this actually meant.

On 4 March 1948, the *Columbia* struck fast on a reef in Warner Bay, where she hung on her side for six days before a Vancouver Salvage Company tug pulled her free and towed her to Vancouver for expensive repairs to both hull and keel. As a sign of the times, a Grumman Goose amphibious aircraft flew to her immediate relief from Vancouver, carrying a salvage expert and emergency pumps in case she threatened to sink. This was the vessel's first major accident in thirty-eight years of service. Despite the setback, the *Columbia* ran 185 ports of call that year, the majority of them floating log camps consisting of floating homes, some bunkhouses, cookhouses, and in one case a floating playground. Thus a whole mobile village would be shackled together and secured to the shore by "stiff-legs" and cables. These itinerant communities were even more ephemeral than the camps built on shore. Picturesque in their utilitarian, ramshackle simplicity, they followed the logging operations up and down the coast and made it possible for loggers to have their families with them. When the time came to move along to the next base of operations, the floating habitations left scarcely a ripple as they hauled in their cables and took slowly to sea. Eventually, new growth covered the logging site and all trace of lives shaped by grinding hard work and isolation disappeared.

Between the summer of 1948 and the winter of 1950, Rollo Boas produced "The Sea Padre's Column" for *The Campbell River Courier*, whose masthead motto proclaimed the newspaper as "dedicated to the progress of Vancouver Island's rich northern fishing, logging, resort and hydro-electric power areas." The motto articulated the newspaper's mandate of incorporating into its communications network such outlying settlements as Heriot Bay, Mansons Landing, Whaletown, Owen Bay and Stuart Island. Blessed with the *Courier's* full support, Boas scarcely could have wished for a better medium for his message. As the paper announced on 7 July 1948, Boas's column "would seek to further bind together this growing community of Campbell River with the many ports of call in this great 'Inside Passage' as they touch the life and work of this little mission ship," *Rendezvous*. Turning out an easy journalistic style, Boas wrote a folksy, down-to-earth, almost entirely secularized commentary on coastal life. Ironically, the newspaper editor seems to have been a more forceful exponent of the Mission's importance and purpose than was the missionary himself. As the newspaper put it:

The regular link between Campbell River and these various points can rightly be claimed by the Columbia Coast

Mission boat, the M.S. *Rendezvous* [which throughout the year] comes in and out of Campbell River bringing patients to the hospital; and the hundred and one other errands of mercy and good will that typifies her task to this up-coast area. Her skipper and Padre, the Reverend Rollo M. Boas with his wife [Kay] and two children find themselves all over this area seeking to bring to communities . . . the message and administrations of the Christian church.

Following the pattern of the Columbia Coast Mission, in her 43-year service to this part of the coast, this mission ship does not confine herself merely to "preach the gospel," but she seeks to enact the fact, in word and deed, that the God she would serve, is interested in the body, mind and spirit of the men and women to whom she comes.

This was about as far as the Mission itself ever went in proclaiming any theological program. And, indeed, settlers long remembered the services rendered by the missionaries and their ships; rarely, if ever, any sermon or statement of doctrine. However, one consequence of the Mission's "service, not services" approach was a tendency to let itself be absorbed by the needs of the secular society, to the point where the Mission's seaborne ministrations were superseded by the constituency it served.

We see this process of gradual secularization reflected in "The Sea Padre's Column." Boas's columns ranged from coastal geography, to correspondence schooling for isolated children, to a hitchhiker's guide to island hopping, to commentaries on tides and currents. He discussed the islanders' reading habits, their social events and their difficulties in buying food and supplies; he explained the basics of boat and hull care, haulouts, and various methods of fishing and logging. In his dual role of columnist and padre-skipper, Boas saw himself as an intermediary between the boom town of Campbell River, with all its supposedly "big city" amenities, and the isolated settlements of the upcoast mission patrol area. As Boas reminded his readers in September 1948, "within a couple of hours steaming from Campbell River we come into an entirely new world. A world of two boats a week, no communication with the outside world [and] fresh food only on boat days" when the Union Steamships vessels—either the *Cardena*, *Chelohsin*, *Lady Cynthia* or *Lady Cecilia*—stopped off with supplies.

Introducing local readers to the wilds of the outback, Boas devoted many columns to descriptions of daunting landmarks like Seymour Narrows, the waters off Cape Mudge and the seven rapids—Okisollo, Surge, Arran and Hole-in-the-Wall among them—which the mission boat *Rendezvous* regularly patrolled. These difficult and sometimes treacherous waters struck him as a metaphor of the Mission, which sought to turn natural barriers into channels of communication. Boas's themes included the ruggedness of his patrol area, the brooding headlands and powerful tidal currents and the need for navigational aids.

Perhaps consciously avoiding religious topics, Boas frequently sidestepped even the most obvious occasions to explain or promote his Christian traditions—even, for example during Advent, the four penitential weeks leading up to Christmas. Only in the edition immediately before Christmas, on 22 December 1948, did Boas finally deliver a Christmas message by suggesting how one might make the festival "a true and sincere commemoration of the birth of Christ." Unless the "Sea Padre" had misjudged his audience, they probably felt more at home with the comfortable homespun musings he delivered than with doctrine or more abstract theological exposition.

In the days prior to Christmas, Boas and the *Rendezvous* were completing the Christmas patrol to the extreme reaches of his patrol area. He described some of the journey in the *Courier* of 4 January 1950. It provided his best summary of the work of the Mission:

> The *Rendezvous* is heading down Toba Inlet after having made its Christmas tour of that part of its patrol. Christmas has begun in earnest for us, as we are seeking to reach as many ports of call as possible before the season passes.
>
> We broke the nine hour journey . . . by calling at the International Logging camp in Humfrey Creek. And

after a great deal of trouble with the sound projector were able to give them at least a bit of sound motion picture . . . The next day it was "head of the inlet or bust" [to reach the Klahoose logging camp].

Here was a whole camp that was meeting the Columbia Coast Mission for the first time. Only a few of them had ever heard of the mission. Now they were seeing it in action. True to the mission's tradition, it was seeking to meet the every need of the people. It wasn't only entertainment, nor fun, nor presents for all the children from the church inland. Nor was it only medical advice and help, nor was it only religious in its interest; and not even confined to the children's needs. It was everything.

When reading such records, one wonders how realistic the missioner's perceptions were, or whether he might not have been overly optimistic in his judgement of the Mission's spiritual impact. Judging by his own account, however, this particular tour changed lives:

As these people saw the colored motion pictures of the life and work of the mission they realized that the Saviour who had inspired all missions, came to save the whole of man.

And for all this, we do feel that we have found friends at the Klahoose Logging camp . . . Only we [regret] as we do with every port of call, [that] we can only call so seldom. The mission boat has to be shared with so many other places. But it is good for people to know that the church is there to be to them as they are able [to share it, just] as it was to them inland. To so many it does mean a return to the church which . . . did not seem to hold anything for them [in the cities and towns]. But out here in the very back woods, where there is nothing but themselves, all that the church would seek to give them comes with fresh meaning. Yet it is the same church, the same message of God's love; only the setting is different.

Boas's reflections never move beyond this level of discourse despite the occasional sermonizing. "Those who ply the waters of the sea, they see the signs of great good and a great God," he paraphrased the Old Testament psalmist. "And from where better may we listen to some of these tales than from some of the happenings around the islands of the inside passage." Boas was keenly sensitive to the majesty of the coastal scenery, which he viewed through the eyes of faith. Though his descriptive passages are often marred by hackneyed phrases, they convey something of the awe with which he viewed his God's creation.

Nothing in "The Sea Padre's Column" reflects the major changes which coastal life was experiencing, and which were threatening to render the Columbia Coast Mission obsolete. Featured prominently in the very newspaper in which Boas himself was writing, were innovations in technology, transportation and communications, and the emergence of what is now called the "social safety net." Thus Queen Charlotte Airways had placed a large advertisement in *The Campbell River Courier* of 1 December 1948 extolling its "Inexpensive Air Service to Coastal and Vancouver Island Points." It offered regular passenger service and air freight for perishable goods. "Fly QCA" would become a byword among the islands. A week later the company was advertising "2 speedy round trips daily" between Comox and Vancouver with limousine service connecting points on Vancouver Island to Comox. Logging companies were running their own float planes, and within three months, the BC Shellfish Company inaugurated a one-day flight bringing fresh lobsters to Vancouver from Halifax. This "marked the beginning of what may be a new air cargo industry." At the same time, ads for the new BC Hospital Insurance Service announced it would be distributing its first cards and urged people to join the scheme in order to experience "freedom from hospital bills and their worry." Its local offices were located in three well-established hospitals on northern Vancouver Island. Significantly, two of them, St. Joseph's Hospital in Comox, and Lourdes Hospital in Campbell River, had been founded by churches.

If medical and air services were rapidly overtaking the work of the Columbia Coast Mission, more was to follow. An article of 8 December 1948 reported the announcement by the minister of

National Health and Welfare that "one of a large number of new projects [was] planned in the field of general public health." In cooperation with the provincial Department of Health and Welfare, a "new division will work toward setting up a province-wide program of dental examination, treatment of children and education." This was what the paper elsewhere called a "Preventative Dental Bureau for BC." A month later, the newspaper featured a quarter-page ad from the BC Department of Finance regarding the new Social Security and Municipal Aid Tax, the 3 percent sales tax. The social security would provide support for "Old Age Pensions, Mothers' Allowances, Child Welfare Service, Control of Tuberculosis, Cancer and Venereal Disease, Operation of Public Health Nursing and Medical Inspection of School Children, Social Assistance, Hospital Grants and Mental Hygiene Programme." And on 19 January 1949, a BC Telephone Company advertisement announced that during the reporting period January 1946–January 1949, "more than 48,000 new telephones [had been] installed despite continuing equipment shortages." The quarter-page ad told of British Columbia's burgeoning population and of BC Tel's expanding communications services. There were other signs of change as well: Boas's article of 29 June 1949 now spoke of summer resorts emerging in the once-isolated islands, while a news item the same day mentioned the appearance of "many yachts" visiting the once-distant Stuart Island.

Clearly, the secular world with its social net, air travel, health programs, correspondence education and communications services was phasing out the church's Social Gospel. The degree to which any of these changes were influenced by the Mission cannot be assessed, though in the course of history the Social Gospel itself can be shown to have brought about change in secular society. For Boas, however, these changes signalled not so much a future to which he or the Mission would have to adapt; they pointed instead to a rugged past that had been much harsher before the Mission and aircraft had arrived. His perspective is best summed up in his article "Nine Hours There, Twenty Minutes Back" in the "Sea Padre's Column" of 31 August 1949. Here he described the journey "by gas boat and aeroplane" to Allison Harbour and Nakwakto Rapids. He concluded:

Yes, we made it. Thirty-six running hours from Vancouver, [a further] 20 hours from Whaletown and [then a further] nine and half hours from Alert Bay. And, onboard the Queen Charlotte [Airways] plane, we returned to Alert Bay in 21 minutes.

As Boas wrote, "it makes us realize just what conditions must have been in that north country before the advent of such airlines as the Queen Charlotte Airways." Significantly, the same page on which Boas' article appeared featured a photo-story of the "world's first amphibious landing gear for helicopters" showing what it called an American army "egg-beater" equipped for medical evacuation.

By this time, the clinic at Whaletown was a well-established institution in the *Rendezvous*'s district. Boas liked to call it the Columbia Coast Mission Medical Clinic and had rallied local assistance in expanding it. Volunteer labour, some donated by local enterprises, helped build on the mission site. The board changed the name to the John Antle Memorial Clinic on the death of the Mission's founder on 3 December 1949, at the age of eighty-four. Antle would always remain an imposing figure, especially for Boas, who had suggested the name change.

Antle's passing deeply affected Alan Greene as well. Greene had just brought the *John Antle* into Secret Cove after an evening transit of Welcome Passage when he learned by radio-telephone that Antle had died. "Welcome Pass—Secret Cove! How deeply significant the names sound tonight when I think of the safe anchorage our old chief has reached," he wrote. Heading homeward, Greene hearkened back to a profound liturgical tradition he shared with his old friend:

And as I plowed the little craft Pender-wards, I repeated [the hymn] "When on my day of life the night is falling," recalling with each line the many times he and I had sung the hymn together, as in the darkness of the Columbia's pilot house he guided her to some safe place for the night. He loved that hymn with all his love for

fine poetry, and as is so true of us all, he found it easier
to give voice to his inner feelings when there was no
need to hide the workings of his face. I discovered the
true John Antle in such moments. His sometimes stern
judgements of others were for the nonce silenced as he
let the gentle rhythm and sense of Whittier's prayer lift
him into a humble one-ness with God . . . How dearly
I sensed in those moments the true spirit of that rugged
man.

Antle was buried at sea from the *Columbia* on 7 December 1949
in Manson's Deep, off Bowen Island, after Holy Requiem Mass
at St. James Church, Vancouver. Greene and Boas were among
the official mourners. John Antle, who had remained a formative
force as "eminence grise" in the Mission for years beyond his
retirement in 1936, continued to influence the Mission's thinking
even after his death. Said Greene:

> He gave to the people of the Coast . . . all his gifts of
> mind and soul. He made friends. He made enemies . . .
> He was a brave man and to the frequent dismay of his
> Board undertook each new venture with scarcely a dollar
> in hand—and by sheer grit and unquenchable conviction
> finished each new unit.

In preparing a eulogy, Greene reflected on the meaning of his
mentor's life, and the shape that life had given to his own venture
in faith:

> I have seen him in all his moods. I have suffered from
> him at his worst—and I have been inspired by him at
> his best. And yet there would break through his darker
> moments flashes of real humour and pure kindliness that
> were proofs of an inner generosity of spirit.

Meanwhile, the tensions between medical and pastoral services were
being worked out in microcosm on Cortes Island. Rollo and Kay
Boas not only had established their clinic, but were planning to

"The Church at the Turn of the Road," as Alan Greene described it. St. John the Baptist, Whaletown (Cortes Island) was consecrated on 13 August 1950.

build a church. Boas often asked himself: "Must we continue to hold our church gatherings in school houses, halls and any place we can use? Can we build upon such foundations a church that will outlive and outserve the popular and easy approach of the 'isms'?" In musing thus, he was echoing one of Alan Greene's major themes. At issue was the need to transform a previously itinerant church with transient ministries into an established community. Rollo and Kay Boas built their church—what Greene called "The church at the turn of the road"—after her brother's design, on a piece of property between the clinic and the government dock. The consecration service of the Church of St. John the Baptist on 13 August 1950 was attended by eighty-five people and gave liturgical expression to the Boas' Christian vision. Sermon, psalms, prayers and hymns like "The Church's one foundation / Is Jesus Christ her Lord" lent thematic focus to the new undertaking.

The official opening of the expanded clinic over a year later, on 8 November 1951, projected a similar sense of personal commitment, with the *John Antle* transporting guests from Mansons

Landing and Blind Creek, and the *Columbia* bringing over twenty guests from Qualicum, Comox, Courtenay and Campbell River. Sixty people joined Rollo Boas, Alan Greene and Bishop Victor Howard in a brief dedication service evoking a rich tradition of liturgical worship. They celebrated the stirring themes of salvation, healing and the missionary response to human need. The reception accented the fellowship and sense of community that bound all together in the grand venture of Christian living.

The work of the mission ships continued unabated with its daily mix of human emotions. The sporadic jottings in the logs give some clues. On Sunday, 18 November 1951, Boas's pencilled notes reveal a sequence of events: "Mr H. Saunders died—attended to matters. Did not go out on patrol. Alone on board. Casket for H. Saunders. Funeral of Henry Saunders: acted as undertaker, registrar, priest." The log reveals the funeral was followed by a birthday party later that day with fourteen children and a film show in the clinic. Then, after a logbook gap of some ten weeks, Boas recorded, twice underscored, "The Death of King George VI—Holy Day" on 6 February 1952. Thereon followed a series of memorial services among the settlements that Boas served. Thus at Owen Bay School, Boas's log noted "Memorial Service re Death of our Late King—Our New Queen," and subsequent meetings with the Cubs, Scouts and the Royal Canadian Legion to mark the event. These would seem to have been the highlights amidst regular rounds of sick calls, pastoral care and acts of good neighbourliness. These latter he would only note in his log when something special struck him. As one of the few entries reads: "Picked up Mrs J McCartney, [her] four children, 2 dogs, 4 rabbits, chickens and baggage"; and on 6 February 1954, "radio telephone and receiver installed." If the settlers were never too far from aid, neither were the mission ships themselves. When the *Rendezvous* struck a rock at the northeast end of Coulter Island, the log entry reveals a "plane spotted us and came down." The little ship ultimately required major repairs in Vancouver.

The uniqueness and romance of the Mission's work made it a marketable item in the media. One illustrated article described Rollo Boas as "plumber, lumberjack, builder, ditch-digger or whatever the occasion requires," and revealed his plan of constructing "several 16 x 22 foot church buildings and putting skids under them so they can be put on floats and towed wherever they are needed." In extolling the work of the Social Gospel, the author revealed Boas as "a versatile chaplain [who] preaches by tide-table"; he set his schedule by wind and weather and steamed to his parishes as the sea allowed. And that was no exaggeration, as one gathers from his report of a typical Sunday in the region bordering on the Yuculta Rapids:

> I have held a Communion Service on board, in the north end of the rapids, because the tide happened to be ebbing north in the morning. Then returning to Big Bay for service there, when the tide changed to flood. And finally, on to the "Landing" [at Stuart Island] on the last of the flood tide, to have a Communion Service with two or three families there.

On another occasion, the powerful currents of Beazley Pass, Surge Narrows and Okisollo confronted him with similar challenges:

> It is difficult to drop in at a given time and hope to arrange for a service . . . If I can have a day's visiting before a service at Surge Narrows on the Sunday morning, then travel three hours to Granite Bay [to] conduct a Sunday School in the late afternoon, and an informal service for the adults in the evening, then visit that night and part of Monday, it has been a good two and a half days work.

If Rollo Boas was the romantic, photogenic missionary for the media, so too was his wife Kay, who was named *Saturday Night's* Woman of the Week in September 1951. An article entitled "First Lady of the Sea" portrayed her as a vivacious forty-two-year old with the "figure of a model, the sort of ankle that gets whistled at and a flair for clothes that tempts other females to break the tenth Commandment." In many respects the polar opposite of the stereotypical parson's wife, she shared with her husband a profound prayer life, and dedicated herself to the Mission's ideals while harmonizing her various roles as "wife, mother, teacher, trained nurse, deckhand, cook, gardener, carpenter, helmsman and double for Dorothy Dix," as the *Saturday Night* article expressed it. In Rollo and Kay Boas, the Mission found a pastoral team. But despite their energy and commitment, the task was seldom easy. Together they nourished both in their marriage and their ministry a life of faith. To be sure, they saw themselves as Anglicans by choice and tradition, but they embraced what Rollo Boas sometimes called a "larger catholicity" which freed them from sectarian bias. He expressed the pastoral ministry thus:

> The greater percentage of "our" people are not Anglicans. They are protestants who are willing to accept the spiritual leadership which they want and appreciate—and at the hands of us Anglican priests. For this very reason, the CCM has been called the "Salvation Army of the Church of England, afloat" . . . This is not for the purpose of proselytizing other people to change their affiliation (which, for most parts, is loosely held), but rather for the purpose of Evangelization in the larger sense of the word . . . I realized that, though I was an Anglican priest, I must be willing to minister to all peoples using only those universal Christian means common to all Christian peoples. Personal evangelism became the pass-word, informal services, the common means of community worship and a readiness to be "all things to all men" that by some means some might be saved. [This meant providing a personal model and making] down-to-earth attempts to present the age-old gospel in every day terms.

In fact, the Boas's "parish" was even larger than this correspondence suggests. Their discussion groups included Roman Catholics, lapsed Lutherans and Seventh Day Adventists, as well as many others whom Boas described as being in "the no-man's-land of non-denominationalism, who are ready to be reached by a church who will meet them on this ground of understanding."

The radical obsolescence besetting the Mission found early expression

(l. to r.) Reverend Rollo Boas, Bishop Godfrey Gower and Reverend Heber Greene, at St. John the Baptist, Whaletown, October 1954.

in Alan Greene's 1952 annual report. Despite his defensive insistence that "in no sense do I feel that our task is petering out," the signs were all too obvious. Threatened with the possibility of having to close St. Mary's Hospital by the end of March 1952 because of a "grave financial situation," the Mission handed over responsibility for its administration to a local hospital board. Greene advised the board that the Mission could contribute no funds beyond the $5,464 the Community Chest of Greater Vancouver provided for the St. Mary's operations. Strictly speaking, therefore, the Mission was no longer running any hospitals on the coast. While the John Antle Memorial Clinic at Whaletown was carrying out "undoubtedly some fine preventative work," any patient in need of hospitalization was ferried by the *Rendezvous* to Lourdes Hospital in Campbell River, run by the Roman Catholic Church.

Meanwhile, ships and staff were aging. Built in 1910 to replace her namesake, the *Columbia* was now forty-three years old. Her skipper for the past sixteen years, George MacDonald, was now seventy. The ship's medical officer, Dr. E. Mountjoy Pearse, was

Lay missionary Ernest Christmas, who ran the Kingcome mission 1942–54 and skippered the Mission's launch Gwa-yee until acquiring his own ketch Veracity.

eighty-one. In Greene's words, it was simply "hard to hold the services of young people eager to get on in their profession." Money to operate the fleet was problematic as well. Indeed, were it not for the $8,000 annual grant for ship operations from the Community Chest, "we would have to terminate *Columbia*'s work" altogether. Kingcome's seagoing operations now posed a problem as well. Mr. and Mrs. Ernest Christmas, who had served as lay missionaries there since 1942, buying their own thirty-seven-foot ketch *Veracity* to replace the Mission's twenty-four-foot *Gwa-yee*, were now contemplating retirement. They would take the *Veracity* with them, of course, leaving the Mission without sea transport between Native villages.

The loss of *Veracity* and the aging of *Columbia* made it clear to Greene that the ships must be replaced. Yet, the board did not agree, recognizing that permanent parishes were replacing transient "floating churches." The Mission owned five church buildings: St. Mary's, Pender Harbour; The Church of the Good Shepherd, Lasqueti Island; St. John the Baptist, Whaletown; St. James, Mansons Landing; and St. George's, Kingcome Inlet. Through Heber Greene's intervention, the Mission had been bequeathed land at Sayward on which to build another; and, again through Heber, a new church was being built at Hardy Bay on property donated by the Alice Lake Logging Company. Doubtless the combined statistics from these small parishes were more impressive than those for the mission boats with their irregular stopovers in isolated hamlets. If figures could speak, the churches would win hands down over ships. "But please bear in mind," Alan Greene urged the board in 1952, "that each ship is a small travelling Church. A dozen people may meet on the *John Antle* or the *Rendezvous*, and often forty gather on the *Columbia*." As always, Greene cautioned that an accountant's approach to their missionary profession obscured the actual value being delivered:

> The Church statistics [on Services like Holy Communion, Mattins, and baptisms, etc.], while not impressive as to totals, have hidden within them, many occasions of real and very precious meaning to those who attended. The endless pastoral visits, whether social or definitely spiritual, have been unquestionably a source of great blessing to many, of all age groups . . . We visit every family regardless of their church affiliation and offer the same services, medical, social and spiritual, to all. If we were to limit the Mission's interest in people to Anglicans alone, one man could do the whole job, so small is the proportion of Anglicans to the total. I still consider that in the 225 small centres the four ships serve, we are ministering to approximately 9,000 white residents and probably 500 Indians.

Despite the lengthening shadows, Greene still took pride in the continued success of the Aged Folks' Guest Houses in Pender Harbour, which now counted ten units and thirteen guests. At a monthly rental of five dollars, they were fully self-supporting.

The third John Antle. Acquired by the CCM in 1945, she was skippered by Alan Greene 1945–53, renamed Laverock II in 1956, and donated to the Diocese of Caledonia in 1957.

Undaunted by fiscal problems, Greene had already begun raising funds to replace the old *John Antle*. A good solution seemed to lie in the forty-five-foot *Western Hope* the Diocese of Caledonia had offered to the mission as an outright gift. Built in 1940, she had outlived her usefulness in the operations for which she had been designed, and needed a complete refit. *Columbia* towed her the 450 miles to Vancouver for a survey to determine the costs of upgrading. For Greene, this was obviously the right ship for the mission's job. In a fundraising article, "A New Ship in the Offing," he assessed the cost of refit at $15,000 and listed a few of the more expensive single items: gum-wood hull sheathing, a ten-foot lifeboat, electric anchor winch and, of course, new engines. Greene did raise the money—including an emergency grant of $5,000 from the Missionary Society of the Church in Canada—despite the fact that the once-generous British Columbia and

*The fourth John Antle (ex-Western Hope of the Prince Rupert Coast Mission)
was dedicated by Bishop Godfrey Gower in Coal Harbour, Vancouver, on 27
June 1953. Alan Greene and Frank Ball (at helm).*

Yukon Church Aid Society had long since dried up as a source. Renamed *John Antle*, the fourth mission ship to bear that name, the *Western Hope* was equipped with modern technology, including a new 165 hp gasoline engine and radio telephone. The third *John Antle* was tied up alongside and held in reserve pending her sale.

Greene had known for some time that Boas was considering moving along to new personal challenges. In anticipation, Greene urged the Board to appoint a younger man who had recently offered to join. Thus, on 14 June 1954, Boas's log records "the ordination service of the Reverend J.G. Titus, new skipper-clergyman for the *Rendezvous*." The change of command took place on Sunday 27 June 1954 in Whaletown. A brief log entry recorded a "Farewell Tea and Introduction of the Old and New"; this was followed by evensong in the little church down the road attended by a small congregation. Although no record remains, those in attendance likely gathered as much to wish "God speed" to the couple who had served them for ten years with so much energy, devotion and compassion, as to welcome their new seafaring priest.

Other signs of renewal were afoot. Looking forward to celebrating the Mission's fiftieth anniversary, Greene had set himself the goal of raising $100,000 to replace both the old *Rendezvous* and *Columbia*, which he sold in 1955 and 1957 respectively. Assessing this new *John Antle* (ex-*Western Hope*) as now good for twenty-five years of service, Greene hoped to hand over to his successor a reinvigorated Mission. "I'd like to retire when I'm seventy, but before I leave the Mission I want to see three first-class ships in operation, good for many years of fine service, and my dream for the year 1955 is the raising of this rather staggering sum and the building of these two ships."

This was a very tall order, particularly as he knew the bulk of the money had to be raised from his usual sources in eastern Canada—from Calgary to Halifax. Only by cajoling and badgering "British Columbia, and particularly the businessmen of Vancouver" could he hope "to convince our Eastern friends that we have the generous backing of those who know us best." The inability to foster grassroots financial support in its own home province had always been a major obstacle to the Mission's corporate success. As the "Greening" of the mission drew to a close, the old money problems lingered on.

CHAPTER 6

Medical Pioneers

On board the mission ship *Columbia* a priest of the Church
of England, robed and vested, had just commenced his
sermon when an urgent call for help came through—some
man was badly hurt in the woods miles away. Throwing
off his cassock and surplice, the skipper dashed to the pilot
house, rang up the engines, and was off within a few
minutes. "That," came the gruff remark from a hardened
old sinner of a logger, who in some manner uncompre-
hended by himself had been cajoled into coming to the
service, "is the best damned sermon I ever heard . . ."

This classic anecdote from John Antle's missionary enterprise
was recounted by Dr. J.H. MacDermot during his lecture to the
Vancouver Medical Association in 1935. Having served at the
CCM hospital at Vananda, Texada Island, in 1907–08, MacDermot
was one of Antle's earliest physicians with the Columbia Coast
Mission. Implicit in the story was Antle's famous biblical dictum
of proclaiming God's Kingdom by healing the sick. In practising
the principle, medical missionaries faced all the vicissitudes a frontier
society could deliver.

"The Early Medical History of the B.C. Coast," as MacDermot
explained in his Vancouver lecture, confronted the raconteur with
an exceptional challenge. It demanded "the journalist's eye" in
order to capture "one of the romantic and fascinating stories of

our time"; it required the gifts of a poet to re-create "the thrilling deeds of patient, quiet, unassuming heroism"; it needed the flair of both the playwright and the spinner of yarns, and finally the dogged support of "a historian who would see and assign to the characters in this account their proper place." Absent from his impressive recipe for narrative success was some record of the players' time upon the stage, some archival trace of their lives.

Antle's medical missionaries have left us a meagre trace of their passing, all the more regrettable because the contributions of medical personnel were fundamental to the Mission's purpose. Sharing the same venture as those on the church side of the operation, they too left a legacy which, as MacDermot expressed it, "cannot be measured in terms of money, but of human life and happiness."

Anecdotal accounts like MacDermot's offer the briefest glimpses of the men and women who provided the medical care. While memories still linger about the "kindly" and "devoted" doctors and nurses who contributed so much to the well-being of patients in distress, little substantive trace of their work with the Mission remains. One can still find statistics on numbers of patients treated and on the number of miles the hospital ships steamed, but scarcely an insightful word about the personalities themselves, and nothing about operations and surgical procedures.

Like the missionaries, the medical personnel had to prove their worth. By way of demonstrating this point, John Antle told a cautionary tale in the first edition of the Mission's magazine *The Log of the 'Columbia'*, published in March 1906. "The Honourable James Dunsmuir, who was opposed to the Mission at the start, had occasion during December last, while up here in his yacht, to use the hospital [at Rock Bay] for one of his men. Having seen both the ship and the hospital, and learnt of the work being done, he generously admitted his mistake, and showed the sincerity of his opinions by sending a cheque for $500, which I received opportunely on Christmas Day."

Thus began a tradition of convincing a sometimes skeptical public that the Columbia Coast Mission was not so much "religion" as it was medicine. For many years, doctors and nurses remained an indispensable component of a mission which advertised itself as ministering to the body, mind and soul. Medicine was an early mode of delivering the Gospel. In the editions of *The Log* that followed, Antle informed his readers of the medical work carried out by the hospital ship *Columbia* and at Queen's Hospital at Rock Bay.

Regarded in its day as a well-equipped cottage hospital, Queen's was situated about two miles west of Chatham Point, and was operated as a joint venture of the Columbia Coast Mission and the Victorian Order of Nurses. The building was owned by the BC Mill and Timber Company. With accommodation for ten patients, it handled medical, surgical and midwifery cases. Antle had already initiated the "Yearly Ticket" plan whereby ten dollars per annum would cover all a potential patient's medical needs. Led by surgeon W.A.B. Hutton, and assisted by nurses "Miss Sutherland and Miss Franklin" (women's first names are rarely mentioned in early church documents), the hospital treated 1,250 cases in its first year. Thirty-three operations were performed in the hospital, and eighteen aboard ship. For the rest, medical staff counselled logging camps and individual loggers on matters of hygiene and first aid. The first nurse-in-charge was Kate Franklin. Described by Dr. MacDermot as "an exceptional woman," she had come out from England after training in St. Bartholomew's Hospital, London.

Working at first entirely on her own as emergency physician—both as "first-aid expert as well as a nurse" as MacDermot put it—Franklin had such a "strong will and firm way with her" that the loggers "gave her an obedience no doctor could secure." Antle quickly recognized that the work could become rather trying for the nurses. Unlike the doctor and skipper, who could get away from it all simply by taking the *Columbia* to sea, the nurses were tied down. They had little opportunity for rest or recreation. Antle therefore proposed "to provide the necessary change of air and scene for both Miss Sutherland and Miss Franklin by taking them on the *Columbia* once in a while to visit the outlying camps and settlements." Unfortunately, the nurses have left us no records. We will perhaps never know whether these well-intentioned diversions actually provided the necessary rest and respite, or whether, like the proverbial busman's holiday, they simply transferred the workplace to another milieu.

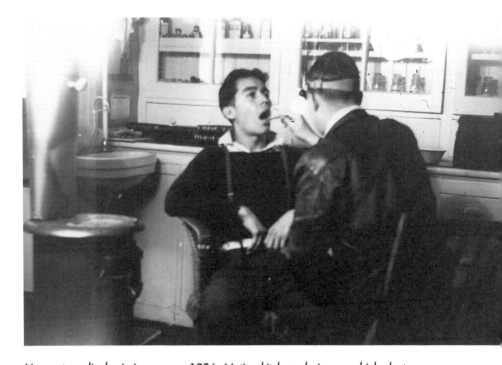

Itinerant medical missionary, ca 1936. Notice kitchen chairs on which doctor and patient are seated next to wood-burning stove. Doctors carried their surgical equipment, dentists a treadle-operated drill.

The medical mission served a vast, rugged area. A typical case from the ship's decklog for 24 February 1906 illustrates the difficulties delivering medical aid to isolated people:

> At Shoal Bay. SS *Cassiar* arrived from Vancouver, having on board Hansen Galnek who split his foot open with an axe at Smith's Camp, near Lund, on Thursday, the 22nd. After the accident he was brought by row-boat 25 miles to Lund, where he boarded the *Cassiar* and came on to Shoal Bay. We took him on board the *Columbia*, where his wound was attended to by Dr. Hutton, and in a few hours he was comfortably installed in the hospital at Rock Bay.

That month alone, the hospital found itself overcrowded with a number of severe cases: three broken legs (one with grave complications), nasty axe wounds and a fatal case of a young man who had been suffering for three weeks with bowel inflammation before he could be brought in.

Death was a frequent visitor in the wilderness. A patient with cerebrospinal meningitis died barely two days after reaching the hospital. Shortly thereafter, Nurse Jean Sutherland was stricken by what Dr. Hutton diagnosed as an extremely painful type of pleurisy, followed with startling rapidity and virulence by other complications, and death. Never robust, yet always energetic and cheerful, the intelligent young woman never spared herself in attending to her duties. In the words of Hutton's eulogy, her medical skill had given the loggers "more than they will ever realize." One of her patients, "with very limited materials at his command, got ready a cedar casket, in which was sorrowfully placed the mortal remains of her, whom so many had known as an angel in their distress." Draped with a Union Jack sprinkled with salmonberry blossoms and spirea, the casket was put aboard the *Cassiar* for transport to Vancouver. Within a year, Hutton himself would be dead, killed in a marine accident. He was replaced by Dr. D.P. Hanington and two new nurses "Miss Miller and Miss Riddock."

Similar stories emerge from the sparse records of the Mission hospital at Vananda, near the northern tip of Texada Island, where Dr. J.H. MacDermot worked. In those early years, he once recalled, the wolf was never far from the door:

[The hospital] was scandalously short of the most elementary necessities. It was a hard winter, and night after night the temperature was below zero, not only outside but in the main ward, where it fell frequently as low as three degrees below, though a red hot stove (outside the door) threatened destruction of the building. It was a small stove and might have been more useful inside the ward. We had an acute rheumatic case who needed heat. There were only three hot-water bottles in the place and one leaked. There were only six sheets (three flannelette) for thirteen patients, and blankets had to do. The water in the pipes froze, and the sanitary arrangements were plugged. It was a tough spot and one had to forget all one's dignity as a doctor of medicine and become a plumber and water carrier. It was very good for one's soul.

Over the next three decades, medical personnel too numerous to mention sojourned with the Mission. Flexibility and adaptability were central to their personalities and their work. Even the buildings had to be adaptable, if not floatable. During the late 1920s, for example, Carriden Bay's cottage Columbia Hospital was loaded onto floats to follow the shifting fortunes of logging camps. Its loss while being towed during a storm was a blow to the Mission, but the work would continue. Like the itinerant missionaries with whom they served, the medical personnel learned to cope with the vicissitudes of coastal conditions.

As we have seen, the loss of the floating hospital was the prelude to building St. Mary's Hospital, Pender Harbour, in June 1930. It was first manned by Dr. I.B. Thompson and his staff, joined within the year by Dr. C.H. ("ol' doc") Ployart, with Bessie Newbold and Antle's daughter Marion as nurses. Like Newbold, who distributed clothing to needy families, many involved themselves in social work in their off-duty hours as well. By May 1931, the Mission was operating three small hospitals: St. George's, Alert Bay; St. Michael's, Rock Bay, and St. Mary's. The annual statistics for the three units were impressive: 7,860 hospital days, 297 medical cases, 293 surgical cases and 3,088 outpatients, of whom 842 were treated by Dr. Gordon Kirkpatrick, the *Columbia*'s doctor. When Kirkpatrick shifted to St. Mary's, he was replaced by Dr. David Ryall.

Few characters or personalities emerge from the paper trail of medical postings, appointments and reports. Records about medical personnel and their practice are exceptionally lean and sometimes ambiguous. When one reads in the Rock Bay hospital file, for example, that "the Doctor and Mrs. Gray are living in one of the family houses while the owners are on vacation," we assume that a certain Dr. Gray and his wife have moved in. Or, when catching the entry that "old Cupid again has performed his duty well, for Miss K. Amer and Mr. Hollister are starting life anew," we suspect a marriage. More difficult to interpret is the notation:

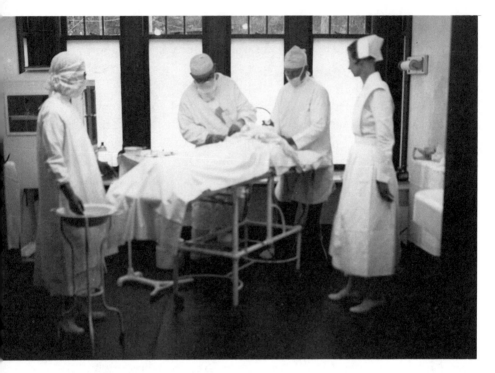

The operating room of St. Mary's Hospital (1936), with Dr. I. Martianoff, nurses B. Moody and G. Lowe, and orderly E. Russell.

"Speed gets 'em . . . so we find Dr. Kirpatrick applying a plaster cast to the victim of the 'high balling.'" Such cryptic commentaries would have been intelligible to locals who understood their allusion, but they tend to leave the outsider amused—or a touch perplexed. Yet, anecdotal evidence does on occasion shed light on the kind of perceptions and human relations that breathed life into the medical ministry. One such entry records the visit of a youngster who informed the attending physician: "Some day I want you to examine me and tell me how I feel."

Other entries in files occasionally hint at situations affecting the Mission as a whole. When Gordon Kirkpatrick became *Columbia*'s surgeon at the beginning of July 1930, John Antle welcomed him as a most promising physician fresh from medical school and master of the latest professional skills. "He can be recommended as one of the younger generation of doctors, trained to the minute, and eager to emulate the work of his predecessor, Dr. [Herschel]

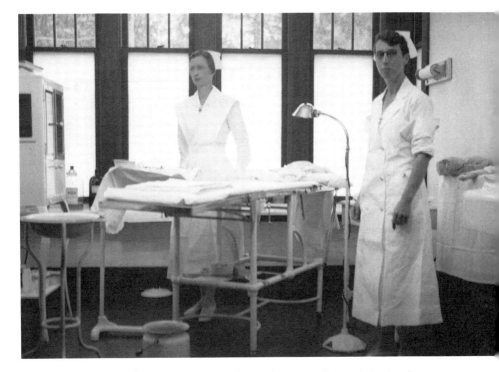

The operating room of St. Mary's Hospital (1936). Nurses (l. to r.) B. Moody and G. Lowe.

Stringer, whose reputation on the coast is hard to live up to." He had left the hospital ship *Columbia* in 1923 to spend four years of graduate work in Britain, and was one of the earliest icons of the medical mission. Frequently mentioned as a benchmark for excellence, Stringer unfortunately remains obscure.

Like his role model, Kirkpatrick established a sterling reputation. When he resigned in 1935 to join the staff of the provincial government's mental hospital at Essondale, the Mission was understandably saddened to see him go. Compared to most, he had remained an exceptionally long time, but his departure underscored a serious problem for the Mission: with its limited resources and facilities, and its inability to match the pay and security of an established profession, it could not hold onto its doctors.

John Antle was not only aware of this particular problem, he understood the difficulty of maintaining a credible medical presence in the midst of a largely itinerant population of loggers. Many of them were as skeptical of health care as they were of religious matters. Writing about the Rock Bay hospital in the spring of 1935, Antle put the matter succinctly:

The hospital barely becomes known to one group of men and their confidence gained, when they move out and everything has to be done over again. An outstanding medical man might cure things, but outstanding medical men cost money, and owing to the uncertainty of [medical] work by way of quantity, it would be difficult to get an outstanding man to remain there even if we could afford to pay him.

Part of the problem lay in the fact that, during the Depression, camp populations could suddenly drop to zero, leaving pastors and doctors without clientele.

With the growing settlement around Pender Harbour, however, prospects for developing a consistent medical practice looked much more hopeful. In 1933 Antle announced the arrival of an ordained medical doctor in whom he expressed the greatest confidence: the Reverend T.A. Lane Connold, MD. Within six months the new medical missionary "had demonstrated his ability to lift [St. Mary's] hospital to its full capacity of usefulness." Just how he managed this feat was never explained. But Antle was doubtless greatly relieved. Whenever the Mission had tried this combination of doctor-priest before, it had proved a failure.

A fervent, even zealous priest as well as a competent physician, Connold added to his professional qualifications by becoming skipper of the *John Antle*. A native of England, where the Mission had recruited him, he emerges from his occasional articles as an evangelistic, if doctrinaire missionary. Thus he wrote of finding great "joy in easing pain, in curing sickness, in comforting souls, in telling of the Kingdom of God to lonely people sighing for the consolation and companionship of Jesus." He readily entered into the life of isolated communities like Lasqueti Island where he lost no time in identifying local needs and promoting the people's wishes for such pastoral comforts as a parish church with a consecrated cemetery.

In his human relations, Connold was not the rigid person his theological pronouncements suggest. He adapted readily to whatever circumstances permitted him to evangelize. His description of his church ministry at St. Mary's Hospital is a case in point:

[It was] so unlike the regulation Church Service as to have an interest of its own. The Church is in a hospital ward. Some of the congregation come in boats and some are in bed. It may be no change for some clergy to know their congregation are abed, but odd to have them in bed and in Church at one and the same time. There is no choir. A nurse plays the organ in the sun porch. We stand to pray and sit to sing for the sake of the infirm. The service is always liable to interruption because the preacher may be required to sew up a wound or tap a wheezing chest. There are no collections; and one can come to Church in pyjamas and dressing gown, or shorts and sea boots as desired.

But behind Connold's outward amiability and genuinely engaging personality lay a knot of anger at how the Mission was being managed. It was not sufficient merely to show forth the love of God through ministrations; one must deliver doctrine. In a private letter to Alan Greene, he argued for more stringent theological teaching, more preaching, the inculcation of "real churchmanship," and increased emphasis on the Sacraments. He attacked the whole concept of medical mission as practised in Canada, and the administration of St. Mary's Hospital in particular:

My experience in [missionary] hospitals in England . . . left me unprepared for the principle which obtains here that the Hospitals of the Missions are operated in the hope of making a profit from fees charged . . . I have been taught that the doctor in a hospital never mentioned "money" to his patients so that he never knew who paid and who did not, and thus avoided any discrimination in treatment . . . It was therefore a source of embarrassment to me to find that Hospital days had to be bargained for, and that a bill saddened the exit of a patient from the halls of healing . . . It is contrary to the spirit of missions and repugnant to its principle, and would not be understood in England if known . . . At present the accounts of the religious and medical sides of the Mission must be kept separate because the various contributing Welfare Agencies are emphatic in their refusal to aid anything religious . . . Would it not be more honest to split the [CCM] into two and run it as Columbia Coast Hospitals, Inc., a purely commercial concern, and the Columbia Coast Mission proper, motivated by a purely missionary spirit?

Connold touched some raw nerves despite his errors of fact and interpretation. The Mission's policy of enacting the Social Gospel called for "shewing forth God's love" by healing the sick, not through trying to convert to Anglicanism or by giving catechism lessons. Connold regarded the Mission's approach as giving rise to "characterless sentimental" religion—not the salvational eucharistic version he was accustomed to in England. Nor had he properly understood that somebody, somehow, had to pay for the medical services the Mission was providing—even at the risk of seeking some contribution from the patients themselves. As Greene once remarked, "some people think we have a lot of fairy god-mothers sending us big cheques or that we receive a fortune from England." Connold's anger at "the system" obscures the fact that the Mission never withheld medical care from anybody because of an inability to pay, even though it had advertised itself from 1924 as "Columbia Coast (Medical) Mission, Inc." An examination of accounts shows that the Mission never tried to make a profit, as Connold charged, but simply to break even.

A medical colleague equally engaged in missionary work was Dr. Keith Wray-Johnston who took over St. Michael's Hospital, Rock Bay, in March 1936. A year later he left for postgraduate work in Britain and was replaced by Dr. J.L. Murray of St. George's Hospital, Alert Bay, who in turn was replaced by Dr. Herschel Stringer, then returning from postgraduate work in the UK. Stringer was "keen to renew his former happy associations with up-Coast people." Wray-Johnston and his wife returned to St. Mary's in 1938 where both he and Ben Drew, the later secretary-treasurer of the board, were appointed lay readers in 1941. Besides his medical work, Wray-Johnston organized the first local Hospital Insurance Plan, taught St. John's Ambulance first-aid courses, organized the Sunday School and was instrumental in starting a Girl Guide group. He and his wife even ran a little newspaper for a while, with proceeds going to the hospital. But despite his commitment, he too had to move on. In September 1941, Wray-Johnston moved to the US to undertake specialist training in obstetrics and gynecology. Returning to Vancouver the next year, he joined the Royal Canadian Army Medical Corps. He died in July 1945, leaving his wife and their six-week-old daughter. Church records do not indicate the cause.

St. Mary's Hospital, meanwhile, was growing. With increasing support from the local population, and the formation of a Hospital Club, new equipment and furnishings became readily available. As the tradition of medical service grew, so too did the number of patients. During the first eight years of the hospital's existence, from 1930 to the end of 1937, St. Mary's had treated 515 patients; in the twenty-one-month period from 1938 to October 1939, it had treated 607. Following a concept put forth by Wray-Johnston, the Mission and the hospital Women's Auxiliary helped establish the St. Mary's Hospital Mutual Benefit Association, which gained contracts from logging companies. By Alan Greene's calculations, if everyone on the Sechelt Peninsula joined the plan, the proceeds would cover two doctors, a reasonable ambulance service and the costs of hospitalization. This could all be done "for the present fee or perhaps for a slight increase." In order to staff the medical services provided to contract members in the logging camps, the Mission appointed Dr. W.A. Holm of Sechelt in the spring of 1940. This step of delivering medical services to the camps not only relieved pressure on St. Mary's Hospital, but also marked the beginning of the physician's gradual independence from the Mission. Many adjustments and variations on the health insurance scheme were attempted before the provincial government introduced its own system in January 1949.

The Second World War drew many doctors away from the

Alan Greene baptizes four children of the Seney family on the shore of Jervis Inlet in 1951. His daughter Catherine (extreme right) was a summer vacation school teacher at the time.

Mission and into the three armed services. Dr. David Ryall left St. George's after nine years to join the medical branch of the Royal Canadian Air Force; so too, did Dr. T.R. Blades of St. Michael's. As already seen, Wray-Johnston joined the Royal Canadian Army Medical Corps. To Greene, these departures were all signs of "the inevitable urge and need of the young doctor to go on to wider service." In the summer of 1944 he made a public plea for a doctor "to relieve the really desperate situation confronting us" New doctors—mostly from Britain—became available to replace those who had left, and Greene could give assurances that "whatever happens in these days of constant change, the Columbia Coast Mission will strive to guarantee efficient, kindly medical service throughout its hospitals and hospital ships." Older retired doctors sometimes helped out whenever they could. One example was Dr. W.A. McTavish of Vancouver, a churchman whose brief service aboard the *John Antle* ended suddenly when he collapsed and died during a stroll ashore. After the funeral aboard ship, his ashes were scattered in Welcome Passage. In Greene's words, this final gesture to a Christian who loved the coast and its people symbolized "a sea-fare into the great open spaces of God's Kingdom."

It was only a matter of time before the possibilities of rapid medical evacuation would demonstrate the growing obsolescence of the Rock Bay hospital. In the summer of 1941, three men suffered serious injuries at Merrill, Ring and Wilson camp just after it re-opened. Snapping and whipping under tension, a wild cable practically tore the leg off one man, savagely ripped his other leg, and struck two more loggers before its thrashing ended. Excellent first aid on the scene prepared the men for a harrowing journey to Rock Bay, which they reached three hours later. Wanting to give their most seriously injured man a fighting chance, the logging firm hired a plane to bring an orthopedic surgeon from Vancouver to assist Dr. R. Blades of the Mission. After a double amputation, the victim was flown down to Vancouver the next day. Airpower supplanted seapower whenever time was of the essence. The preferred means of transportation of the future was quickly establishing itself.

On 4 Dec 1945, St. Michael's Hospital, Rock Bay, closed permanently. The decision was forced upon the Mission by the diminishing amount of medical and surgical work, and the withdrawal of further support by the budget committee of the Community Chest of Greater Vancouver. The Mission deplored the fact that St. Michael's had to close for lack of funds. Within a couple of months of its closing, a serious accident occurred in the woods that seemed to demonstrate the folly of not keeping the station open, cost what it may. Falling logs had crushed a man's leg. Writing in *The Log* in January 1946, Alan Greene berated readers for their insensitivity in having withheld financial support:

Picture the journey—step by step. Packed out of the woods, loaded into the camp gas-boat, a thirty-five mile, five-hour run to Rock Bay. No hospital there in operation. Phone calls to Campbell River for the ambulance. Hours lost waiting for the arrival at Rock Bay. A man suffering unrelieved agony on the journey out over bad roads. The ambulance drivers phoning from a far-away point to Campbell River asking Dr. Bathurst Hall to come out by car and give the poor chap a sedative. The meeting in the wood. A good heavy shot of morphine—

and relief for the rest of the journey—and finally the casualty reaches Lourdes Hospital Campbell River. Thirteen hours after the accident. Other cases have made this long, exhausting and sometimes agonizing journey. And there will be more of them.

It was a dark prediction, doomed to be fulfilled.

The wartime social revolution which expanded employment opportunities for women in the armed forces, industry and commerce impacted on the Mission as well. Its first female physician was Dr. Florence L. Nichols. Drawn to the wilds of BC in August 1944, the Ontarian was "accidently or providentially introduced to the Columbia Coast Mission" in Vancouver. Planning to visit friends in Bella Coola, she was offered a lift aboard *Columbia* as far as Alert Bay. Nichols's transformation from vacationer to medical missionary crystallized on reaching Pender Harbour, where she and the ship's crew received the traditional hearty welcome from St. Mary's Hospital staff. "I felt ashamed to be on holidays while nurses were carrying on alone so courageously without a doctor. In the morning I was so conscience-stricken that I sought out Reverend Alan Greene and offered my services for the month of September." Greene's reaction is recorded by inference. "I gathered that Mr. Greene was rather dubious about employing a woman [and he] wondered if I was aware of the existing prejudice against women doctors." (This was about the time Greene had tried to dissuade the Reverend Rollo Boas from taking his wife, a nurse, along with him aboard *Rendezvous*.) For Dr. Nichols, it was a challenge, and Greene found himself in no position to refuse her the chance. She delighted in recounting anecdotes about the insecurities of male patients who had never even entertained the possibility of submitting themselves to a female physician. "I don't see why a lady shouldn't be as good as a man anyway," an elderly rheumatic logger once conceded. "I know you're a human doctor, but I wonder if you would [also] see my dog."

By all accounts, Dr. Nichols fell in easily with the *Columbia* and her crew, and delighted in what turned out to be a grand adventure. The medical side of her journeys—the usual broken legs, gashes and tooth extractions—seems to have been less striking than the opportunity of experiencing the Native villages, where she attempted to undertake a program of inoculations against diphtheria and smallpox. Some voices in the non-Native population warned her that the Native peoples were difficult and uncooperative in matters of health. She rejected this jaundiced view. "The Indians were far more cooperative than the whites [and] were anxious to have their children protected; whereas for the most part the whites declined." Only her own schedule prevented her from staying longer.

Despite the arrival of the first woman doctor, Greene continued to face extreme difficulty in finding permanent medical staff. Throughout the spring and summer of 1945, medical officers on loan from the armed forces spent a week or two as their regular duties permitted. Greene's hope that demobilization would bring great numbers of recruits to the Mission was disappointed. Physicians like Grant A. Gould, who had just completed three years with the Royal Canadian Navy Volunteer Reserve, filtered themselves through the Mission en route elsewhere. Dr. Gould's appointment was doubly attractive; his wife, a graduate nurse, was prepared to volunteer her services as unpaid relief nurse whenever occasion permitted.

Nurses were in high demand in the spring of 1945 when the longest serving nurse, seventy-year-old Kathleen O'Brien, retired after twenty-five years at the Village Island Indian Mission. Described by Alan Greene as a woman of "amazing spirit" and of "splendidly balanced" temperament, she had struggled under sometimes appalling conditions to improve the health of the Native population. In 1934 she had expanded her work by building a T.B. cottage or small sanatorium for tubercular Native patients. Known as "Hyuya-Tsi" (Place of Rest), it drew principally from children at St. Michael's Residential School at Alert Bay. As Greene portrayed the scene in 1944, the settlement then consisted of little more than "a straggling row of small shacks, with one or two fairly decent houses of the White man's design, with the remains of huge community houses, the marks of a passing age in Indian life." Having served with a Miss Nixon, a Miss Dibben and others in this isolated post, Kathleen O'Brien had become the Grande

Dame of the coastal nursing community. Greene saluted her "pluck and determination" in committing herself to living out her "Christian love for her child-like flock," and he regretted the lack of young women to take her place. For her many achievements in health and Native day-school education, she was awarded membership in the Order of the British Empire.

Pay was an early issue in attracting and holding medical personnel. By providing doctors with fixed salaries, the Mission paid all it could afford. Compared with earnings outside the church, this was admittedly very little. Even when the Mission earned medical income in excess of what it paid a doctor, it channeled the revenue back into the hospital's operational account. Doctors were actually subsidizing the Mission. When St. Mary's and St. George's became established institutions with a regular contracted income and some government subsidies, physicians sought a change. They began asking for recognition as private practitioners with hospital privileges and the option of using hospital offices as their headquarters. In effect, this turned the Mission into an intermediary between doctor and patient. The hospitals collected fees and raised funds, paid the doctors for services rendered, then charged them for hospital and office privileges. This separation between mission hospital on the one hand, and medical doctors who provided services within the hospital precincts on the other, signalled a fundamental shift in Mission policy and purpose. It took the CCM a step closer to what Dr. Connold had somewhat derogatorily suggested in 1937 might ultimately split the Mission into two: "Columbia Coast Hospitals, Inc., a purely commercial concern, and the Columbia Coast Mission proper, motivated by a purely missionary spirit."

In the fall of 1946, the Mission engaged a Dr. Warringer of Sechelt as a private practitioner. Although acting as the medical member of the hospital board, he was not a staff member. Yet he found the job required an inordinate amount of work for very little remuneration, and he left six months later to take up private practice in Vancouver. The Mission then cancelled its Hospital Contract Plan (the successor to the St. Mary's Hospital Mutual Benefit Association) because its dollar value depended both on membership levels and on monthly rates. In an attempt to break even, the Mission had been edging up the rates. For practical purposes, the system now depended upon user fees. Doctors and Mission, meanwhile, worked towards establishing a new plan for group health and accident insurance for the Pender Harbour area. Eventually known as the North Pacific Health and Accident Insurance Plan, St. Mary's Hospital officially recognized it in the spring of 1947.

While the Mission explored new financial arrangements and plans, it completed a fundraising drive to build a staff residence beside the hospital. It was officially opened on 21 August 1948. In developing future policy, Greene earnestly sought the hospital board's "fullest co-operation in making it a Hospital worthy of our Church and of the generous support so many friends have given us." When the provincial government's own hospital insurance scheme commenced in January 1949, he had everything in place. Although the new doctor, A.J. Tripp, joined as a private practitioner (a working arrangement he had enjoyed elsewhere for the past ten years), the relationship seemed healthy. He supported the CCM's concept of medical mission.

In the long run, however, the St. Mary's project enjoyed only precarious success. By 1953, the Mission's executive committee feared that a combination of low occupancy and the resultant low revenue would force them to close the hospital by the end of March that year. Having reached a point where further support from Mission's funds was impossible, St. Mary's welcomed the creation of a local hospital committee to raise funds to assure its continued operations. Even if the Mission could have operated St. Mary's financially on its own, it still could not attract and hold its doctors.

The twenty-fifth anniversary year of St. Mary's in 1955 was marked by what the Mission's board saw as hopeful signs. After two years of "endless problems and many set-backs [the operation was] getting out of the woods by degrees." Increased occupancy rates resulted as patients on the Sechelt Peninsula chose St. Mary's over Vancouver. The Mission ascribed this trend as "obviously due to the confidence the public have in Drs. Playfair and Swan, and their initiative in going out to places like Vancouver Bay, Egmont and Halfmoon Bay for regular clinic days each week."

The "old" Columbia, built 1910, and the new Columbia, built 1956, nesting at Vancouver in 1957.

The hospital was now moving toward incorporation like St. George's, Alert Bay. In surrendering control, the Mission could be proud of having pioneered the hospital system. It was gratifying to see the community it continued to serve become the custodian of a hospital founded by the Social Gospel.

The secularization of St. Mary's left the Whaletown clinic and the hospital ship *Columbia* as the Mission's sole dispensers of medical care. The clinic was serviced by physician Bathurst Hall and dentist Trevor Harrop, who dropped in from their private practices in Campbell River. The ship depended mostly on very short-term retirees to serve as the medical members of the crew: three old faithfuls, Drs. G.H.J. Ankenman, W.R. Simpson and H. Wetsclaar from Victoria, served in as many months in the spring and early summer of 1955. Dr. Molly Towell joined briefly in 1956 before returning home to England, leaving Greene once again to impress on his board the difficulty in obtaining permanent help. Towell herself seems to have been particularly valuable, for she had "thrown herself into her job as ship's doctor with all her might and has won the confidence of everybody." Her departure underscored the ongoing stresses and strains of the medical mission.

In this case, however, a congenial turnover took place when her successor, Dr. Mary Woods, joined the *Columbia* in Vancouver on 1 February 1957. Recruited in England, she was attracted by the opportunities for adventure and exploring new horizons. Looking at the little ship, that seemed a miniature of what her imagination had conjured up, she suffered a twinge of dismay. But after a quick tour of the *Columbia* with Towell—and hearing tall tales of shipboard life and the exhilarating dangers of seafaring—she found herself "Queen of all I surveyed." Happily, this seemed precisely the challenge Dr. Woods had come to find: independence, opportunity and immersion in a new culture. Her lilting reports exude an energetic brightness, a sense of excitement at contemplating the natural beauties of the coast, and a sympathetic absorption in the alien world of logging camps and secluded settlements. Checking that the ship was "in all respects ready for sea," Greene quipped about the new member of the crew: "And I give her 100% on the trimness of her cabin 'up forrard'. It's slightly different from that of my brother Heber 'back aft.'" A notorious clutterbug, Heber's sloppiness was legendary.

An enterprising woman, Woods not only played the organ at impromptu services, but took every opportunity to develop the Mission's mandate. During her first stop at Bull Harbour, for example, she surprised the CCM by signing medical health contracts with all the families at the Department of Transport's wireless station. After seven months with *Columbia*, however, she reported a symptomatic slump in her practice. Logging camps had for the most part failed to open, patients had no real complaints, and those that did come had only done so in order to make use of their medical coverage on the contract plan, and "were unable to satisfy my professional appetite." On average, she saw one and half patients per day. And in the Native villages she found "just a few old aches and pains, and the inevitable teeth to be extracted." Little had changed by the end of 1957; twenty-five polio shots and sixty chest-rays were done as part of the provincial government's public health program.

Mary Woods returned to England in the early summer of 1958. Her place was filled temporarily by a retired physician, A.E. Riddell, who had frequently substituted as relief surgeon whenever needed. This next trip in *Columbia* was to be his last, though; he died suddenly at home on North Pender Island, thereby bringing another important association to a close. With the death of Dr. Darrell Hanington on 8 March 1958 at the age of seventy-three, the Mission lost one of its few remaining links with the earliest days of the medical ministry. A devout Christian and loyal churchman all his life, he had succeeded Antle's first medical doctor, W.A. Hutton, as surgeon of the first *Columbia* in 1906. A native of Yale, BC, where his father had practised medicine for seventy-five years, Hanington had taken his medical degree at McGill before returning home to join Antle. He later served as surgeon at Queen's Hospital, Rock Bay, where he met and married Janet Riddock, a nurse in the Victorian Order of Nurses.

The first female physician to join after Patrick Ellis became superintendent in 1960 was Dr. Joyce Davies. Early in 1961, she took over from Dr. A.E. Dale who was moving on to medical mission in Inuvik, NWT. With a rather gauche attempt at humour, Ellis's welcoming remarks published in *The Log* may reveal his own discomfort at having a woman join as ship's surgeon:

> We have had women doctors on the *Columbia* before and I gather that they have been quite a success. I know that many of the women welcome the idea of having another woman in this professional field to whom they can talk, but I suspect that there will be many bashful men who will have to be dragged into the surgery before they will face a woman doctor! Anyhow we extend a very warm welcome to Dr. Joyce Davies . . . I am sure that you will all come to love her and that you will benefit from her skill in the medical profession.

While Superintendent Ellis was in eastern Canada on another of the fundraising lecture tours which had characterized Mission public relations since John Antle's day, Dr. Davies was learning the ropes of seagoing ministry at the toughest season of the year. Gales in the northern region whipped up tumultuous seas and lashed the ship with razor-sharp rain and sleet—followed by those wondrous lulls when mariners contemplate their bearings. Dr. Davies described one scene:

In the midst of winter Gales the Pacific Ocean suddenly remembered its name early in February for a few hours, and allowed the doctor and chaplain to visit Pine Island Lighthouse. There was some swell, especially in the narrow cove the keepers call "Grand Canyon," so we were glad that they lowered their [own] larger boat by engine and cable. We visited the families of Mr. Pen Brown and his assistant Mr. Ranger, and our sack of mail that we'd brought from Port Hardy was naturally well received.

Yet for all the adventure such work provided, it offered little that was medically interesting, and doctors continued to come and go. W.R. Simpson, a retired physician from Victoria who had filled in frequently before, spent a few weeks at sea in 1962. He was succeeded in 1963 by Dr. Cezar Heine, who punctuated his medical ministrations with innovative educational programs directed towards alleviating specific health problems among the coastal population. As physician and public health mentor, he appeared in camps and in print. Dr. Heine's popular columns in *The Log* presented clearly written discussions on nutrition, obesity and the risks of smoking. After two years aboard *Columbia*—an extraordinarily long time for the period—he left with his wife Jan and toddler Andrew to work with the Native peoples in Hazelton. Ellis observed on his departure that "we could not have asked for a more wonderfully devoted Christian doctor to serve with us."

Because of the shortage of doctors, Ellis was unable to announce Heine's successor. "But we pray that God will stir the heart of some doctor to carry on the valuable work that has been done so that the health of our people will not be jeopardized." Dr. Monica Shackleton arrived in 1965 but left before year's end—earlier than expected. Obviously, the work was medically unchallenging. Having advertised for doctors, the Mission could do little more than pray that somebody would take her place.

The Mission's Diamond Jubilee in 1965 was a time of reassessment, particularly of the medical work. Although the altered circumstances brought about by the industrial and social development of the province were now all too obvious, the CCM clung faithfully to its tradition. Human need and loneliness must be addressed wherever found. Writing in *The Log*, Cecil FitzGerald captured the mood of the board's deliberations:

> There remains as the work of the Columbia Coast Mission the Mission Ship *Columbia* and her medical and spiritual ministrations. This ship works in an area still difficult of access and still requiring a special form of ministry.

The *Columbia* ran without a physician until the autumn of 1966, when it was joined by Dr. Fred Wiegand and his wife Helen. A thirty-three-year-old Montrealer who had just completed his surgery specialization at that city's Royal Victoria Hospital, he doubtless felt the Mission would provide excellent opportunity to practise his newly acquired skills. Indeed, the Mission sometimes looked very challenging on paper with its promises of wilderness medicine and adventure. Wiegand had worked variously during his student days: as a roughneck in the Alberta oil fields, in the iron mines of Labrador and in the eastern Arctic. On arrival he acclaimed "the rugged beauty and magnificence" of the British Columbia coast. But the work disappointed him. Emergency calls often required far less than he was trained to give. In late October 1966, for example, the *Columbia* lay at anchor in Kelsey Bay when an emergency call summoned him to attend a difficult childbirth at Gilford Island Indian Reserve. Fortunately, he recalled, "an ABAS [Alert Bay Air Service] float plane was nearby, so [I] scrambled to get necessary supplies, jumped into the plane, and landed at the village only about half an hour later." But by the time he arrived, the baby was stillborn; the doctor had little to do as its mother was fine. The only other emergency that month left his surgical skills similarly unchallenged: transporting a patient to St. George's Hospital in Alert Bay. Now run by an independent incorporated board, the hospital put Wiegand's patient into the care of its own medical staff. Beyond finding three hungry and wet runaway children and returning them to St. Michael's Residential School at Alert Bay, Wiegand had little to do that month but help conduct the funeral for the stillborn child, and lend a hand trying to refloat a stranded gillnetter. Small wonder that medical doctors moved on in search of broader professional prospects.

Yet Wiegand was not despondent. He saw the Mission's medical service as having done precisely what it should have been doing from the very beginning. "Certainly, the goal of every medical mission is to work itself out of a job," he wrote. The Mission's record "will ever be a source of pride." In establishing its distinctive medical service, the CCM not only met real human needs and alleviated suffering, but helped lay the foundations for a province-wide health care system which counted "high quality and far-reaching public health nursing, and the availability of regular float plane air service" among its attributes. Wiegand also noted the significant population shifts from wilderness to towns, and the major impact they exerted on the fate of the medical mission. Though he did not use the term, he was in fact commenting on the process of secularization, a major theme in the Mission's history.

The *Columbia* was now drawing its potential patients from a population of about four hundred people. The key to successful emergency treatment clearly lay in an ability to transport patients swiftly to medical centres with modern diagnostic and therapeutic facilities. In this light, *Columbia* was like a slow-motion shuttle-bus which no longer required a doctor. With Wiegand's departure at the end of 1966, the medical work of the Mission ceased. He had served barely four months.

In fact, the medical mission had a far greater impact upon coastal people than the story of purely medical treatment might suggest. It was a major instrument of the institution's larger function of "ministering to the body, mind and soul," the motto which graced some of the early annual reports. This larger role was achieved in a variety of subtle ways. It was rooted in St. Luke's words that served as the CCM's enduring motto: "Heal the sick . . . and say unto them, The Kingdom of Heaven is come nigh unto you." The healing process often involved restoring people's feelings of self-worth; it meant integrating them into a caring community which, no matter how far away, was always with them in spirit; it meant sharing the joys and sorrows of their common humanity. Among the few remaining testimonials lies an appreciative letter of 1966 from the inhabitants of Pine Island Light, a weather-beaten outcropping jutting into Queen Charlotte Sound, where Mr. and Mrs. R.P. Brown had lived for ten years:

We agree with the view that a public health nurse making tours on the *Columbia* is the right thing now, but we shall miss your doctors. There have been some wonderful people, who have been both a help to us in time of need and wonderful company for their occasional visits.

None had the sparkling personality of Dr. Wiegand, what a marvelous person. The late Dr. Riddell, fascinated by our resident auklets, was hauled ashore with difficulty, Dr. Stevenpiper—keen on gardening and poultry; Dr. Davies—a yachtswoman to whom small boats were no terror; Dr. Woods—very understanding of women's problems; Dr. Onhauser—with real appreciation of natural diets; and Dr. Shackleton; Dr. Heine—really quite special, but how he suffered from seasickness; Dr. Dale—who suffered such tragedy, and then the terrible fire he was in; Dr. Tafton and the Dr. from Courtenay with a heart condition—don't remember his name, but my wife had strained some muscles near her heart from too much mattocking and heavy garden work, and he was able to pinpoint that trouble right away and tell us what she should not do and how to mend it. All devoted doctors, wonderful men, and I imagine true servants of Christ.

This letter bears witness not only to the high regard in which the medical services were held (including the fine women despite its concluding praises for the "wonderful men"). It also attests to the staffing difficulties which dogged the Mission from the start. In the course of their ten years at Pine Island Light, the Browns had benefited from the ministrations of no less than eleven doctors.

With the passing of the medical personnel, it became increasingly clear that the state was taking over the services and facilities which the church had pioneered. Yet at times, the transfer of control from church to secular society seemed poignant indeed. The process was underscored graphically by the fate of the buildings in Pender Harbour once known as St. Mary's Hospital and Chapel. When it was announced in June 1971 that the long-empty and deteriorating "Hospital Gets New Life," the Pender Harbour newspaper, *Peninsula Voice*, explained it was to become a hotel, with the church turned into a cabaret. Perhaps this was a fitting transition for a building which had served its community so well. Rather than suffer the wrecker's axe and disappear altogether, it would remain a central, lively presence overlooking the harbour to which so many had once come seeking help.

CHAPTER 7

Potlatch and White Man's Prayers

Nothing has done more to popularize the work
of the Columbia Coast Mission among the Native peoples of
British Columbia than Margaret Craven's novel *I Heard the Owl
Call My Name* (1973). Based on the work of the Reverend Eric
Powell at Kingcome Inlet, and on Craven's visit there in October
1962, it is a haunting story sensitively woven with Native and
European lore. Ultimately it reveals the spiritual journey of a young
priest who, listening deeply to the voices of the Native people
among whom he ministers, is transformed by the experience. The
novel captures not only the transformation of a missionary, but a
turning point in the Columbia Coast Mission itself. Yet, neither
the real-life missionary nor the perceptive novelist was alone in
trying to participate in a dialogue and learn the wisdom of the
First Nations. In celebrating the Mission's sixtieth anniversary in
1965, Bishop Godfrey Gower spoke of the Native people's gift to
a radically secularized non-Native society which had once deemed
itself the sole bearer of "true religion and piety":

> Twentieth century man has forgotten his Creator; he
> thinks that he is very self-sufficient, and he thinks he
> can handle things very much to his own satisfaction. At
> least the Indian has not done this. True, he must adapt
> himself to this technological age—to scientific things. He
> must have an education; but I hope there is one thing
> that the Indian will never lose—the sense of the Spiritual

—the sense that there is something beyond which you can taste or see or handle. The sense of standing in the presence of something infinitely bigger. The sense of awe in the presence of even the movements of nature. We must give and we must receive. Here is one thing the Indian can contribute to our rather sophisticated and secular society.

As with other missionary groups, the Mission's early involvement with the Native peoples of the British Columbia coast shows little inclination toward the concept of dialogue. In fact, the Mission's ministry was strongly marked by a paternalistic approach which was itself cast in the mould of British imperialism. For Powell, this was the dark side of the Mission's history. Yet, so deeply rooted was this attitude of cultural and religious superiority that many early Church of England missionaries were scarcely aware of their ingrained bias. Sincere in their belief that they were toiling in the Lord's vineyard for the cure of souls—what they sometimes called "childish" and "depraved" souls—their imposed benevolence often smacked of cultural indoctrination. ⸴

To be fair, church relations with the Native peoples reflected both the attitudes and legislation of the British and the Canadian governments. Following on the Civilization of Indian Tribes Act (1857) and the first Indian Act (1876), successive legislation actively promoted assimilation of the Native into non-Native society. Indian culture was deemed to be no more than a transitional condition which must be transcended by inculcation of White-European values. "Civilizing" the Natives aimed at the virtual destruction of their culture. To this end, traditional Native practices such as the Sundance and the Potlatch were officially suppressed. Even today, the current Indian Act of 1951 remains an essentially Victorian statute that continues to resist change.

If the missionaries' early attitudes now seem misguided, there is no denying the Mission's abiding concern for the welfare of its Native charges. Early records reveal compassion, commitment, care—and an often hard-nosed conviction that the Native peoples had to be equipped with British culture and manners if they were going to cope with the demands of the twentieth century. However gently they expressed such ideas, most missionary workers had little doubt about what was best for the Native people in their charge.

The Mission began its work among the indigenous peoples as an exclusively medical venture when the first *Columbia* included them in her regular patrol. Typically, it involved about fifty-six ports of call between Port Hardy at the northern tip of Vancouver Island, and Pender Harbour in the south, stopping off at logging communities known by such unofficial names as Ben Willet's Camp, Geo. O'Brien's Camp, Scott's Camp and Anderson's Camp. En route to these and other outposts, the vessel visited the isolated lighthouse communities of Pine Island and Scarlet Point. Problems of Native health in Alert Bay prompted the *Columbia* to begin calling at the Native settlements of Village Island, Karlukewees, Kingcome, Fort Rupert and Nahwii. Quite independently, two nurses—Miss Kathleen O'Brien and Miss Nixon—took it upon themselves to provide medical services on Village Island. Soon convinced of the need for general education for all Native children, as well as of the need for nurses, teachers and missionaries, the two women purchased and repaired a float house at their own expense. The *Columbia* towed it to other locations, eventually bringing it to Alert Bay where the Reverend M. Comley, who was in charge of the Anglican Church's Indian work, had erected the first schoolhouse, building it virtually single-handedly. By 1927 the Columbia Coast Mission formally assumed responsibility for the villages beyond Alert Bay, and Misses Nixon and O'Brien (the latter then fifty-two years old) officially joined the Mission. Alert Bay, which was becoming a vital focal point for coastal trade and fishing, also became the major centre of the church's medical and educational mission to the Indians.

The other major focus in those years was farther north at the Kwagiulth village on the Kingcome River at the head of Kingcome Inlet. Kingcome was originally a ward of the Church Missionary Society of England, and the Reverend A.W. Corker became its first Anglican pastor in July 1889. The Native population at the time shifted between their winter settlement of Gwayasdums (Gilford Island), where Corker had built a school in 1891, and the summer settlement at Kingcome. Lying within the bounds of the Diocese of New Westminster, Kingcome's medical and pastoral needs were placed in the hands of the Mission in 1930. John Antle described the rugged adversity which his two lay workers, Miss Eva Dyer and Miss Davies, faced:

Here the physical conditions are all but unbearable. Floods are due in the fall and the spring, and the swift-running water often creeps up to the floors of the school and things look more than discouraging. But Miss Dyer and her companion stay with the job. Children are taught, the sick are visited, and the Indians, both men and women, are gathered together, especially on the Lord's Day, for spiritual refreshment. Then . . . every two weeks, the *Columbia* comes to the mouth of the river [whereupon] a launch containing the Doctor and Padre comes buzzing up the three miles to the village, and for a brief period [the two women and the villagers] are in touch with the rest of the world.

Antle admired self-sacrifice and quite typically could not help using *The Log* to chide the well-heeled church-women back in civilization: "Think of this, you women who live softly in the city, with your electric servants which make life easy, and realize that it is women of this kind, the Florence Nightingales, that still keep alive our veneration for your sex." Nor did he want people to forget Miss Victoria Cadwallader who single-handedly operated the Indian school in Fort Rupert:

This is supposed only to be a school where children are taught to speak, read and write English, but it is more than that. Victoria knows their language and is looked up to by the young Indians, and her influence among them is incalculable.

Little was being done in the remaining villages except to send the children up to the so-called big school, the Indian residential school in Alert Bay. The reports and correspondence of these years reveal strong differences of opinion concerning Native schooling, perhaps even a full-muscled tug-of-war, between the Anglican Church and

Village Island, 1938.

the Columbia Coast Mission. The church supported the government and the Indian agent without question; the Mission did not. Church and government authorities were content to remove Indian children to the residential school for months at a time, thus breaking up families and alienating children from their culture. The missionaries, beginning with John Antle himself, advocated the village day school, with pupils living at home in their own culture.

In the summer of 1930, the principal of the Indian residential school in Alert Bay, F. Earl Anfield, toured the day schools in the outlying villages as far as Bella Bella. He was highly regarded by the Natives for the work he had done among them in Alert Bay and on Village Island. Chief Jimmy Sewid respected him as a man who trusted the Natives and was "a great worker for the church." Anfield reported the day schools were "without exception, well built, well equipped, and, best of all, in the hands of quite well trained and devoted teachers." To his mind, however, a principal problem lay in the day schools' being used as feeders for the residential schools, which "take away the best of the children to the larger centres," abandoning the less educable and less motivated to village life. Most of the parents placed little value on

Village Island, 1938.

"white" education. As Anfield tried to impress upon them, "if day schools were properly supported by the parents, there would be no need of primary class rooms in our residential schools." Ultimately, he saw the day schools "as an agent in the introducing of Indian children to the routine and life of the larger schools." Significantly, Jimmy Sewid moved from Village Island to Alert Bay precisely because of better educational opportunities for his children.

"The front line of Indian education," Antle explained, was the day school teachers. "These noble workers, often in the loneliest and most disheartening places," performed their "heroic" tasks "in face of real difficulties and often hardships and loneliness." Antle's thoughts highlighted the tough conditions under which such women spent years of service. The record is not clear as to just how long the lay workers endured, though we do know that Kathleen O'Brien remained for twenty years on one station, retiring in 1945. Her maternalism towards the Native people encompassed moral as well as medical concerns. As she once wrote to Alan Greene: "I have been reproaching the leading [Native] Church members that this year God has not been put first, and they accept the reproach. They really are rather dears, for they always seem nicer to us when I have felt it necessary to point out what I feel has been wrong." As a valedictory note explains, she had endured "as well by reason of the merry wit as the wisdom and balanced mind which this selfless and tender-hearted woman brings to bear on Indian and all other problems surrounding her since, one Epiphany-tide in England, she sought Divine guidance to the Mission field—and was led to Village Island."

The Mission also differed with the church over the potlatch, which had been banned by the Department of Indian Affairs in 1885. In tradition and jurisprudence, the potlatch is a very complex issue. Suffice to say that, whereas church and government sought to eradicate, under pain of fine or imprisonment, the "primitive" and "heathen" practice (whereby Indians would give away all they owned in the course of weeks of bountiful celebrations), the Mission appealed to the Superintendent of Indian Affairs for more compassion and understanding. Indeed, the Mission regarded the outlawing of the potlatch as akin to the liquor prohibition laws of both Canada and the US, pointing out they had led to even greater excesses than the practices they had been introduced to control—bootlegging by whites, among them. According to the Mission, prohibiting the potlatch completely led "altogether to the detriment of the Indian and any work, medical, social, or religious, that his well-wishers may be trying to do for him." In the July 1930 issue of *The Log*, Antle expiated further:

> The old customs handed down through the generations are very dear to the Indian. Some of the things connected with the potlatch are not in accord with our Christian civilization and the Indians realize this and are willing to forego them. There is also much in the potlatch that is well worth preserving . . . Frankly, our sympathies are with the Indian, and our hope is that the authorities will go carefully into the matter and devise some modification of the present condition [of sweeping prohibition of the practice]. This will . . . gain the gratitude of the Indian, and the respect of all white men who know enough of the situation to fairly appreciate it.

In the fall of 1930, John Antle reported on one of his many trips to the Kingcome Indian village, where the potlatch survived to a greater degree than anywhere else on the coast. Comprising some two hundred inhabitants, the village originated with the merging of three different Kwagiulth tribes drawn together by the convenience of communal fishing. Having chosen this site for its bush hospital, the Mission first bought a makeshift shack from the Powell River Paper Company. It scarcely survived the journey overland and upriver. By 1930, however, "with the help of the Indian Department and the Diocese, a fine building [stood] large enough to combine a dwelling for the staff with a room capable of seating all the inhabitants of the village."

Two lay workers, who transferred from St. George's Hospital in Alert Bay to spend a winter in Kingcome, had the task of opening up the house after it had stood empty for most of the summer. Rain had seeped in, the stove had rusted and pipes hung loose. In the fall of 1930, nurse Margaret A. Solomon and her teacher-colleague, E.H. Adams, arrived aboard the *Columbia*, bringing enough groceries to last until fresh supplies came from Vancouver in the spring. Trained together at the Church of England Deaconess House in Toronto, the two women looked forward to the enterprise, despite its hardships. The ever helpful homesteader Ernest Halliday provided them with fresh produce and, in Solomon's words, "took us up river in his canoe and assisted us in getting a fire lit."

In January 1931, Antle officiated at what Nurse Margaret Solomon described as the most important event of the month: the baptism of twenty-four Natives of all ages, including "several Indian chiefs." Sensitive to the interface between cultures and faith, she was especially struck by the conversion of Mr. and Mrs. Jim Punquiet, an elderly couple thought to be almost one hundred years old:

This old couple received instruction in their home, with the aid of an interpreter. They opened their hearts to us and told of having heard the gospel message in their youth at Fort Rupert. Since that time they had believed in a personal God who could and would help them in

Kingcome village gathering, 1 May 1937. Note the red ensign and the placard (left rear) "God Save the King."

times of sickness and in perils when canoeing, and they had never ceased to pray to Him for help and guidance.

The Native peoples' commitment to the Christian faith was nonetheless fraught with serious difficulties. Conversion largely implied a rejection of the old ways of Native life. As a number of Kingcome's leaders explained to the missionaries at the commencement of confirmation classes that year: "if it was considered wrong to carry on some of their Indian practices, then they would not be confirmed because they could not give them up." The Natives therefore withdrew to ponder their situation. Just which practices they felt at risk is not stated, but the Natives clearly had aspects of the potlatch in mind. Hearsay among the non-Native population associated the potlatch with drunkenness and debauch. On his next visit, John Antle placed the matter firmly in the context of church and state, and in Solomon's words, "showed that certain practices would be a sin against God [simply] because it was against the present laws of the country." Once again, the "certain practices" were not defined.

Speaking during a special evening service for the Indians, Antle preached on the text "Render to Caesar the things that are Caesar's, and to God the things that are God's" (Mark 12:17). Regrettably, the argument he developed from this text is not extant. Although Antle's preaching notes are missing, we do know the meetings went on for days. For lay missionary Margaret Solomon, it seemed that battle lines had been drawn between two Native camps: the "staunch Christians" of the village on one side, and the "anti-Christians" on the other, with "Satan making a last stand." When it came for a decision, Margaret Solomon reported, the people met in the mission house:

> As usual, we allowed the people to choose the hymns. From the first we felt it to be an unusual meeting. Everyone was keyed up. All the old staunch Christians were there. As the meeting progressed the hymns chosen led to a climax . . . hymn 403 "Art Thou Weary, Art Thou Languid"; [hymn] 755, "Come, Ye Sinners, Poor and Wretched"; [hymn] 781 "We Have Heard the Joyful Sound, Jesus Saves"; [and hymn] 562 "Nearer, My God, to Thee." Then Mr. Tom Dawson was called upon to give the message that had been sent to him during the last few days . . . The message was given in the native tongue and afterwards interpreted for our benefit . . . Imagine our suspense! But then imagine our surprise and joy . . . when we heard the text in English, Ezek[iel] 18:17: "When the wicked man turneth away from his wickedness that he hath committed, and doeth that which is lawful and right, he shall save his soul alive" . . . Following this message, Mr. Dick Webster, an Indian chief . . . called upon the meeting to help the mission in every way and cooperate with us in the various lines of work undertaken in this village.

In January 1931, the bishop of New Westminster visited Kingcome for the first time to conduct the first confirmation service ever held at the village. Eight persons presented themselves. Not a huge number, but the resident nurse found the occasion uplifting:

"Although a very stormy day, the Indians came in large numbers, nearly filling the church hall. All were eager to welcome their bishop and were honored to think that he had given up a part of his busy life to hold a service in their midst." The nurse's somewhat condescending description leaves no hint that this kind of work was precisely the kind of thing to which the bishop ought to have been devoting a good part of his time. In the absence of any Native records or memory of such events, we are left with a skewed picture.

It is clear that John Antle and some senior leaders of the Anglican Church were far more sympathetic to the traditions of the Native peoples than either the government or its agents. Writing in November 1931, Antle spoke of Bishop Schofield's visit to Kingcome to discuss questions of Native traditions and culture with Native representatives. In contrast to what Antle decried as the government's heavy-handed assault on Native culture by legal and administrative fiat, the bishop had simply come to listen, to learn and to share. "Perhaps if there had been more heart to heart talks of this kind in the past," Antle mused, "there would not be so many non-Christian Indians in the Quagutl [sic] tribe as there are at the present time." Supporting his bishop's view, Antle argued "that intolerance and the use of the big stick never yet advanced the cause of Christ, nor helped to spread his message." Once more, the maverick minister came down on the side of the Native peoples. He virtually accused whites of cultural imperialism, the abuse of law and theft:

No one with [even] the smallest amount of love for his fellow man can fail to sympathize with a people on whom like a bolt from the blue, the mandate of the law has fallen, sweeping away customs which have been practiced by them through the centuries, upsetting their whole social system, and laying ruthless hands on family treasures valued by their owners above rubies. The potlatch would pass away in time anyway and no one knows this better than the Indians, but why outrage and embitter a people whose only crime is to love their own people,

and their own customs and who wish to be let alone
to enjoy what is theirs in their own way.

Antle hoped dialogue between Bishop Charles Schofield and Native
leaders might help heal some of the wounds. The Natives "deserve
of the White man, who is fast absorbing the country which was
once all theirs, at least a square deal."

In February 1932, the Mission published "A Plea for the Modification of the Law Prohibiting Potlatches." Analytical and sharply
critical of "citizens who sit back and look with contempt upon
the red men, once supreme in this province of ours," the plea
accused the dominant white population of having degraded the
indigenous peoples by exploitation and the abuse of power. Even
the gentlest paternalism of the Mission's own members was not
spared: "One missionary, the Reverend Holmes, late of the Columbia Coast Mission, once reprovingly remarked in his kindly
manner that Indians are like little children, they have to be taught."
But in teaching, the article continued, "so many white people
omit to practise the very things they preach." The government's
brutal repression of the potlatch was simply the most salient case
in point:

> Before white men crowded them so utterly into the
> background, [and began] passing laws that deprived the
> Natives of every liberty, every custom that meant so
> much to them socially—for social standing was the key-
> note to nearly all their ceremonies—potlatching took a
> very prominent part . . .

According to the Mission's plea, white culture had torn Native
culture from its roots and robbed the Native peoples of their
self-awareness, the distinctiveness of their culture, and their self-
esteem. "Completely stripped of their background," the Natives
had been left with "no traditions to keep up, no family pride to
help them, for that very pride of their ancestors has been cruelly
shamed and forbidden under the white man's compelling law."
White culture had therefore cast the younger generation of Natives
into a wilderness diaspora with neither cultural memory nor a

Kingcome village, 1938. (l. to r.) Mrs. H. Johnson, Mrs. B. Sandy, Mrs. B. Robertson, Mrs. P. Scow.

healthful sense of self-identity. The Mission argued that dialogue with the Indians, and genuine compassion with their condition, would reveal ways in which they themselves would curb any improprieties in potlatch practices. At the same time, it continued, dialogue and compassion would have nurtured those positive aspects of the potlatch—generosity, hospitality, ceremonial and symbolism—which expressed the inner spirit of their culture. No records suggest how this plea was received.

In Kingcome, meanwhile, the anglicizing (or "anglicanizing") of Native culture continued. Teachers taught the British Columbia school curriculum as far as possible, while spiritual and social life were organized according to Anglican tradition: a WA (Women's Auxiliary) for the women; a JA and GA (Junior Auxiliary and Girls' Auxiliary) for the girls; and scouting and cubs for the boys, based on the principles of Lord Baden Powell to "Do your Duty to God and the King." Reports revealed successes. One year the Native community raised $120 to buy lumber to build church pews; another year they had raised $90 for a bell and built a bell tower. Sunday School had enrolled thirty children and, the nurses reported, "our Wednesday night prayer meeting shows that the Indians are really seeking after God."

Native life focussed on its traditional activities of fishing, gathering and hunting, with villagers sometimes leaving for weeks at a time in search of their livelihood. Poor seasons, like the fall and winter of 1933, created particular hardships. Where the normal seasonal catch of fish was about four hundred per family, some fishermen were returning with nothing, and the salmonberry crop was also a failure. An exceptionally high river and three floods added to the misery. And yet, to judge by Margaret Solomon's notes, fundraising for a new church building remained a priority. One searches in vain to discover who it was that established the order of priorities in such times of physical deprivation and indeed, whether the Mission played a role in supplementing the meagre food supplies.

While buildings seemed to offer a sense of permanence and stability to the work of the Mission, personnel shifts spelled uncertainty. At Kingcome, missionaries came and went. By the spring of 1934, the village's three missionaries had resigned: Margaret Solomon for mission work in the Arctic, her sister L.K. Solomon for the Okanagan, and E.H. Adams to work in South Africa. The three were replaced in August by two energetic young women: Amy Wakefield as nurse, and the teacher Phyllis M. Arrowsmith, who forwarded a preliminary report:

> [We] arrived at . . . 3 a.m. on August 31st [and were] heartily welcomed by Mr. [Ernest] Halliday and Mr. Reg Halliday, and taken to the home of the former where we found a bedroom already prepared for us . . . Later, in the afternoon, we were escorted by Mr. and Mrs. Reg Halliday in their gas boat *Marylea* to the foot of the Reserve, where we transferred to a large Indian canoe, in which was the Chief and two other Indians. We landed at the lower end of the village and were conducted to the mission by the Chief, while the canoe took our trunks . . . direct to the mission . . . We are now installed and the year's work has begun . . .

If Kingcome was the most settled enterprise, then Village Island was perhaps the least. Here, two nurses and a teacher tried to cope with a shifting and transient Native population. Whole families simply disappeared for months at a time, removing large numbers of children from the day school. Faced with difficulties of control and administration, Murray Todd, the Indian agent at Alert Bay, contemplated reorganizing Native life by concentrating the various bands and their six villages into two large communities. Accordingly, he sought the best sites for the amalgamated villages. Significantly, Chief Jimmy Sewid approved of this move, as did John Antle. It "would enable the [Indian] department as well as the Church to concentrate their energies and their funds [thus resulting] in very much improved equipment, and much better opportunity to influence the life of the Indian, especially the rising generation, both as to his social and religious life," Antle wrote. Moving from backward, poorly equipped villages into more "progressive" ones was Sewid's view too. Antle saw in Todd a man motivated solely by his conviction that the day school and Christian faith were the mainstays "in the training and development of the Indians on this Coast." Sewid saw him as "a wonderful man [who] was just like a father to me." Others saw Todd as a manipulative and insensitive man bent on enjoying whatever power his office could afford. In the event, his attempt at amalgamation failed.

Years passed, but patterns of life remained constant. While many Natives were absent from the Kingcome reserve each winter, trapping and clamming, and whole families were absent fishing in the summers, the Mission station continued its medical and educational work. Visited every two weeks by the *Columbia*, the three laywomen now responsible for the station pursued their goals. The end of 1938 saw the completion of three major projects in Kingcome. Men of the village had designed and built St. George's Church using lumber purchased with funds raised by the village Women's Auxiliary and a matching grant from Archbishop DePencier. They also built an assembly hall, and levelled a regulation-size sports field. External support came from various sources. The Indian agent donated toward the purchase of a stove, the Girls' Club of St. John's Church in Strathroy, Ontario, provided embroidered altar linen, and many others had contributed in both money and kind

King George V Totem Pole at Kingcome (1938) with hand-carved plaque proclaiming that the deceased king, "who ruled so kind so gentle with wisdom from above," is still alive in British hearts.

to complete the much-needed facilities. Officials of church and government attended the inaugural celebrations which honoured the work of the Mission. Along with medical clinics and church services in both English and the Native tongue, Kwakwala, the Mission offered regular primary education and Sunday School. Eventually, music lessons were introduced for the young, including attempts at forming both a kazoo band and some vague nucleus of a brass band with instruments donated and bought.

In 1936, carvers erected in front of the mission house a forty-foot totem pole—the first in many years. The government had forbidden the raising of totems, "and the Church, bless their English hearts, went along with it," as Eric Powell later observed. But Bishop DePencier outmanoeuvred officialdom by "blessing it [in 1938] as 'the King George V [memorial] totem pole' as a slap against the government; for as the King George totem pole it had to be okay." The missioners sent a photograph and description to George VI and were delighted to receive a letter in acknowledgement. This they framed and put on display. Yet apart from this tactical deception understood by only a few, the church (and later the Mission under Alan Greene) largely rejected Native culture.

When Archbishop DePencier arrived at Kingcome in May 1939, in the *Columbia*'s dinghy, accompanied by a staff correspondent from the *Vancouver Sun*, he had every reason to rejoice. Much progress had been made at the village. St. George's Church was freshly painted in honour of the first anniversary of its dedication, the playing field was "newly mown by hatchet," and over seventy Natives gathered to attend his service. As the reporter recalled, "no congregation the world over sang with more vigor and yet devoutness that grand old hymn 'Stand Up, Stand Up for Jesus'." A village committee informed the archbishop of their plans to erect a cottage hospital in the village and impressed him with the deep spiritual bond between the villagers and the church. The reporter concluded:

As the *Columbia*'s dinghy was about to start downstream, Chief Dick Webber led a party of his villagers down to the shore where under the greying twilight they bared their heads and sang in their native Kwakwalla [*sic*] "God Be With You Till We Meet Again."

Standing amidships in the dinghy, [the] Archbishop . . . was deeply touched by this spontaneous . . . token of affection. Their song ended, he gave them his blessing and the dinghy swept away downstream.

Beneath this veneer of civility ran currents of discontent. Thus, at the request of a number of Natives and chiefs who still held to their old traditions, a conference was convened at Kingcome Inlet on the weekend of 7 April 1940 under the auspices of the Columbia Coast Mission. The government sent Inspector Coleman of Indian Agencies in British Columbia and Murray Todd, the Indian agent in Alert Bay; the church was represented by the Archbishop. Present as observers were L. Earl Anfield, the principal of St. Michael's Indian Residential School at Alert Bay, and Kingcome homesteader, Ernest Halliday. As Alan Greene later wrote, the primary reason for the conference was Native reaction to Section 140 of the Indian Act. This section dealt with the practice of Native dances. As expressed in Greene's account, the section had been "framed years ago with a view to removing from the life of the Coastal Indians the evils of the potlatch, and more particularly the endless giving away of gifts in kind or in cash and the repeated impoverishment of the giver."

On this issue, the Indian Act expressed complete insensitivity to Native culture. It was oblivious to the fact that giving and sharing were central to Native culture; even the Chinook transliteration of the line in the Lord's Prayer—"Give us this day our daily bread" (*Potlatch konaway sun nesika muckamuck*)—underscored this view. In the rather one-sided discussions that passed for dialogue, the Natives gained nothing by pointing out that the whites frequently gave gifts and held parties at such festive occasions as Christmas; nor did it help to remind the white authorities that Jesus himself had enjoined his listeners to "give to him that asketh of thee" (Matthew 5:42), and "sell all thou hast and give to the poor, and thou shalt have treasure in heaven" (Mark 10:21). Even when quoting from the white man's scriptures, Indian arguments fell on deaf ears.

Ever the paternalist priest, Greene expressed "profoundest sympathy with the older indians who claim that these celebrations are the only form of entertainment they can possibly enjoy." But in doing so, he seems to have regarded Native customs as essentially theatrical rituals. Of Native culture he wrote, "the Indian is a born ritualist and in his love of gay colours shows a rare gift of interpretation as he portrays the cycles of nature, and the habits of animals and birds." Condescendingly sympathetic, Greene's descriptions reveal no real appreciation of the Natives' spirituality, no perception that the Natives might have had an important indigenous ethos or religious dimension of their own.

In the end, the amendment which he helped the Native delegation draft allowed them to continue their dances and associated gift-giving as long as gifts were limited to community dance prizes rather than the free bestowal of one individual's wealth on another. Greene claimed it took a day and half of consultation to formulate the amendment, for "the old Indians cannot speak English" and everything had to pass through an interpreter. (That did not prevent Greene and the archbishop from holding a church service entirely in English that evening—without an interpreter). Although Greene and the Native delegation spent two hours deciding how best to present the amendment to the government representatives, and though the Indian Inspector assured the assembly he had come "to listen, [and] to convey to his seniors the exact wishes of the Indians," Green's account leaves little doubt that it was the Natives who listened while the authorities preached law and order. Greene had hardened the Mission's position to the point of rejecting Antle's conciliatory approach to Native culture. Here as elsewhere, Greene argued that God and the king agreed with one another. King George VI and the Church of England required of the Natives essentially the same thing that God Himself demanded: unquestioning obedience to state authority.

> Inspector Coleman from time to time stressed . . . that the Church of England with its missionaries at Kingcome had for years . . . taught them the Law of God, and that it was their duty to live up to the Church's teaching . . . I, as I listened to this blunt-speaking layman, felt

it was a fine thing to have him rather than one of us parsons tell them just what it was the Church had been trying to do in their midst all these years.

Ultimately, Agent Todd committed himself to nothing but a vague promise: he would convey the Native peoples' wishes to Ottawa. By way of emphasizing the context of deliberations, "a very happy interlude" highlighted the conference. Everyone moved to the memorial totem that had been erected two years earlier, ostensibly as a tribute to the late King George V. And now "with due ceremony Inspector Coleman and a few of the chiefs laid memorial wreaths" while the archbishop offered prayers. In the absence of Native records, we can only infer the delicious ambiguity this ceremony projects: reverence for the English king, or mourning for a culture in decline. But as Greene later wrote, this commemorative obeisance to the Crown was of crucial importance. "It was a reminder again of the inherent loyalty of the Indian to the great Ghikumi, which means, one's chief," the Great White Father in England. This part of the conference no doubt served as an admonition that, whether they liked it or not, the Native peoples were subjects of the British Crown through the agencies of Indian Affairs and the Anglican Church. The church rarely missed an occasion to make this point.

While Mission life continued virtually unchanged with its emphasis on health care, day school, and church-focussed parish activities, there was an increasing split in the anglicanization of Native culture. While older Natives still depended on their own language, the younger ones were reported as growing increasingly indifferent to Native traditions and more accepting of the English tongue. Symptomatic of this, by the spring of 1941 the Mission offered two Sunday services at Kingcome—one in each language.

Whatever the success in turning the Kwagiulth into Anglicans, the Mission remained an unstable venture: the Natives still left from time to time to seek their livelihood elsewhere. Day schools came and went, and for a period of over eight months, from spring 1941 until the beginning of 1942, the Kingcome mission was virtually closed; even the lay workers had gone.

Bishop Godfrey Gower and Ernest Christmas heading up the Kingcome River in an outboard-powered dugout canoe, 1954.

By January 1942, however, the mission was again running with the arrival of layman Ernest Christmas and his family. They had been farming in Margo, Saskatchewan, for fourteen years and were seeking a new life. As Alan Greene announced, Ernest Christmas, his wife and fifteen-year-old son Edward were "all three deeply interested in the Church's work" and were eager "to undertake evangelistic, social and medical service." Judging by Mrs. Christmas's lengthy letters and reports, evangelism was a special priority. Greene reported at the time that the "Indians of the four Kingcome tribes are returning to the Mission, glad that schooling and religious guidance is available for them and their children." Again, there is no record of the Native point of view.

But that year, Natives in the parish of Alert Bay did express their views about the *Columbia*—very negative ones. So persuasive were their opinions, in fact, that the executive committee of the Diocese of British Columbia decided to withhold its annual grant to the Mission until such times as the ship improved the quality of its spiritual work. Parish minutes record that "Indians have never been satisfied with the work of *Columbia* since Reverend J. Antle left" in 1936, and that there existed a "noticeable gap between the CCM and the Parish of Alert Bay—Indians notice these things—the lack of co-operation is evident to all with eyes to see." They complained that the ship's captain—rather than the pastor or the physician—decided on the schedule. "The Chaplain has no say and cannot plan any worth-while work as far as the Church is concerned," one observed. "At Knights Inlet Cannery," reported another, "the Chaplain prepares for a service—the *Columbia*'s whistle blows, the Captain pulls out with the boat." In an acerbic letter to Bishop Harold Sexton, the Reverend Max Andrews, who had just completed seven months with the *Columbia*, added further fuel to the fires of discontent. He had found captain and crew "the most uncongenial men one could imagine for this type of work [who] haven't the slightest interest or sympathy in the Church life of the ship." They not only carped publicly about the church, but belittled the competence of *Columbia*'s medical personnel and hampered the work of the doctor and priest. He complained that the skipper visited favourite haunts for long periods of time, where there was no scope for the Mission, stopping only for the briefest times at places where the Mission had much to do. From Andrews' perspective, the *Columbia* was little more than a private yacht for the captain's convenience, and "not the fine piece of work which so many of our liberal contributors are led to believe." Frustrated by Alan Greene's lack of attention to his appeals, Andrews placed his proposals before his bishop. If *Columbia* was to be a real mission boat, both the physician and the clergy- man must help draw up the sailing schedule. Better still: "Dis- pense with the present crew and put Christian men on the boats."

Despite the comments of priests with similar complaints, Alan Greene did not take the bull by the horns. This was not the first case of Greene's failure to back up his clergy, resorting instead to a self-serving diversionary tactic: "You and other members of the Diocesan Executive Committee overlooked the fact that in spite of the rather sketchy spiritual work accomplished by the *Columbia*, there are still going on in many communities in your Diocese, the religious ministrations of the Church through my activities as skipper-parson of the *John Antle*," he wrote in August 1942. Ul- timately, Greene had to concede that "you may be right to some extent as to the time having come for a readjustment of the *Columbia*'s work." Greene shrugged off Max Andrew's serious complaints as little more than a petty squabble between *Columbia*'s skipper and crew on one hand, and Reverend Andrews and Dr. Simpson on the other. Replace these two men and all would be well. "If a self-denying missionary young priest could be secured, there is a vital work for the Church through the *Columbia*." In the best of all possible worlds, he implied, one should have ordained skippers in command.

Meanwhile, the wartime economy was offering Native people greater opportunities for employment outside their traditional occupations and territory. Fish canneries, for example, employed them in great numbers. Indeed, as the Reverend Heber Greene naively observed: "The fact that their fishing fleets have been augmented by the Japanese withdrawal from coast fishing has made great inroads on village life and upset the children's schooling." He offers no hint here of the federal government's War Measures Act, called into effect at the instigation of racist British Columbia politicians. Within twelve weeks of the Japanese attack on Pearl Harbor on 6 December 1941, the Act had sanctioned virtual deportation: the forcible removal of Japanese-Canadians from within one hundred miles of the Pacific coast, their detention in camps, and the confiscation and cheap resale of their homes and fishing boats. This was done despite security reports that Japanese-Canadians posed no threat to national security. This was no "Japanese withdrawal" as Heber Greene claimed even as late as 1946. The removal of Japanese-Canadians had been a public event, and passers-by could see their fellow citizens confined behind the barbed-wire fences of Vancouver's Exhibition Grounds, where they were guarded by Canadian soldiers with fixed bayonets.

Far more disturbing to the missionaries was the Native peoples' desertion of village life in favour of better-paying opportunities elsewhere. This semi-nomadic lifestyle struck the new Kingcome missionaries, Mr. and Mrs. Christmas, as entirely counterproductive. They saw a need for "spade work by the Columbia Coast Mission and its superintendent to get the Indian families reassembled in their ancestral, but somewhat remote, valley." Just what the missionaries had in mind is unclear, and Mission work continued much as in the past. It focussed on health care, day school and the propagation of the faith and of fealty to Britain. On ceremonial occasions, the community trooped to the King George V totem pole in front of St. George's Church, where they said prayers for the Empire. Patterning their work after the Church of England, missionaries soon added a Church Boys' League to the parish-oriented groups, and set the village on fund drives, either for the Red Cross or to contribute cigarettes to the army overseas. By 1943, they had sent eighty thousand cigarettes to eight Canadian regiments.

Despite the enhanced activity, it became clear to the Christmases that they would have to shift their operations to remain in contact with the Indians during seasonal fishing or foraging. Following the seasons, they too moved for long periods of time to the fish canneries at Glendale Cove in Knight Inlet. The correspondence of Mrs. Christmas gives the clear impression of a dedicated nurse struggling desperately to convert the Natives from paganism. Described by a journalist as a "cheery, courageous woman, [she] had been fighting blindness for years, yet no one who met her would have known it." She set herself the goal of writing a letter a night to the superintendent of the Mission discussing the issues of each day: ever "fighting under Christ's banner," despairing over the waywardness of her "childish" charges, rejoicing in the opportunities "in the Lord's vineyard," and "living the life of Hope." The potlatch caused her special anguish. Although to her mind the Natives did not practise this "excess" as they had prior to the enactment of federal law—she apparently did not know of the arrests in the 1920s—they occasionally held lengthy intertribal visits highlighted by dances, singing, ceremonies and "endless formal orations." Mrs. Christmas recognized that opinions were divided about how the Potlatch Law should be applied, and rejoiced whenever she thought she found evidence that the younger generation of Natives seemed indifferent to the old customs and traditions. Yet she remained convinced of "the real need for the Church to wean its charges from the pagan drag." The practise of such traditions, she wrote, "results in a withdrawal from mission life as such, including lapse of church attendance." The winter of 1943–

1944 seemed to her a particularly bad year for Native celebrations which, whatever their actual character, she now put down as "the Potlatch."

At last the superintendent of the Mission took action. Apparently without having inquired further into Mrs. Christmas's allegations, Greene involved the bishops of the Dioceses of New Westminster and British Columbia in a forthright condemnation of "this ancient practice" of potlatch. In a pompous formal declaration, Alan Greene concentrated all the elements that had characterized so much of the Church of England in Canada: paternalism, racial superiority and cultural imperialism. It is by no means clear that the Mission's founder, John Antle, nor many of its ordained ministers, would have supported Greene had they known the direction he was taking. Drafted on 29 February 1944, the document reveals little trace of the "great deal of thought and years of study" Greene claimed to have devoted to the potlatch issue. Although he suggested parenthetically that it might be possible to "plan some way by which all that is good in the Potlatch may be kept," he focussed primarily on its eradication. His document aimed at convincing "the Indians" of the White Man's altruistic benevolence in all things:

> If in the mind of your Sovereign, King George, and his Government here in Canada, it is best that the ancient custom should end, surely you like us White people will obey Him, and at this great and critical point in our history make any sacrifice that offers you a grand chance to step forward.

In conjuring up this "critical point in our history," Greene was alluding, of course, to the commitment of Canadian troops to the war in Europe. This was utterly irrelevant to the question of the potlatch. It also disregarded the fact that, by 1944, many Native people were also serving overseas in Canada's combat forces. (Jimmy Sewid's memoirs describe his own "call up.") Greene argued that Natives owed obedience simply because "we White people in the British Empire are making tremendous sacrifices of liberties and things we hold dear in order that we may save the

British Empire from destruction." This great service of "our sons and daughters far from home" was vital, for if the enemy won the war, the Indians would be "ruthlessly overrun [and] would be governed by a people that would treat you with very little love or respect." The Indians would "become dirt under their feet and ALL your liberties would be treated as nothing." Shown in this light, the sweet benevolence of both the Canadian government and the Anglican Church was meant to be abundantly clear to even the most obdurate proponents of the potlatch. So, too, was the church's role in colonial rule:

> The Church supports the State in this matter [of eradicating Native customs and the potlatch]. She never wishes to hurt you. She wants to lead you on step by step to the day when the Indians prove to the Government of Canada and its citizens that they are wise people, eager to learn from the wisdom of the White people . . .

Much of "white people's wisdom," like many "white people's prayers," had a political agenda. Thus, in the spring of 1944, while the Allies were preparing for the Normandy Invasion, lay missionary Ernest Christmas was watching the home defence unit of Natives known as the Pacific Coast Rangers "drilling and marching" in Alert Bay, and longed to form his own unit in Kingcome village. Just as hopeful as his wife in their cause of civilizing the pagan, he visualized a dream:

> It may be we shall have a contingent [of Rangers] yet "dressing by the right," forming "column of company," and other drill, right on our old football field, while their fathers look on and consider the change from their forefathers' day of pounding tom-toms and the age of potlatches.

CHAPTER 8

Two-World Tensions

"THE PEOPLE CONTINUE AN ATTEMPT TO LIVE in two worlds at once—the ancient one and the one which contains such modern advantages as they would no wise wish to relinquish," lay missionary Mrs. Christmas wrote from Kingcome. Throughout the 1940s, she continually deplored the Natives' "open reversion" to their old ways. Whether she meant a falling away from the Christian faith, or a tendency to Native rites and social practices, is not clear. One thing was obvious: the Natives had to lead a "nomadic life"; they had to move between the remote settlement of Kingcome and the more accessible village of Gwyasdums (Gilford Island), and to the fish canneries like those at Bones Bay and Glendale. In response, Ernest Christmas chose the nomadic life for himself. In what he called "a venture of faith," he had the Mission purchase the twenty-eight-foot motorboat *Bob*, which he renamed the *Gwa-yee*, the Kwakwala word for the Kingcome village site. In December 1944, the boat made its first run from Vancouver to its patrol area, where it tended to the medical and pastoral needs that could not await the *Columbia*. Themselves nomads, the Christmases wrote of "going thirty-six hours without sleep in a winter storm and shepherding a very collapsible harmonium over epileptic logs." Ernest Christmas captured the rugged isolation of his first season aboard the *Gwa-yee*:

> Except for falling snow we should have been to Gwayasdums to have a Christmas service and party about

New Year's Day, as promised. Even after starting we were delayed first by minor engine trouble and then rough weather, so had to tie up at the head of the inlet four nights; to paraphrase the 'Wenceslas' carol, we were underneath the mountain right against the forest trees, by four rushing fountains; instead of [the carol's] frost and snow we had high winds with heavy rain, but inside our small [five by seven-foot] cabin we were able to catch up on Christmas mail. From the boat we could touch the mountain face down which the waterfalls poured in tons per minute and upon which flourished firs which were seedlings in Wenceslas's time.

Under more favourable weather, *Gwa-yee* eventually reached Gwayasdums. There the Mission needed buildings for its pastoral and medical services. For the time being, however, the Christmases were happy to accept the Native peoples' hospitality:

. . . for our big "Xmas" get-together we managed with the old-time big house—earthen floor, roof open to the sky above the central fire, and the original seating accommodation of a low platform along each of the side walls; the place is roughly 75 ft. long by 36 ft. wide, with giant totems in due position. To one of these, its grotesque features peering through the tinselled branches, our 15-ft. "Xmas" tree was lashed . . . About 150 persons were present . . .

First we had a service—a strange setting for the reading and teaching of the Bethlehem story—and Christian prayers, with the glow from the fire falling on the speaker's face and picking up the dimly-seen congregation along the walls. We had a gas lantern for use by our portable organ, and, although numerous adults were absent clam-digging, young fellows and girls were there who had learnt the Church's carols at St. Michael's School and at Kingcome, and the singing went up as lustily as the flaming sparks through the open roof.

By all accounts, the "experiment" of following the Native migrations in the *Gwa-yee* was successful. "Going out to the people," as Ernest Christmas described his work, was, after all, the traditional missionary approach—far better than waiting for the people to come to the church. Alan Greene spoke with pride of the Christmases commitment "of real service to their Indian flock." He was encouraged by plans "to build a church hall which will be part mission house, part church and, if needs be, a temporary day-school should the Indian Affairs Branch decide upon a school there." The government's need to exert some control over a migratory population meant providing more than merely a school. Indian Agent Murray Todd in Alert Bay had passed on his department's approval of the plan, provided it "fit into a comprehensive scheme" that he himself had in mind "for the remodelling of that entire village." To both church and state, this seemed the only means to contain the Natives. At Kingcome, village life was all but abandoned as Natives sought employment elsewhere. The government tended to cut subsidies to smaller settlements as a means of forcing Natives into larger enclaves. Yet wherever the federal government slashed its subsidies to small, "uneconomical" day schools (as it had done in Kingcome in 1944), the Mission stepped in to pick up the slack.

On the surface, therefore, relations between the Mission and the Indians seemed poised to continue much as they had before. But within the wider context of Canadian laws, there were undercurrents of resentment and dissatisfaction. Although proud of its special relationship with the Indians, the Mission was siding more and more with the forces of government and administrative control.

Apparently unknown to the Christmases—and disregarded by the Columbia Coast Mission—Native leaders had become conversant with what Alan Greene once called "the wisdom of the White people." They began to join forces to rally political will as a means of claiming their lost rights and determining their future. Deeply frustrated by the inaction of the federal government, Native peoples realized that their primary challenge was to organize strong political associations beyond the band level, to present a united front at the negotiating table. For too long, they had remained

Kingcome villagers gathering for worship in the garden, 1947. Note (right) table set as an altar, and portable organ.

divided and had spoken with weak voices against the powers of combined federal and provincial law. Working in isolation, the Christmases favoured the principle of assimilating the Natives, while the Natives' grassroots movement was vying with the paternalism of church and state.

Native activism already had a long history before the Christmases moved to Kingcome. As early as the 1890s, the Nisga'a began their campaign to obtain government recognition of their aboriginal land rights. By 1911, Native activist Peter R. Kelly (1885–1966) was distinguishing himself in the Native land claims issue. In 1916, the Allied Tribes of British Columbia were formed in an unsuccessful attempt to force the British Privy Council to make a judicial decision on land claims. Then in 1927, as president of the Allied Tribes, Kelly testified on Indian grievances before a special parliamentary subcommittee in Ottawa. Rejecting these grievances, the Canadian government undoubtedly contributed to the organization's collapse. But the Allied Tribes was succeeded in 1931 by the even stronger Native Brotherhood of British Columbia, in which Kelly played a prominent role for a decade. He was a key figure in the consultations of 1940 which forced a revision of the Indian Act. It is perhaps an irony of history that Kelly was also an ordained minister who served as skipper-chaplain of the United

Church's mission boats *Thomas Crosby III* and *Thomas Crosby IV*. Likewise, Nisga'a chief Frank Calder (born in 1915) entered the lists. Variously employed as fish plant tallyman, trade unionist, machinist and entrepreneur, Calder was an organizer for the Native Brotherhood, and in 1944 became president of the North American Indian Brotherhood. In 1949 he graduated from the Anglican Theological College of the University of British Columbia and eventually became the first Indian member of a provincial legislature, and the second Canadian legislator of Indian origin after the Métis, Louis Riel. The famous "Calder case" of 1973 galvanized an issue the Nisga'as had long championed, arguing the existence of their aboriginal title to lands they historically occupied. Though Chief Calder ultimately lost his case, the decision motivated the federal government to begin negotiating land claims.

Significantly, the CCM's journal *The Log* made no mention of Native political activities until rather late in the day. The Kingcome missionaries, Mr. and Mrs. Christmas, never referred to them in letters. This changed when the Sixteenth Annual Convention of the Native Brotherhood was invited to contribute to the revision of the Indian Act. The convention took place early in 1946 at Fort Simpson, the largest Indian village on the BC coast. Speaking at the opening memorial service for the late Haida president of the Native Brotherhood, Alfred Adams of Masset, who had attended Heber Greene's ordination in Masset over thirty years earlier, Heber Greene invoked the memory of "this fine Christian father and leader in both State and Church," and urged that "if we forget the past we cannot forge a future."

Heber Greene's account of the convention published in *The Log* dwelt at length on the speech given by the Indian Commissioner, Major Donald MacKay. It was motivated by imminent changes to the Indian Act. In his speech, MacKay cautioned the Native Brotherhood that it "will be judged" by whether or not it made "sane observations and suggestions." He rehearsed in glowing terms what the eighteen agencies of his department had accomplished for the welfare of its 25,000 Indian charges. Reeling off figures without context, he showed that two hundred of four thousand Natives were in high school (seventy day schools and thirteen residential schools accounted for 50 percent of the children). The commissioner credited the various churches with the genesis of Native education. He then listed government involvement in medical services—again, pioneered by the churches. He referred to new government initiatives, including a grant of $5 million nationwide for hospital and medical facilities, and a further $2.5 million national building program to assist the "homeless and penniless." Central to the commissioner's address was a stout defence of the Indian Act. To his mind, it had been subjected to "cheap criticism" by people ignorant of the legislation. Admittedly in need of fine tuning, he conceded, the Indian Act remained for him a sterling piece of legislation: "No statute in Canada provided better protection for a minority group." The commissioner's views notwithstanding, the Native Brotherhood remained unconvinced that the status quo dealt adequately with the many injustices governing their lives.

The Brotherhood pursued the theme in Masset early in 1947, during its seventeenth annual convention. In welcoming the delegates representing Natives, churches and government, Mrs. E. Yeltatzie, a daughter of the distinguished Haida Chief Henry Edenshaw and president of the Church of England Women's Auxiliary at Masset, recalled the genesis of the Native Brotherhood. It was "a program embodying all the ideals of Christianity of a higher standard of life." She then set the stage for deliberations:

> The natural resources that supported the Native life in former times are depleted, restricted, or hampered by the ever increasing competitive environment of the present. And it is time indeed that we make a serious effort to meet the challenge of our heritage as Canadian citizens, though long denied by our Christian Government, in spite of their democratic principles . . . The Haida expression we use to encourage one another in critical times, I wish to pass on to you: "Take courage—take courage." Take courage in your undertaking and be not afraid of your own convictions, if they be for the advancement of your people as a whole . . .

From now on, *The Log* made a point of covering Native issues, however lightly. Nothing suggests that Kingcome's lay missionaries grasped the larger strategic picture of Native political development. In 1947, they still saw their villagers as "feckless, illiterate and untrained in sound values." The Christmases were particularly unhappy that the Natives of BC might be granted the franchise, a right not actually accorded until 1960. The Christmases' judgement of Indians in general was skewed. Even if their unflattering description reflected the true image of the small populace of their village, Kingcome was not necessarily the norm. In fact, the Native movements were increasingly championed by well-informed, well-educated and articulate leaders.

If the Native population was changing, so were Ernest Christmas and his wife. Slogging on in the isolation of their coastal mission, they logged over a thousand miles a year in the *Gwa-yee*, frequently living aboard in wretched winter conditions. Much of village life was extraordinarily primitive, with missionaries and Natives alike toting their daily water from the river in shoulder yokes. Yet, living so close to the Natives of Gwayasdums and Kingcome, the Christmases gradually entered into a new life of dialogue and self-understanding, which they began to articulate in 1948:

> . . . it is not merely that Indians have a racially tranquil way of taking life one day at a time, but that the methods hitherto adopted by the "white" Government, of keeping them in wardship, have (however unintentionally for the most part) had the gradual effect of stifling [that] which must once have existed in many more members of a free race than now. It is when any of us live with them long enough, with an open mind to comprehend these things, that we grow readier to work for them, with them—knowing that only so will they come to work with us for each other. Above all, they must feel that Christians are sincere.

In February 1949, unusually heavy snows destroyed the Mission buildings in Kingcome. Only its very steep roof saved the church from destruction. The Mission established a Kingcome Restoration Fund and sent out appeals for financial help. In May, while struggling to renew the village and to support its medical and educational needs, Mrs. Christmas grew exasperated at the meagre progress being made and laid the blame on the government: "how slowly compared with what should and could have been done ere this by the Indian Department and its large resources."

Perhaps the Department of Indian Affairs felt it had enough to do elsewhere. It had already begun investing in the village of Gwayasdums in an effort to concentrate the Native population in a more easily administered centre. By the end of 1950, the Christmases reported after a pastoral visit to Gwayasdums "the clearance of old houses and erection of new ones by the Department, plus large school premises . . . with 110-volt lighting." All gave Gwayasdums "a new interest in life." By the summer of 1951, the Indian commissioner promised the Mission that funds would be forthcoming for upgrading Kingcome as well: renovations of houses, a water system and new day school. As Mrs. Christmas observed, this "long-withheld" financial assistance enabled "desperately necessary [changes that] could not be afforded without the Indian Department's aid."

For the older Natives, much of this was coming too late. As one chief observed: "Many of my people have looked for the better things we have been promised in earlier years for this place we love, but many men and women have died seeing nothing changed." The record of visits at Kingcome for this period—the Indian commissioner, the superintendent of Health and Welfare, the school inspector and the TB mobile chest clinic—suggests that officialdom was taking renewed interest in the Native settlements. Mrs. Christmas wrote in January 1953 that "never before, in our eleven years of observation and written comment concerning needed official health and welfare measures for Kingcome, has there been a fraction . . . of the recognition such as has now begun." The newly amended Indian Act of 1951 was undoubtedly the reason for improved funding and services. As a first consequence of the changes, the Kingcome villagers elected a village council by secret ballot, their first exercise of the democratic franchise.

In the spring of 1953, the Native villages began attracting the interest of American medical evangelists—the Marine Medical

Mr. and Mrs. Ernest Halliday, Kingcome homesteaders since 1894. Pictured here ca. 1954, they had been "unfailingly hospitable to our missionaries."

Mission operating out of Seattle with their missionary ship *Willis Shanks*. The 136-foot converted US navy minesweeper and her crew first came to the attention of the Columbia Coast Mission when they arrived in Bella Bella in 1950 to attend the twentieth convention of the Native Brotherhood of BC. Heber Greene was impressed not only with "their fine quartet who sang Negro spirituals," but with the imposing presence of the ship itself:

> The *Willis Shanks* . . . has been converted into a hospital ship. With a Doctor aboard, two nurses and seven beds for patients, it is able to meet a great need on the Alaskan coast—the Panhandle section. In their chapel they have a Hammond organ and piano. It is run by two 500 HP engines and is equipped with Radar. It is pilot-house controlled. It is a faith venture.

Innocent enough on the surface, the incident sheds light on the character of the Mission's ministrations to the Indian reserves.

Whereas the Columbia Coast Mission of Alan Greene's day was largely content to function among the non-Native population as a nondenominational servant of the Social Gospel, its relationship to the Natives was decidedly sectarian. For this reason, the *Willis Shanks* loomed large, not only as unfair competition, but as a threat to Anglicanism. As soon as Greene got wind of what he regarded as an unconscionable intrusion into Anglican territory, he reacted with almost unbridled anger. Writing to Captain C.F. Stabbert of the Marine Medical Mission on 7 June 1953, Greene in effect told him to "get off Anglican turf." Tough-minded and utterly exasperated by the apparent American impudence, Greene briefly sketched the history and principles of religious ministry to the Native peoples:

> In Canada the rule as regards Indian communities has always been that the Church which began and maintained Missionary work in any Indian Reservation is the Church responsible for that group, and the Roman Catholics, the United Church, and the Church of England have never encroached on the field occupied by the other. The Dominion government, while not putting this into so many words in the Indian Act, has looked to us all to carry out this tradition . . .

Accepting as fact what he had been learned from his brother Heber and from hearsay, Greene repeated the evidence against the American mission: that Stabbert had attended a recent convention of the Native Brotherhood and had impressed the Natives with all he could do for them; that the Americans were well equipped for medical mission; and that they intended to offer summer Bible school in the villages. For Greene, the Americans' "rather pretentious programme" amounted to nothing less than an underhanded attempt "to raid Canadian missions." The American threat seemed all the more unpalatable because Stabbert had consulted neither the Church of England nor the Dominion Government about his project. The Church, Greene stressed, had invested far too much money and effort to let the Americans go unchallenged:

It will be most embarrassing for the Christmases, our Lay Missionaries, to have you visit Kingcome. Long and costly work has been done there by our Church in an effort to hold the Indians true to their [Anglican] Faith . . . The Indian naturally makes comparisons and is deeply impressed by the large scale show you put on through funds given generously to your ship and its work . . . There cannot and we feel must not be divided loyalties, or years of hard work go by the Board, and the Indian, who is very ready to accept everything offered to him, may end making odious comparisons between the rather lavish scale of your work and the simplicity of ours.

The crux of the problem for Greene was that the Americans had declared themselves a nonsectarian mission quite disinterested in proselytizing among the Natives:

The lack of your identity as a particular Church ends up in the Native saying: "Why worry about our old church if we can have this?" And they inevitably begin to feel that Churchmanship is a small matter. "Any Church is good enough for us as long as they give us this or that." And the reaction against the actual missionary on the job is sometimes tragic.

Without having taken the trouble to research the question himself, or even to verify the vexing rumours about the Americans, Greene exploited the occasion to fire off broadsides without consulting his bishop on the matter. In effect, he was taking on the bishop's responsibility for stating Anglican policy, just as he had done with regard to the potlatch. His bishop supported Greene's aggressive letter to Stabbert. "I am in entire agreement with you regarding the proposed activities of the Seattle Medical Marine Mission," Bishop Sexton replied, "and will go to any lengths to support you in the stand you have taken. It seems to me that the Canadian Immigration Department might be able to stop it, and I am getting into touch with the officials at once." The American medical

Twenty-fifth anniversary of the King George V Memorial Totem Pole, Kingcome, 18 June 1963. (l. to r.) Commander Smith (AdC to Lt. Gov.) Captain G.H. Hayes (Commander, 2nd Canadian Escort Squadron), Stanley Hunt (chief councillor), the Honourable George Pearkes, Patrick Dawson (councillor), the Reverend Eric Powell (in Native regalia and clerical robes), Bishop Godfrey Gower, and the Reverend Ian Barry.

mission never did get established on the coast. Whether this was due to the bishop's intervention or the American missionaries' desire to avoid conflict is not clear. Certainly, legal obstacles could easily have been invoked to prevent the Americans from working and practising medicine in BC if the case had been pushed. Ultimately, the incident shows that Greene was in this case more interested in maintaining control than in Native well-being.

In December 1954, the Christmases left Kingcome aboard the mission's ketch *Veracity*, which they had purchased to replace the

Gwa-yee. They looked forward to service in the more comfortable posting of Pender Harbour. The task they had undertaken at King-come had been daunting, the hardships often extreme. Yet, harsh as their life had been, they had remained steadfastly optimistic. What concerned them most, after more than a decade in isolation, was the Mission's difficulty in finding replacements. Problems of financing, lifestyle and motivation were making it increasingly difficult for the Mission to engage both pastors and doctors.

A landmark appointment revitalized Kingcome in 1955. Eric Powell, a student at Anglican Theological College, joined for summer employment. As Alan Greene noted, he "had thrown in his lot with the Indians at Kingcome in good style, particularly among the young men." With three years of study still ahead, Powell spent only his summers and Christmas holidays at Kingcome, leaving the mission to its own lay leadership throughout the winter. Years later, Powell characterized his approach as that of listening closely to the voice of Native culture and spirituality, and thereby deepening his own faith. That approach lay at the root of the Powell legend, which some of his successors in the CCM tried to live. When the Columbia Coast Mission's first aircraft pilot, the Reverend John Mellis, encountered Native culture in 1971, he too underwent what had been Eric Powell's experience of deepening self-understanding. Bringing his own cultural baggage of race relationships in the US, where he had grown up, Mellis was at first apprehensive about "crossing the boundary" into Native territory. "But the more I got to know the Indian people, the more I came to really love them and appreciate them and find my own sense of personhood affirmed by them."

Eric Powell first encountered the Mission as a nineteen-year-old deck hand aboard the second *Columbia*, when Alan Greene was superintendent. He recalled going to sea "with some really gruff orang-outang characters." Captain MacDonald, an admitted agnostic more interested in boats than mission, skippered the ship at the time, with Heber Greene as chaplain. After serving for over a year and a half as deckhand and cook, Powell took a teaching job in a logging camp in Warner Bay, Seymour Inlet, where he tutored ten children in correspondence courses and learned the life of the outback. He saw at first hand how the loggers felt about the Mission and, like them, looked forward to the *Columbia*'s arrival every six weeks. Whereas the loggers had never been particularly attracted to the religious side of the Mission's work, they appreciated it for its service to their families. The mission boats brought news of the outside world, medical treatment, books and periodicals, sometimes even movies. During this time, Heber Greene encouraged Powell to enter the priesthood; but he had to first complete university studies before entering theological college.

While attending university during the 1950s, Powell had spent his summers deckhanding and cooking on forestry boats, and his path frequently crossed the *Columbia*'s. On one occasion, he found himself working in the Kingcome area after Ernest Christmas had left. The *Columbia* was elsewhere paying its occasional medical and pastoral calls. "I noticed that the church was in terrible repair and was a bit of a mess, and so was the mission house," Powell recalled. When job hunting the following summer, he approached the bishop of New Westminster for permission to paint the church in Kingcome, thus launching himself on a mission to the First Nations which would change both his life and theirs.

Powell's first reports from Kingcome communicate zest, excitement and adventure. A casual visitor might have been struck by the "one-way street, new and old houses with gardens and lawns, a school, a large playing field, and a little white Church called St. George's." In this respect, Powell observed, it was much like any other small, spruced up coastal community. But Powell saw more. At Kingcome, he experienced a vibrant, caring, bicultural and bilingual fellowship unfolding in monastic isolation, "surrounded by majestic mountains" and into which the Christian way of life had struck deep roots. Powell's Christmas message in *The Log* in 1957 evoked Kingcome as a model for effective Christian living: "in His love, all men and women of different races can dwell together in peace."

These bonds seemed accentuated in 1958 when Eric Powell and the Kingcome mission hosted the week-long visit of a Japanese priest. On the eve of the centenary of the Holy Catholic Church in Japan (Nippon Sei Ko Kai), the Reverend Christopher N. Yazawa, Rector of St. Paul's Church in Nigata, Diocese of Mid-Japan, came to share in the experience of mission. Drawing on

St. Paul's analogy between Christendom and the human body, each with its interdependent members, he took as his text "those members of the body which seem to be more feeble, are necessary" (I Corinthians 12:22). Reverend Yazawa pointed out that membership in the Japanese church was only about forty thousand out of a population of ninety million; in a quantitive sense, his church was "very small and feeble." Yet it served a vital purpose. In steeping itself in a burgeoning economic and industrial market—thereby accepting the material side of Western culture—Japan had lost its spiritual centre. He saw his church functioning as a much needed leaven of change. Implicit in the analogy was that Natives could act as leaven in Canadian society. Listening to Yazawa, Powell was struck by the aptness of the text to his own work in Kingcome, and to the possibilities for Native spirituality to bring about change beyond its own culture.

Ordained on 1 May 1958, Eric Powell took up permanent residence in Kingcome—the first ordained minister to do so—and committed the Mission to a fundraising campaign for a new mission boat. This necessity had been on Alan Greene's mind for some time. In fact, he had announced the drive well before Powell had graduated: "So, my friends, get ready for another appeal. This time probably for a maximum of $10,000 with which to purchase a suitable ship for the then Reverend Eric Powell." Powell recalled Greene's first having mentioned the new ship:

> "We're building your ship for Kingcome. Do you want it fast or slow? Fast, or slow and comfortable?" [Of course] I said I wanted it both, obviously. Well he said, "You can't have both." But he suggested that it be slow and comfortable because "when you go from one village to another, one camp to another, the problems will always be there; they won't go away and you'll need time in between to think and pray." And he was right.

When Greene launched the fund drive, the headline in *The Log* trumpeted that "The Superintendent is at His Old Tricks Again." Greene had raised the ante to $15,000:

"The old man of the sea." Reverend Alan Greene, ca. 1958.

I have assured Mr. Powell that the Mission will give him a suitable one-man ship for his work. By that I mean a ship about thirty feet overall with all the appointments and equipment on her to give him safe and comfortable going as he serves the Indians in the upper reaches of our Mission. His base will be the Kingcome Indian Mission, and from there he will go out to the Indian communities such as Gwayasdums (Gilford Island), Village Island, Turnour Island, New Vancouver, and Hopetown. On all these voyages, he will live and sleep on his ship. There will be days when the going is rough,

and I want him to have a really sea-worthy ship, equal
to the rough voyages he will have to make . . . We
have the MAN. We need a SHIP.

Powell did not know the new ship's name until the day of its
dedication, when Greene casually turned to him and explained:
"Oh, by the way, just thought it would be a good idea of mine
to name it the Alan Greene." In deciding to name the last ship
before his retirement after himself, Greene revealed the same strain
of confident self-worth as his predecessor, John Antle.

The *Alan Greene* was launched from Bissett's Boat Building Yard
in North Vancouver on 14 November 1959. She was christened
with champagne by Mrs. Christmas in recognition of her thirteen
years at Kingcome. A large crowd turned out, despite a heavy
snowfall. Driven by a 65 hp Perkins diesel, the thirty-five-foot
vessel with a ten-foot beam would always "look faster than she
really is," and seemed an encouraging sign of the CCM's renewed
commitment to Kingcome. Greene developed this theme in his
dedication address:

> In the area served by this ship, the Anglican Church,
> with Alert Bay as the old missionary centre for eighty
> years, has been the recognized Church to serve the Na-
> tive population as other churches do, in their respective
> areas on our Coast. Therefore the Natives in this ship's
> territory are the children of the Anglican Church and
> the basic reason for the building of this ship, is to assure
> these sterling folk that with a ship, and now, a Missionary
> Priest who will give all his time to ministering to them,
> they will be carefully and adequately shepherded by the
> Church of their fathers. [Powell] will take young men
> from the Kingcome Indian Mission as his ship's helpers.
> It is our earnest hope that this will eventually lead to
> these young men offering themselves as candidates for
> ordination in the sacred ministry, and then serve their
> own people.

This hope presaged a more equitable relationship between the

Mission and the Native people. When Eric Powell took the *Alan Greene* on her maiden voyage to Kingcome Inlet, his assistant, Ernest Willie, was indeed one of the Natives who would be ordained a few years later. But, contrary to Greene's vision that Indian priests would "serve their own people," Willie's ministry was carried out within the mainstream of Anglican church life.

With the launching of the *Alan Greene*, the Mission decided to care for the Indian villages near the Kingcome Mission with a boat specifically dedicated to the purpose. "Thus, each week," Eric Powell wrote, "the little Mission Ship plies her way in and out the inlets visiting the scattered and isolated villages which make up the parish of St. George," in the Diocese of New Westminster. Powell recognized that his "Kwakiutl brothers and sisters in Christ" were experiencing a changing culture. His description of Kingcome Inlet illustrated this point:

> In the village are the remains of the old long houses where the people lived and where the ceremonial dances took place only twenty years ago. The big totem poles still stand in the village lane reminding us of the legends and folklore which are often still told by the old men to the young children. Soon, our old people will have passed away and a new and different generation of men and women will take their place. These are the students of St. Michael's Residential School, Alert Bay. They have been trained from their youth in the meaning of the Christian family and they have been taught the skills and the trades of the modern home. Thus, the old buildings are decaying and coming down while new and modern bungalows are taking their place. Therefore, in what was once a picturesque and ancient village, a new and modern fishing community is emerging.

Powell saw the church as the very centre of the community, both structurally and spiritually. The village priest was not so much the mentor as the catalyst. As a team player, he assumed various roles: assistant counsellor, nurse, postman and umpire at baseball games.

Yet as missionary, he also had to push back old boundaries and break new ground:

> Once on a hunting trip one of our men shot a bear and I was very curious to discover where the animal was shot. On a quick examination the bullet wound could not be found and this therefore made me all the more curious. Then a very stoic fellow spoke up and said: "This bear was not shot, it died of fright. It is the first time a bear has ever seen a white man this far up river, let alone a missionary." I had no reply.

In May 1961, Eric Powell was posted to St. David's in Powell River, while retaining responsibility for overseeing the Kingcome mission as priest-in-charge. He was succeeded both at Kingcome and as skipper of the *Alan Green* by layreader Ron Deane who, with his wife Dorothy, had begun his association with the village two years earlier as maintenance man. Deane confessed to having "felt a mixture of alarm and humility" at being called to follow in Powell's footsteps. When American author Margaret Craven flew into Kingcome in the fall of 1962 to work on her novel *I Heard the Owl Call My Name*, it was Deane who first welcomed her.

Focusing on Powell's personal encounter with Native spirituality, Craven largely overlooked the political context in which Kingcome village was obliged to work out its destiny. In reality, there were many occasions when the symbols of church and state authority converged. One example was the twenty-fifth anniversary of the King George V totem pole on 18 June 1963. The Canadian destroyer HMCS *Mackenzie* brought Lieutenant Governor George R. Pearkes to Kingcome to attend the memorial service conducted by the bishop of the Diocese of New Westminster, Godfrey Gower. Attended by naval personnel, members of the RCMP and Indian Affairs, and leading representatives of the Mission, as well as almost all the adults of the village in ceremonial robes, the service concluded with the obeisance before the totem pole. In a scene re-enacted over the years with various VIPs, the lieutenant governor stood with bowed head before the pole, on which hand-

Twenty-fifth anniversary of the King George V Memorial Totem Pole, Kingcome, 18 June 1963. (l. to r.) Right Reverend Godfrey Gower, the Honourable George Pearkes, elected Chief Stanley Hunt and Councillor Pat Dawson.

carved letters on a weathered wooden plaque dedicated to "Our Noble King" proclaimed its own political truth: "He slumbers only in his stately peaceful rest / He is not dead, in your in my heart he lives on / And many million men shall tribute and honour / In years in time to come, to our noble King. / He ruled so kind so gentle with wisdom from above / He gave his love his kindness his noble service too / To his British Subjects who loved him and still do / So let us now pay tribute to our noble King." On that day, Pearkes was made an honorary chief and named Na-g-ya-gu, "Big Mountain," symbolizing his vice-regal power.

The autumn of 1963 saw the end of what Superintendent Pat

Dancers ready to perform the Dance of Life and Death and Rebirth, in front of the Long House, Kingcome, June 1963.

Ellis, who had succeeded Greene in 1960, called "a very remarkable ministry to our Native People up the coast which has spanned something like ten years." Eric Powell was leaving for studies at St. Augustine's College in Canterbury and Ron Dean was also leaving for England. Kingcome once again had reached a critical point in its community life. Ellis's public tribute to Powell focussed on his capacity for outreach, empathy and transformation:

> Few men have done more for the Natives than Eric has, and he has rightly earned for himself a place of affection in their hearts . . . He has been to them a true Pastor and shared with them the wholeness of their

lives, and given of himself and his means to bring them into a fuller life. Wherever he goes he brings with him the presence of Christ and the joy of a life lived with Him. Only once have I seen him depressed, in spite of his own physical sufferings, and that was not because of his own discomfort but because he saw a temporary lapse among his people when they were given full rights for the use of liquor.

Powell had been Ellis's "inspiration through many times of difficulty and depression." With the additional departure of Ron and Dorothy Dean, Ellis had lost "a team that has given their all in the service of God." They would, he reflected, "leave a tremendous gap in the family circle of the Mission." Yet the *Columbia* continued her medical patrols with regular stops at Kingcome, soon under the pastoral care of the Reverend Gene Diespecker, who remained there with his family until 1967.

As he made clear in an interview in 1989, Eric Powell always felt that the history of Kingcome was an essentially different story from that of the Columbia Coast Mission. Of course, Kingcome had "played a very important part in the early life of the Mission," if only because "it was a drawing card" for encouraging support from funding agencies both abroad and in eastern Canada. The Mission had focussed specifically on Kingcome to show "how the Indians were to be dealt with in terms of education and their health and particularly their spirituality." Yet despite much that was good, Powell insisted that the church had been misguided about a lot of its work. It was often more noteworthy for what it had left undone than for what it had actually accomplished for the Native peoples. Most Indian villages in the southern region of the Mission's territory, from Campbell River across to the mainland, were ministered to by the Roman Catholic Church; as for instance, at the settlement of Church House. Powell felt that was probably reason enough for Anglicans not to encroach. But he considered the settlements in the northern region to be potentially Anglican missions, yet of these only Alert Bay had been developed. The reason, to his mind, had less to do with lack of strategic vision than with attitude and style. "The skippers on board the *Columbia* itself did not like tying up at Indian villages. They preferred to tie up at logging camps." And besides, there was "a healthy racism on the coast," including among some members of the Mission.

Kingcome had fared very poorly indeed. Looking back over thirty years since his ordination, Powell observed: "As far as the village of Kingcome was concerned, there were dedicated missionaries there as lay people. Many were school teachers, some were nurses, some were misfits . . . But the church went along in the 20s and 30s to do away with Native culture and help suppress the potlatch." And he recalled the "letters from Mr. Todd, the infamous Indian agent at Alert Bay, to Alan Greene impressing upon Greene to help put down the potlatch in Kingcome and in the villages—which the Church did." In short, Powell remained convinced that "the Church deserted [the Indians] repeatedly." Even when he himself had sponsored Natives wanting to enter the ministry, their candidacy was rejected. Without naming names, Powell spoke of certain bishops who saw no need to ordain Natives, simply because there was only one village to which they could possibly be posted. The thought that ordained Natives might actually minister to white settlements was anathema. Natives were regarded as little children, "probably the most derogatory thing you can say about any culture or nation," Powell observed. "They were objects of the Church to be cared for as little children of Jesus . . . 'Gentle Jesus meek and mild, look upon a little child,' [according to the Sunday School prayer]. And so we never developed any Native leadership along the coast in terms of missionaries."

This was not quite true. On 3 May 1967, a former carpenter from Kingcome Inlet, Ernest Willie, received his degree in theology from the University of Saskatchewan. In struggling to complete senior matriculation at night school, then catching up on university subjects while adjusting to Saskatoon's predominantly white society, Willie had asked no quarter and given none. Those who understood the difficult road he travelled wondered at each step just how he would manage. When announcing in *The Log* that "Ernie Makes It," the principal of Emmanuel and St. Chad College extolled the achievements of this Tsawataineuk student who was subsequently ordained in Christ Church Cathedral, Vancouver, where he ministered to a mosaic of Canadians:

> He has challenged our white complacency and inspired us with his sermons in the College Chapel and in parish churches. We have wrestled together—and sometimes wrangled—at bull sessions, at our Co-Op breakfast, and in class. Ernie is proud to be an Indian, proud of his own people's history and heritage. Not too proud to learn from the white man's history and heritage too. But honest and independent enough to challenge our presumptions, and to question sometimes our white man's interpretation of God and His creation . . . Though he has reservations about many of the white man's interpretations of Christianity, he is not likely to apologize for being a Christian.

The rhetoric of the principal of the theological college—"white complacency, white man's history, white man's interpretation of Christianity"—was intentionally discordant. It provided the only means for addressing the type of two-world tensions that had characterized relationships between the church and the First Nations since the earliest days. By being ordained and having "married a white girl," in the principal's expression, Willie (and his bride) bridged a cultural gulf. Accompanying him across that bridge at his ordination were several members of the Columbia Coast Mission: Eric Powell, Alan Greene, Pat Ellis, Gene Diespecker and Lance Stephens.

This was not the first time the image of a bridge was used to discuss intercultural relations within the Mission. In *The Log*'s special 1967 issue celebrating Canada's centennial and the Columbia Coast Mission's sixty-third anniversary, the Reverend Ivan Futter spoke metaphorically of crossing a bridge in order to create a multicultural, pluralistic country. This indicated a major change in perception since John Antle's 1906 article in *The Log*, where he wrote of the Indian reserve as "a bridge by which a somewhat intractable race may cross in safety the gulf between its own and the white man's civilization." By 1967, both the Mission and the country had come a long way, and Futter's use of the bridge metaphor reflected a desire "to cast out [national] traits which are undesirable, to make opportunities for men of all races, colour and creeds to live side by side with one another." Indeed, it meant living together "as God intended that man should, each worshipping God as he thinks best." The theme was developed further in a lead article by the editor of The Log. Quoting at length the late Governor General Georges Vanier's prayers for Canada's next century, the Venerable J.W. Forth, who succeeded Ellis in 1965, endorsed Vanier's concept of Canadians as "a people of many origins," and his expression of tolerance, mutuality, openness and pluralism. Forth continued: "These prayers . . . we also pray for our Mission . . . that we may grow as we ought to grow, without fear of the future . . . without contention and without arrogance, striving constantly to pursue righteousness and serve our Lord and His church."

Significantly, the centennial edition of The Log abandoned the conventional image of Natives as marginalized wards of church and state, featuring instead an engaging cover portrait of a self-possessed, contemplative young Native woman in her traditional garb. Captioned "The Indians Were Here First," the cover communicated a startlingly fresh approach to ministry, where Native culture now offered its wisdom to white Canada. Or, in the title of Ernest Willie's feature article, "We speak; They listen."

The Reverend Willie's article addressed three major themes: education, land claims and secularization. He wondered aloud why it had been necessary to uproot children from their homes by sending them to residential school, severing them from their own traditions and culture. He saw land claims as an attempt to redress "the exploitation of [Native] lands and natural resources." He recognized secularization as a process in which "the church has withdrawn its active support and has given way to government organizations." This meant, that "with the government taking over the church's responsibilities, Native Indians now have to clear away the red tape of the great white father in order to reach the cross of Christ." In other words, administrative convenience and bureaucratic fiat had replaced the works of a caring community.

Lucid, conciliatory and tough, Willie's words set the tone for what he trusted would be the path his people would follow:

> . . . while we Native people must fight for our recognition, we must avoid fighting against the white man to gain it. We have indeed been victims of grave injustice, but if we are to emerge from the wreckage we must do it together with the fullest cooperation on both sides . . . [Only thus] are we ever going to regain our former position, knowing our identity, worth and dignity which will enable us to take our place in any given society.

CHAPTER 9

Overtaken by Time

T HE HALCYON DAYS OF SKIPPER-CHAPLAINS had passed when the Reverend Joe Titus joined the Mission in 1954 to assume command of the *Rendezvous*. Many signs were already pointing to the Mission's obsolescence. The question remained just how to keep pace with a developing province. The quandary about whether to choose slow boats or fast aircraft was simply the most obvious aspect of the changes transforming coastal life. Struggling to maintain its relevance to a culture in transition, the Mission sometimes saw renewal more as a threat than a challenge. Just how well the Mission coped depended upon the manner in which the individual missionary melded his expectations with current reality. Even more importantly, success depended upon the particular vision of the Mission's leader. Alan Greene, by now a canon in the Diocese of New Westminster, responded to change with a boat-building boom, drawing young Titus in his wake.

Brought up in Saint John, New Brunswick, Titus first heard of the Columbia Coast Mission as a child in Sunday School. In 1952, he served with the CCM as a student missionary. By his own admission, Titus "didn't have any particular training in operating vessels, but had learned a lot back east on the fish boats" where he worked as deckhand during summer breaks in his university studies. Both he and his wife Joan, whom he married in August 1954, two months after joining the Mission, regarded this first appointment as an adventure. A registered nurse, Joan Titus had much to offer their joint ministry. She always travelled on patrol with her husband in the summertime, and one winter worked as deckhand—"the best deckhand I ever had," her husband recalled. Alan Greene disapproved. He "didn't like women to go on the boats," Titus recalled. "He thought this macho stuff—this was a man's world." Indeed, this was also Greene's attitude to female physicians on board, though he had to soften his line once he realized that male physicians were no longer volunteering their services. When left on her own, Joan found Whaletown a very lonely outpost, relieved only by the monthly clinic when the *Rendezvous* brought the doctor and dentist from Campbell River and ferried patients in from local ports. Given all this pastoral concern for those in need, it is ironic that Joan gave birth to their first child in Whaletown, alone, in the middle of the night.

The *Rendezvous's* patrol was still bounded by Savary Island, Lund, Johnstone Strait, Rock Bay and Greene Point, and Titus essentially continued the pattern Rollo Boas had established:

> I would arrive in an area Friday afternoon or maybe Thursday night and would spend [the next two days] visiting . . . There was always a main community [where] I would have a church service on Sunday morning, and then [I'd go] to other isolated spots, maybe individual homes, where I'd anchor or tie up at their float or maybe two or three families in a small jippo logging outfit. [Monday through Wednesday] visiting in these areas and possibly having a church service in their home or on board the boat—frequently just Morning and Evening prayer because a lot of them weren't Anglicans or didn't want to receive Communion . . . Then perhaps Sunday School in the middle of the week [somewhere else].

With the exception of the monthly clinic and the occasional emergency run, the *Rendezvous* patrol was still essentially a pastoral service. Whatever might have been the religious practice or faith of the coastal peoples, "they were very much part of the worshipping congregation of my services and in a sense were parish people of the Columbia Coast Mission." Of course, large numbers of people claimed no church affiliation whatever, but many none-theless identified with the Mission. Their reasons for being drawn to it were as varied as the personalities themselves. As the Native people in his area came under the Roman Catholic Church, Titus ministered with few exceptions to the non-Native population, as in Boas's day.

And Titus was left as much on his own as Rollo Boas had been. His only restriction was to keep out of Alert Bay, the preserve of the *Columbia* and St. George's Hospital, and Heriot Bay, then being ministered to by provincial government services. Of course, Greene required his usual monthly operational reports consisting of baptisms, religious services and miles travelled, and visited the Whaletown station from time to time. "He didn't visit that often," Titus recalled, "but when he did it was not the threat of the boss coming. It was a real joy." Greene's charisma continued to impress those he met. Titus spoke for many on the coast in remembering him as "a very warm personality [who looked] older than he was." A robust man, he exuded "a delightful sense of humour and a deep faith he didn't push at you."

Titus quickly set about orienting himself to his new parish. Two months into the job he reported: "They have been two memorable months for me. I have fallen heir to a very comfortable house, a Model 'A' Ford, a cat, a wonderful old ship, a sizable parish, an honourable tradition and, above all, a host of new friends, chief among whom is my bride." An old timer offered him the intriguing advice that he would have to experience three things before being properly initiated to the coast: run out of gas, run aground, and secure the ship on a short taut rope with a falling tide. Titus did all three. The first jottings in his log show the rough transition from ceremonial change of command to working-priest: "The *Rendezvous* officially is handed over to the Reverend Joe G. Titus . . . Mr. N. Harrington and Joe Titus install port-side gasoline tank. Some job!" Later, after a service on Savary Island in the home of a Mrs. Ferris, where forty people attended, he recorded in his log the early litanies of self-taught seamanship:

> . . . getting dark. Some rain . . . trouble anchoring in
> Blind Creek. In rain had to haul anchor and go into

Gov't float. Hard rain. No trouble. Long night. New experience.

Subsequent entries reveal the self-deprecating irony with which he viewed the stages of his learning process: "found out the engine won't run on air." Even four years later, he still had the landsman's difficulty of distinguishing between ship's speed in knots and distance-run in nautical miles. Such nautical lore had yet to be mastered when reporting that the *Rendezvous* had "logged 1,380 knots in 163 hours of running time."

The chores of being a skipper-chaplain quickly became plain: ship maintenance, scraping and painting the dinghy (and indeed the *Rendezvous* itself), punching through stormy seas to make appointments, and ferrying patients and medical personnel to and from the clinic. On 13 July 1954, barely one month into his work, Titus recorded his first ceremonial occasion in command of his new ship: "visited by Dean Beattie and Mr. Henderson on HMCS *Porte Quebec* for a few minutes." His reflections on these opening days merit quotation at some length. As one of the very rare occasions when a skipper-chaplain actually committed his thoughts to his log, the entries shed light on the round of social visits which constituted much of missionary work:

This was the beginning of a week's cruise in [the] NW corner of the patrol. The weather was good throughout with the exception of a westerly in Johnstone Strait on July 21 [1954]. We started up the Straits from Rock Bay to Mayne Passage. We travelled for 25 hours and 2 minutes, averaging about 200 miles. I was warmly received everywhere I went. The boat was new to many people. To others it was well known. Many had known her in their youth around Quathiaski and now were glad to see her again. It was good to meet old friends of the Mission and to make contacts with potential new ones. Owen Bay now has only 5 families. Rock Bay too appears to be very low in population. There seem to be only several families there. There is a fairly large camp at Elk Bay which should have more frequent visits.

Titus's early notes reveal warm receptions at the camps as well. This was certainly the case in Bute and Toba Inlets, and when stopping off for a "courtesy visit" at the Native settlement of Church House, which was served by the Roman Catholic Church. Figuring he had been taken at first for a Catholic priest, he quipped about the Natives' response to his arrival: "The dirt was soon washed off and the hair combed when 'Father' was seen coming." Titus's log continued:

> We overlapped the *Columbia*'s patrol [area] at Blind Channel, but the *Rendezvous* is known there, and a warm welcome was received. In the immediate area of Blind Channel there were 2 small [logging] camps where the *Columbia* had not visited. At Blind Channel I met an old crippled widow who had been married nearly 50 years ago by John Antle. Her loyalty is for the Mission.

Despite the pleasant reception throughout his patrol district, he noted ample signs that the population was dwindling, and that those who remained evinced a distinct indifference to religious matters:

> There are very few Anglicans. Some are R.C. Others, the large majority, have no Church connections what-soever.
>
> Many of the camps, of 8–12 men, have no families, or perhaps only 1 or 2. In these places [mission] work is largely among adults. Only in larger spots are there any children to speak of. Many of these receive S.S. [Sunday School] by Post. Of these, very few give a response [to it].
>
> Only in one place was I warned that I would not be received as a Clergyman. Told that if I would leave Religion outside, I would be welcomed. I accepted. Better to get one foot inside the door than a door slammed in the face of the Church of God. Some day that man may reveal why he does not even wish to discuss it.
>
> Other people take it lightly. Joking over some fanatic

[churchman] who made a jack-ass of himself. These people have no concept of the Truth. Their only impression is some experience [of church people] that has filled them with humour. A few will lightly make brushes at Religion, but they are not eager to pursue it at any length. Perhaps they will as time goes by.

Very few welcome the chance to discuss things pertaining to Religion. I met no "sectarians". At least they did not reveal it to me if they were.

Only in a couple of places were prayers said. Once [where they were] asked for, and the other I suggested, knowing they wanted me to.

This was primarily a trip to get acquainted. I think it was successful. Also, I cannot help but feel that in some places some good in the name of Christ was done.

Titus's log reveals the impact of air service on the Mission's patrol area. Once, unable to start his cranky engine to get to Surge Narrows for the Royal Canadian Legion's Remembrance Day service, he arranged by radio-telephone for a repairman to fly in from Campbell River. Help could also have reached him by water taxis, those high-powered, seaworthy boats now linking island communities. Indeed, one doctor preferred to use them for the run from Campbell River to the Whaletown clinic, especially when a strong sea was running. In such conditions, "the water taxis get up on a crest and just fly," leaving the mission boat to wallow along, taking every wave over the bow. Joe Titus was quick to reflect on the possibilities for change. "And I thought that either of these two systems of transportation might be superior to what we already had." But as Titus reflected, "Alan Greene couldn't see this. He had been born and brought up with these heavy boats and slow boats, and this is what he saw as needed." Be that as it may, Titus's claim that he would have had no difficulty sleeping aboard a water taxi alongside the dock would have startled Alan Greene, especially the claim that he "wouldn't have been any less comfortable than aboard the *Rendezvous.*"

Meanwhile, the *Columbia* continued her patrol pattern from her base in Alert Bay: from Bull Harbour in the north, to Seymour

John Antle (IV) at a float camp.

Inlet in the east, down to Rock Bay, Cordero Channel to Stuart Island. Nearly all the people served were in logging. Thinly populated as the inlets of Loughborough, Knight, Drury, Kingcome and Seymour now were, the mission ship continued to seek out their isolated settlers in addition to visiting the eight Native villages at the mouth of Knight Inlet. After six weeks on patrol, *Columbia* would return to Vancouver to give her crew shore leave. During the typical period from 22 April 1955 to 10 July, she made fifty-three ports of call, bringing medical services to "169 White and 87 Indian patients." The statistical division between "white" and "Indian" reflects the Mission's compliance with provincial government rules that paid different rates for each group. As well, the Mission was working under contract to the Public Health Service, administering preventive inoculations as part of a government health program.

The Mission's 1955 annual report reflects the changing circumstances of operations. For example, it no longer included the medical returns for St. George's Hospital, Alert Bay, and St. Mary's

Hospital, Pender Harbour, these institutions now being managed by independent local boards. The report thus comprised three sections. The first, "social services," covered the Aged Folks' Guest Houses in Pender Harbour, which housed fifteen senior citizens. The second, "evangelistic," reviewed the number of religious services provided by all three ships. The third, "medical," reported on the John Antle Memorial Clinic at Whaletown (for which Greene could provide no statistics), and the achievements of the "Hospital Ship *Columbia*." The latter, travelling 12,308 miles, had paid 1,173 visits (thirty of them in response to radioed emergency calls) and had treated on board "570 White and 279 Indian patients."

Equally revealing, the 1955 financial report showed just how little support was derived from the dioceses within which the Mission operated. The Diocese of New Westminster provided only $1,500 in 1955, and the Diocese of British Columbia $1,000. By contrast, the Toronto-based Missionary Society of the Church in Canada offered an annual grant of $7,000; the Community Chest of Greater Vancouver, $8,000 for the *Columbia*; the Community Chest of Victoria, $1,000 for the *John Antle*; the Women's Auxiliary throughout the country raised some $4,300; and the New England Company of London (England) provided Bishop Godfrey Gower with funds to cover the Kingcome operations. As Alan Greene recognized, "the greatest weakness in our Finances is the relatively small sum contributed by those we serve with the three ships." Income from medical services and church collections together amounted to only $6,621.56. Of this, medical income formed the major share. As the Reverend Titus recalled years later concerning Mission finances, "the Dioceses of New Westminster and British Columbia fed peanuts into the Mission. It was financed mostly from WA [Women's Auxiliary], and business and churches mostly back east who heard the romantic story from Alan Greene, who's the only one who ever went and talked about the Mission." In short, Titus claimed that the two dioceses within which the Columbia Coast Mission operated regarded it as an entirely separate operation, and "didn't give a darn what was going on."

Yet the *Columbia* struggled on, playing whatever role it could in a changing coastal society that still resorted to inventive, makeshift solutions. Gilean Douglas captured the pioneering spirit in her account of an upcoast wedding:

> It would be rather overwhelming if a whole city turned out to a wedding. But upcoast it's the usual thing for an entire community to be present . . . Sometimes the ceremony itself is held in the cabin of a mission boat, with as many guests crowding in as possible and the rest standing on deck or dock. But every now and then a logger, used to solving knotty problems, comes up with a better solution. At least 150 guests were expected to be at this wedding, so the Sullivan Bay community hall was put on a moving float borrowed from a nearby camp and a fleet of gas boats brought the church to the bride . . . All the old time logging spirit was there, bottled and otherwise. Some of the guests arrived on the *Columbia*, others by the Queen Charlotte or B.C. Airlines. But most of them came in their own gas boats, until a whole fleet was tied up around the hospital ship at the camp float.
>
> The community hall's bareness had been masked by evergreen branches, flowers and crepe paper. It was filled with people and when the ceremony was over the health-drinking, cake-cutting and serious eating began; what seemed a thousand sandwiches, cakes by the dozen, gallons of tea and coffee. By the dawn's early light there would be more coffee, mounds of toast, eggs, flapjacks, sausages and good old porridge. Then chug-chug-chug would go the gas boats, zoom would go the planes and the guests would be on their way back to making a living.

The *Columbia* was now forty-five years old and failing. Yet in the mid-1950s, mainlanders continued to respond to the Mission more as an exotic and romantic enterprise than a ministry of substance. Not surprisingly, Greene disagreed with the skewed popular image:

> Actually, it is not a very thrilling life, romantic or colourful as it may appear to outsiders, and I think the

Launching the third Columbia on 13 October 1956 from Star Shipyards, New Westminster, BC.

people served owe a lot to *Columbia* for its persistence
in slogging on at a sometimes thankless task. But we
can assure all those the ship serves that we want the old
Columbia—and next year the new—to play a useful and
enriching part in their lives.

While continuing with his shipbuilding enterprise in order to
renew his fleet of mission ships, Alan Greene also pressed on
with his plan of developing parish churches. Canon Heber
Greene had been executing his brother's policy of establishing
permanent links wherever he could. Through him, the Alice
Lake Logging Company, a subsidiary of the Powell River Company, had donated not only property for a church at Sayward,
some forty miles north of Campbell River, but also considerable
free labour. In fact, so much money was being raised locally
that Alan Greene did not anticipate having to use the $1,000
loan which the Diocese of British Columbia had offered. Built
as a replica of the Church of the Good Shepherd on Lasqueti
Island, the church at Sayward opened on 11 November 1955.
By the spring of 1956, St. Saviour's by the Sea, Cortes Island,
was also nearing completion with a view to its being dedicated
that autumn by Archbishop Sexton.

Behind all the shipbuilding and parish expansion of the 1950s
lay Alan Greene's commitment to ongoing ministry, combined
with his energetic fundraising enterprise. With the new *Columbia*
in mind, for example, he had once again headed back to eastern
Canada in 1956, where he persuaded the Missionary Society of
the Church in Canada (MSCC) to donate yet another $10,000.
Then, to sell the idea of a new hospital ship as a necessary adjunct
to medical care, he visited Paul Martin, the federal minister of
Health and Welfare, who matched the MSCC donation with a
further $10,000. Another key to continued operations was an x-ray
unit for the new ship. A gift of the Tuberculosis Society of British
Columbia, the unit enabled the Mission to work for both the
provincial TB clinic and Ottawa's Indian Affairs branch. Greene
also wrote nine-hundred letters to potential private donors. In all
"I did manage to raise about $100,000 more by dint of a lot of
hard work . . . and as the Jubilee Fund grew [I] felt my original

Launching the fifth John Antle on 26 January 1957 from Star Shipyards, New Westminster, BC. The Union Jack draped over the bow shows that the CCM still regarded itself as an arm of the Church of England.

goal was not a pipe dream after all, [and] $125,000 became the final goal. All I can say is 'PRAISE GOD!'"

The new *Columbia* was launched 13 October 1956 from the slips of Star Shipyards, New Westminster, just a hundred feet from where the original *Columbia* had been built in 1910. Sixty-seven feet in length, she had a 182-hp Gardner engine, a diesel generating plant and heating unit, a propane sterilizer in the hospital cabin, propane range and refrigerator in the galley, and a Spilsbury and Tindall radio-telephone. Christened with champagne, she gave every assurance that the seagoing Mission was as vigorous as ever and would endure for many years. Less than four months later, on 26 January 1957, the same shipyards launched the new forty-four-foot *John Antle* with her General Motors diesel engine and similar equipment. Significantly, a Toronto man completely outfitted the pilot house with furniture and navigation gear as a memorial to his granddaughter, Anne Birkett, who drowned just before she was to take a post with the Mission as a vacation school worker. Both ships were sheathed with gumwood along the water-line as a protection against ice. When christening the vessel, Greene recalled, "we did something quite original . . . Our daughter Catherine sent us a magnum of Atlantic Water which we mixed with Pacific Water, and on the same day of the launching, a telegram reading, 'From Sea to Sea Greetings and God's Blessing on the new *John Antle* as she goes to Sea.'" Onto the new ship Greene packed "little Jimmy," the portable organ that had served him for forty-five years.

In 1956, the old *Rendezvous*, in service since 1924, was renamed the *Laverock II*, and the old *John Antle* became the *Rendezvous*. *Laverock II* served the Mission for a year before being donated to the Diocese of Caledonia. Although Joe Titus effectively got a new ship out of the switch, he was disappointed he had not been invited to attend the launchings of the new *Columbia* and *John Antle* (*IV*). But he accepted the fact that these events were really Alan Greene's show. "He liked the limelight and that was ok. He left us alone, so that was fair exchange."

Like other missionaries, Heber Greene was also left on his own; so much so, that Alan Greene could often not find his brother when he wanted to. "I find it impossible to follow my brother's peregrinations," he once wrote. "He's a very honest chap, but his leaps in various directions leave me quite dizzy." Trying to trace his brother was what Alan called "Heber-hunting." Judging by reports, many a "parishioner" of the Mission must have felt the same way about this lovable priest. "I fully appreciate how exasperating his remarkable ability to get wholly detached from his ship with no clue as to where to pick him up, might be to his shipmates," Alan Greene remarked when announcing his brother's retirement. "But he invariably turned up somewhere and settled down to ship-life in a cabin that was a veritable museum of clerical junk."

Although removed from the day-to-day operations of his seagoing mission, Alan Greene jumped eagerly at any opportunity to take a ship to sea. Thus, from 20 July to 9 August 1957, he served as skipper of the new *Columbia*, until relieved by her regular master, Peter Holden. Alan Greene seems to have put the ship through her paces. "Our new skipper, the Superintendent, had us on the run everywhere," his brother Heber reported in *The Log*. "In 20 days he covered the whole district, barring Drury Inlet and Mackenzie Sound. Granted, most of the small camps were shut down." But what Alan Greene's successor would call "running about in boats" masked a rather harsh reality. The new physician, Dr. Mary Woods, reported a slump in medical work in *Columbia* throughout the spring and summer of that year; in fact, she insisted that very little medical work was being done at all. Convinced the patrols were too random, she introduced the policy of establishing fixed schedules (as Boas had done with the *Rendezvous*) so that people knew when to expect the hospital ship. As Heber explained, "we now hold central clinics at the different villages, saving the doctor a great deal of time and effort. I act as chaser of business for Dr. Woods and hold services and talk to the school children where possible. It is producing better results."

The Mission's 1957 annual report seems to bear him out. *Columbia* alone "treated 781 white and 543 Indian patients, a record number in the history of the ship." During this time, the hospital ship was operating with a provincial government grant of $2,000, a federal grant of $1,500 (for medical services to Native peoples) and a $7,000 grant from the Community Chest of Greater

Vancouver in support of medical work. As necessary as such non-church support was, it marked a dependency on sources not necessarily committed to the Mission's spiritual ideals. And Greene anticipated the Community Chest's grant would be substantially reduced in future, since it had not reached its own fundraising objective. In the meantime, the Mission established the new parish church of St. Columba at Port Hardy in 1957, and was contemplating a 1958 dedication of St. Philip's on Hardwicke Island. For Superintendent Alan Greene, the Mission's achievements gave continued cause for celebration:

And in and out of this colourful pattern of life [on the BC coast] little ships called "God's little fleet" taking their orders from One who long ago said "Go into all the world. Heal the sick. Preach the gospel." And beyond a doubt it is because these little ships are ready to turn aside as word comes to them by radio or from a passing ship of someone in dire need, that men listen with respect and patience and sometimes, humility to the gospel these skippers preach.

Besides facing financial challenges, the Mission was also finding it more difficult to find permanent staff to run the vessels. When Peter Holden resigned as skipper of the *Columbia* in 1958, Greene managed to replace him temporarily with an experienced British naval officer. Captain Lawrence Goudy, RN, had been the chief engineer on the battleship HMS *Prince of Wales* when she was sunk by Japanese forces off the Malay coast on 11 December 1941; he was also a qualified upper-deck watchkeeper. In Greene's words, "Captain Goudy has two tickets, as a navigator and as an engineer." Yet the days when the Mission could simply put whomever it wished in command of vessels offering public services had gone. As Greene explained with considerable irritation, "the Department of Transport had classed [the new *Columbia*] as a passenger ship and put us to great expense installing all that is called for on a passenger vessel and also demanding, according to the Canada Steamship Act, annual taking-down of two cylinders on the main engine and the hauling-out of the ship for inspection of outlets,

Elizabeth Goudy at the chart table of Columbia, *April 1958. She was the daughter of the skipper, Captain Lawrence Goudy, engineer officer of HMS Prince of Wales when the ship was sunk by Japanese forces in December 1941.*

propellors and what-not." Nor, to his chagrin, was that all. "Their requirements also call for certified masters and engineers." Judging by the diary of Elizabeth Goudy, who accompanied her father for a month, *Columbia*'s patrol into Queen Charlotte Sound in the early spring of 1958 proceeded uneventfully despite these technicalities. The journey offered both father and daughter fascinating vignettes of coastal life:

> After lunch we turned south again and visited Pine Island. Father kept the ship off the rocks by circling just off shore while the whole party of us went ashore in the lightkeeper's little boat. We had to catch the waves at the right moment and jump onto the slippery barnacled rocks. Kathy [another passenger] is rather a frilly female and likes to be helped and pampered at times. We climbed the lighthouse and had a good view and inspection of

the light reflections. Then went to hear the fog horn blown to which father replied from the *Columbia*! Then we went to the house which Mrs. Lightkeeper has fixed up with beautiful modern danish furniture and expensive art books! We went back on board again and headed back for Bull Harbour.

Since Goudy did not meet Canadian civil regulations, his appointment was short. Greene had to temporarily recall the *Columbia*'s seventy-five-year-old former skipper, George MacDonald. First appointed by Greene in September 1937 as master of the second *Columbia*, MacDonald had served the Mission for nineteen years until breaking his hip in a fall. Now he returned just long enough to allow Greene time to find a permanent skipper. Not until the late spring of 1959 did Captain William Nicholson, for years an officer with Union Steamships, assume command of *Columbia*. By that time, the ship no longer carried a doctor, relying instead on the services of Helen Hope, RN, a public health nurse. Further changes followed. In July 1959, Joe and Joan Titus left the *Rendezvous* to return home to Fredericton. And from Vancouver and Victoria, the two bishops began to visit their mission stations by aircraft—and occasionally by ships of the Canadian navy.

If it was difficult to cope with the constant turnover of Mission staff, it proved especially challenging to compensate for the loss of key missionaries, whose personalities and infectious sense of commitment had shaped the life of the Mission. One whose departure was deeply felt was Heber Greene. After sixteen years of service, this most gentle of pastors retired on 30 June 1958 at the age of seventy. For Heber, life as the *Columbia*'s chaplain had meant a total commitment he himself best characterized in the words of St. Ignatius Loyola's prayer for perseverance: that one might "give and not count the cost, toil and not seek for rest, labour and not ask for any reward" save to do the will of Christ. Alan Greene was convinced "that my brother in his long ministry on the *Columbia* fulfilled the spirit of this great prayer." Among Heber's many pastoral achievements, Alan mentioned with pride that "nearly a thousand children have been taken into his kindly arms, as, in baptism, he 'received them into the arms of the

Reverend Heber Greene, who retired in June 1958 after sixteen years as Columbia's chaplain, having "baptized nearly a thousand children."

Church.'" On Heber's death on 31 May 1968, Archbishop Godfrey Gower said:

> I was taken by his gentleness and I admired his simplicity. He had that rare gift of interior discipline and was never far away in his thoughts from the presence of God. He was remarkably well read and was one of the few clergy who could read his daily New Testament lessons in Greek. The physical hardship of his work he took in his stride and never complained. Thinking of him there comes to

mind the words of the hymn: "By day and night, a
heart that still / Moves at the breathing of Thy will."

Heber proved difficult to replace. Canadian priests could not at
first be found to take up the challenge. Heber was replaced temporarily by Charles Osborne, a theology student from the Anglican
Theological College, Vancouver.

If the Mission travelled east for most of its money, it frequently
reached back to England for its priests. But as Greene revealed to
a candidate in October 1958, this involved a degree of risk: "It
takes a Canadian to understand our coastal people. With the very
best intentions in the world, some of the English workers we have
engaged simply could not deal with our people understandingly,
and their work ended in disappointment for everybody and we
had to start all over with new workers." On 9 March 1959, the
Reverend Trefor C. Williams, an experienced merchant-marine
officer and yachtsman who had been recruited in England by
Bishop Godfrey Gower during his trip to the Lambeth Conference,
arrived in Vancouver from Liverpool. Within a couple of days,
he was steaming toward Pender Harbour aboard the *Columbia* with
Alan Greene in command, and the crew recounting the lore of
the Mission and the coast. Williams found an adventure in both
culture and language-learning. "Often Canon Alan Greene and
myself . . . looked like a couple of hobos instead of 'gentlemen
of the cloth,' but our appearance has made no difference" to being
accepted everywhere. Indeed, their casual appearance doubtless
eased their acceptance in the coastal world. Williams acquired the
new language more slowly:

I should have been provided with a dictionary of the
language on joining the *Columbia* . . . To the non-logging
person such words as choker, cat-skinner, whistle punk,
half-breed donkey, mutt and jeff, dutchman, are absolutely
meaningless, but to the logger they have a meaning, and
their use means an economy of words.

He found life in floating villages no less surprising. Coming from
a centuries-old established culture, Williams had imagined floating

towns as clusters of dilapidated dwellings "far worse than house-boats where the dust was swept between the cracks in the floor." Instead, he discovered "the most up-to-date homes with washing machines, dryers, suds-savers, fitted carpets, and many more things that a man does not [usually] notice."

Within his first year Williams served on three of the four Mission ships, first as chaplain of the *Columbia*, then as skipper-padre of both the *Rendezvous* and the *John Antle*. The latter being the faster and newer of the smaller vessels, she was transferred to the Whale-town base and given a larger patrol area: Strait of Georgia, Discovery Passage, Toba, Bute and Loughborough Inlets, and occasional visits well to the south of the traditional patrol zone.

The retirement on 31 December 1959 of the seventy-year-old Canon Alan Greene, the Mission's superintendent of twenty-three years, marked a watershed in the Mission's history. And the departure of such a key figure inaugurated a critical period of transition. Indeed, many years later, Joe Titus somewhat bitterly reflected that Greene's successor was bent on wrecking what Greene had built. The new man's mandate struck Titus as licence to close down the Mission. "They started to sell off their assets [as] soon as he appeared, and so now [in 1989] what have they got? A bank account, I guess." Eric Powell shared this view. The Mission "had to be closed down because it was not viable economically. Simple as that. And so the Church decides that you leave an area because it's economically unviable. Bad theology in my opinion. Terrible theology." Titus and Powell were correct as far as they went. As will be seen, however, the new superintendent's choices were not so clearcut.

The task of extolling Alan Greene's years of devoted service fell to the new editor of *The Log*, Cecil FitzGerald, a long-time friend and servant of the Mission. FitzGerald had first signed on the *Makehewi* as a deckhand in 1924, then transferred the following year to the newly launched *Rendezvous* skippered by Greene out of Quathiaski Cove. (In the twenties his father, C.H. FitzGerald, had helped Greene on the *Rendezvous* while the family lived in Campbell River.) John Antle had then spirited Cecil away almost immediately as engineer of the *Columbia*, where he stayed for almost twelve years. Cecil FitzGerald's first editorial in *The Log* appeared in the edition following Greene's retirement. He praised the life of Alan Greene, the old "Master Mariner" who had enriched the lives of all with whom he had come into contact: "His knowledge of the Coast with all its swirling, racing, treacherous channels is surpassed by few, and this knowledge backed by courage and kindliness was ever at its best when helping others." There can be little doubt that this heartfelt eulogy reflected the admiration and affection in which Greene was held by all those he had ministered to with great constancy and vision.

On 19 April 1960, members of the board hosted a reception in Vancouver's Georgia Hotel where they presented Greene "an over-sized illuminated cheque for $3,000," a contribution towards a boat he wanted for his retirement years at Redroofs on the Sechelt Peninsula. The *Talisman*, a twenty-two-foot Chriscraft driven by a six cylinder 135-hp gasoline engine, cruised at twenty knots and slept two. Some board members were amused that the old proponent of "comfortable slow boats" had finally experienced a sea change.

To some observers, both outside and within the Mission, it was obvious that time was overtaking "God's little ships." Yet for Cecil FitzGerald, nothing was further from the truth. In *The Log*'s 1961 Easter edition, he set out to counter "comment in certain quarters that in this so-called 'modern day' the role of the Columbia Coast Mission is drifting into obsolescence." By recounting illustrative anecdotes, he tried to demonstrate the Mission's uniqueness. No other national institution, he argued, could respond to the situations the Mission regularly dealt with on a daily basis: loneliness, isolation and human need. "It is true that the Mission no longer operates four base hospitals as it did a few years ago; today's economics preclude this, and reliance is placed on air transport to Vancouver for all the more serious cases requiring specialist treatment." Nor, he added, did the half-dozen major logging camps any longer rely on the Mission for medical aid; they had their own float planes standing by for rapid direct transport to Vancouver. But in other respects, the Mission's constituency had not really changed. It still comprised the small logging camps of four to twenty men, and small settlements of isolated families. Such people "rely on the four ships and men of the Columbia Coast Mission to be that precious link between them and the outside world for that spiritual and medical aid that has no boundaries." In short, "the role of the *Columbia* and the importance of the Mission have not changed. They are as important now in the social life of the Coast as they were on that day at the turn of the century when John Antle first rounded Cape Mudge." FitzGerald might have added that it was not only the "men of the Columbia Coast Mission" who were holding it together, but the women as well. That same edition welcomed the *Columbia*'s new doctor, Dr. Joyce Davies, who was joining not only a ship, but a growing tradition of women physicians. Change in the midst of constancy seemed to be the order of the day.

What often held the Mission together, especially as far as people on the coast were concerned, was the sense of tradition the Mission built up over the years. Names, boats, remembered stories—such were the strands which bound a mission and its people together, weaving a common lore. Only by identifying with this lore could newcomers in the mission field find their way. Groping his way into the unaccustomed world of coastal culture, one new missionary reported that by using "certain code words"—such as "Columbia," "Heber," "Alan"—he could step right into the world the Mission had been serving since 1904. Indeed, some old timers still remembered John Antle. The board of the Mission must have found it very difficult to choose their third superintendent, for they must have known he would inherit not only all the Mission's traditions, but all its problems.

The Venerable Patrick Ellis began his five-year appointment as the Mission's third superintendent in 1960. As he recalled many years later, "the Board came to the conclusion that somebody other than the two people who'd been connected with it from the beginning should assess the thing, [and so] I got landed with the job." These remarks denote less a sense of commitment than a realization that a job simply needed doing. In the words of a fellow missionary years later, "his task was basically to close the Mission down. Dreadful thing for him to have to do and I think he suffered consequently because of that." In fact, Ellis seems to

The Reverend Patrick Ellis, successor to Alan Greene as the third superintendent of the Columbia Coast Mission, 1960–65.

have been ready to resign not long after he was in. Given the Mission's fifty-year legacy of faith, physical and spiritual courage, and devoted service under the inspired leadership of Antle and Greene, it would have been difficult for Ellis not to have felt "the pain of having to close the Mission down." Greene had initiated him into the Mission during the summer of 1935, at which time *The Log* touted Ellis as his mentor's "very able lieutenant." Now, burdened with ill health, Ellis was already under stress when he assumed the leadership.

But officers of the Mission were attempting to make a bold face of it. In welcoming the new superintendent, Cecil Fitz-Gerald explained the four-month delay in appointing Greene's successor. He stressed the difficulty of finding "a man endowed with the ability, fortitude and dedication" for the job. Acknowledging that the task entailed a thorough review of Mission administration and operations in the light of harsh economic realities in the church and the province as a whole, FitzGerald heralded Ellis as the man of the hour. A graduate of both the University of British Columbia and the Anglican Theological College, the forty-eight-year-old Ellis had spent several summers with Alan Greene aboard *Rendezvous* before the war, and had served with the RCAF from 1942–46. He had been rector of St. Paul's, Vancouver, for the previous nine years, and a member of the Mission board for some years. He brought to the job "a spirit of energy and drive and a pleasing personality."

More importantly, Ellis had a vision: rationalization and relevance. He was a realist who understood the difficulties of succeeding to the leadership of a unique mission that had been run by two charismatic leaders: John Antle and Alan Greene. He also knew that changing times had made the Columbia Coast Mission virtually redundant. Once-isolated coastal populations now gravitated to major centres, while permanent settlements had replaced nomadic camps. People were now linked by radio and telephone communications, and were well served by air and hospital services. Private speedboats were commonplace, and logging operators flew crews in and out for short periods of work on station. Thanks to improved transportation, Pender Harbour was no longer an isolated outpost, and community needs had changed accordingly. Even Greene's charitable enterprise, the Aged Folks' Guest Houses, was almost at the end of its usefulness. Some residents had moved away when the hospital was relocated to Sechelt. While "most of the frontiers had been changing," the CCM head office had remained in the Province Building in Vancouver, and the Mission had not kept pace. Part of the problem, as Ellis saw it, was that most members of the board "had never really been up the coast and had never really been that involved" in the front-line work of the Mission. They depended "completely on whatever the Superintendent told us, and of course John Antle and Alan Greene were both very enthusiastic about the Mission."

In short, Ellis confessed to having "got the feeling that we were doing work in areas which should have been established parishes . . . instead of being done by this rather expensive method of rushing about in boats all over the place." The Mission had been necessary in places like once-remote Echo Bay, he conceded, but this was no longer the case. Mobility made the difference. When Ellis became superintendent in 1960 "there wasn't a great need for just socializing or going and taking services with odd people who were able to get out and around." More pointedly, "what the hell are we doing with a missionary work on Vancouver's doorstep," where all kinds of medical and social resources are available.

As a first step, the new superintendent followed the board's recommendation and shifted the Mission's headquarters from Vancouver to Campbell River. Ellis recognized the need for further major restructuring. Like Greene before him, he wanted to shift the accent from itinerant preaching, to established parishes. This was a crucial shift. As he told the 1962 annual board meeting, the Mission suffered from "lack of men, money and facilities to provide the Spiritual needs of these new growing communities."

As if an omen of difficult times ahead, the *Columbia* struck a reef in the spring of 1960 while negotiating Schooner Pass at the entrance to Seymour Inlet in heavy rain and severely reduced visibility. Floated free at high water, she was drydocked to effect repairs to her keel. FitzGerald took advantage of the occasion to remind "us ordinary folks and landlubbers who read of the journeyings of the sea-going missionaries and missionary doctors" of the perils of seafaring:

> We are reminded of the fate of many vessels not so fortunate; and where a small mishap has turned to tragedy

through a shift in tide or wind. We think of the sturdy
ships that have gone to a watery grave off Cape Mudge
. . . We think of running the Yuculta Rapids on a full
flood tide, white water with sucking whirlpools and surging boils, known as "devil's dish-pans" . . . We think
of Queen Charlotte Sound with tiny Pine Island lighthouse standing defiant against the roar and surge of a
Pacific storm, monstrous seas pouring in from a thousand
miles away. The coast is fraught with danger for those
who "go down to the sea in ships." It would be well
for us in our warm snug homes on a stormy night to
offer a prayer "God help the sailors on a night like this."

A major part of Ellis's work was fundraising, just as it had been
for Antle and Greene. But "where do you get the money from
to run something which is in some ways redundant?" he asked
himself. Recognizing that he lacked the public-relations skills of
his predecessors, he nonetheless trod the same path:

I used to travel down east for six weeks every spring
trying to get people to divvy up the money . . . [But
with indifferent success]. That was Alan Greene's great
forte, of course. He could go back all over Canada and
tell his marvellous stories and everybody loved him. And
everybody loved his stories and so they forked out the
money . . .

As Ellis saw it, the Mission of the old days had been "a sort of
romantic thing" which promoters like Antle and Greene exploited
to the full. They could "show slides and tell stories about people
living on float-houses and this kind of thing," and appeal to some
idealistic vision of frontier life which the established churches had
been cajoled into evangelizing. But for Ellis, a self-confessed prag-
matist, too much had changed to go on indulging in that sort of
dog-and-pony show; "the romanticism had died out," and being
superintendent in the 1960s was "a thankless sort of job." Indeed,
fundraising and promotion—the principal tasks of his office as he
saw it—formed "probably the most undesirable part of my ministry

[though] I certainly learned lots of things from it." He saw himself neither as a leader, nor as an animator or supervisor. "The people in the ships knew far more what had to be done than I did. I was just sitting back there [in Vancouver and, later, Campbell River] trying to keep the thing running." The extent to which this perception of his role affected the Mission is unclear. He gave his own people a very long leash. The board, in its turn, granted the same to him.

Certainly, Ellis had sound reasons for doubting the Mission's effectiveness. The *Columbia*, for example, was far too slow for medivac service, and Alert Bay's physician, Dr. Jack Pickup, already had expressed the view that the medical mission had outlived its usefulness. Pickup was so concerned about logging accidents that he learned to fly and bought his own Seebee amphibious aircraft. Consequently, as Ellis claimed, *Columbia* was receiving no emergency calls at all, and her work "was just a routine business of going around taking the doctor to the Indian villages and logging camps, if they happened to need a doctor there." To his mind, "if you didn't need the doctor, you didn't need a 60-foot ship to plow around the country on." Nor was Ellis always convinced that volunteers' reasons for wanting to join the Mission were sound. Although unable to recruit from within Canada when he wanted to, he seemed particularly uneasy about so-called immigrant doctors who applied to the Mission as a stepping-stone into the Canadian profession. "Sometimes you'd get one who may have had a problem of some sort in their life and wanted to get away" from it all by joining the Mission. "Trying to get a doctor who was allowed to practice and who wasn't hankering to get a well-paid job somewhere [else was] a very hit-and-miss sort of deal; clergy were much the same."

Given Ellis's perception of the Mission, it would have been easier to close it down altogether were it not locked into certain situations. One such commitment seemed inescapable: "we were really providing the medical services for the Indian villages." Although many Natives were leaving their old villages and gravitating to Alert Bay and major centres like Campbell River and Vancouver, the Mission still felt responsible to those who remained.

The Mission did, however, reduce and transform its operations through gradual attrition of personnel and resources. In May 1961, for example, the 1940-built *Rendezvous* (ex *John Antle*) was retired from service and sold as a yacht to the layman who had skippered her for over a year. That autumn, barely halfway through his five-year appointment, the Reverend Trefor Williams left the Mission to become rector of the Campbell River parish the Mission had founded. While his new appointment was in line with the general restructuring at the time, Williams was gravely concerned for the seagoing side of the work. His parting words made a desperate plea for help:

> I wish that I could hand on my Master Mariner's Certificate to my successor, as I know the Superintendent [Pat Ellis] is having difficulty finding a priest with those qualifications. If none is found, or a priest for the *Columbia*, then the Superintendent will be the only priest in the Mission, and that means none afloat. Surely there is some priest with sea experience somewhere who could take on this great work . . .

Looking to the future, it remained a moot point whether the Mission really needed "some priest with sea experience"—or one who could fly.

Aircraft had been revolutionizing coastal life, from exploration and medical evacuation in the 1930s, to air patrols in logging and fisheries, followed by scheduled air services in the 1940s. Even as early as April 1932, the cancellation stamp on a letter sent from Victoria to Surge Narrows via the Columbia Coast Mission had urged "Save Time—Use Air Mail." When the Reverend Joe Titus finished his five-year contract in 1959, he had long been accustomed to the regular use of aircraft by police, welfare workers and medical doctors. With a plane, he could have reached any point in his patrol area "within a half hour" from his base in Whaletown. He could have met Mission needs with greater efficiency and his family would not have been so isolated. Larger communities on his route had even offered to build him an adequate shelter for the plane. "I think that if they had introduced aircraft or fast boats that might have delayed my thought in leaving," he admitted. However, Greene staunchly insisted that slow boats were the answer to the special kind of ministry the Mission offered. But his successor had rather different views on the matter.

CHAPTER 10

Mission on Wings:
End Game

Lifting easily off the waters of Campbell River in a
Cessna 170 float plane in the spring of 1962, Reverend Patrick
Ellis surveyed the Mission's magnificent territory spreading out
beneath him in ever expanding grandeur. This was his first, and
"entirely unofficial," tour of the region under his pastoral charge.
During the exploratory flight, he reached beyond the boundaries
of what had once been Mission country in order to experience
the rugged West Coast and points well beyond the tip of Vancouver Island. "From the air it was nothing but beauty with the
glorious sandy beaches . . . and the blue-green of the water, the
rocks so treacherous to ships . . . and surrounded by a crown of
white from the ceaseless breaking of the swells." Beside him at
the controls was the aircraft's owner, Ernest Antle, son of the
Mission's founder, who had flown in from Vancouver to provide
Ellis with a practical grasp of the challenges he faced. Judging
from Ellis's descriptions, the overflights and short stops provided
an exhilarating experience:

> History repeats itself but changes with the passing of the
> years. Nearly sixty years after the Rev. John Antle sur-
> veyed the mainland coast and the islands of the inside
> passage by means of a tiny sailing boat and engine, his
> son took me to the west coast in a plane and completed
> in eight hours what his father could not adequately have
> done in the same number of weeks! But the spirit in

father and son remain the same, and the desire to bring the ministrations of the Church to the people remains the same, it is only the mode of transport that changes in order that the Gospel may be made available to all people.

Whether the Mission should run ships or take to the air continued to be debated for some time, with both sides of the argument offering credible positions. Recognizing the expansion of air and road travel into once virgin territory, and the concomitant development of new logging and mining enterprises, Ellis grasped the need to minister to areas not yet settled. His imagination was captivated by "those places whose romantic and tongue-twisting names have long been familiar—Ceepeecee, Esperanza, Zeballos, Nuchatlitz, Fair Harbour, Kyuquot, Ououkinsh." Clearly feeling himself in competition with other denominations for the evangelization of this part of the province, he found it "a humiliating experience to find the Roman and United Churches strongly established here [around Nootka] and no sign of the Anglican Church." It seemed abundantly clear "that the Anglican Church is neglecting its duty if it does not bring its ministrations to these people." The corollary to this, "the second thing that I am convinced about, if I needed any convincing, is that the Church must take to the air."

Obvious as this was to Ellis, a long tradition of practical experience suggested to others that ships remained the better bet, or at least, that the Mission should not dispense with them altogether. A serious fire at Kingcome Inlet in 1963 seemed to demonstrate the point. In the middle of the night an overheated oil lamp exploded, completely destroying a Native family's wooden frame house, burning three young children to death and seriously injuring two others. Seeking medical aid for the two child survivors (one with burns to 40 percent of her body, another with burned arms), members of the Tsawataineuk band paddled a dugout canoe to an emergency transmitter at Halliday's Landing, to call the *Columbia*. The hospital ship immediately undertook the fifty-mile journey in the dark without radar. On arrival, Dr. Cezar Heine and the Reverend Ian Baird ventured three miles upriver by canoe to tend the victims. In the words of Cecil FitzGerald, editor of *The Log*, "this is another case where the Mission hospital ship has proved its worth because, since the accident occurred at night, aircraft could not be used. As is always the case, *time* is the vital factor in getting medical aid to the victims at the scene." He cited the case not as an argument against aircraft medical evacuation, but rather as a plea for prudence in evaluating the Mission's future direction.

Meanwhile transportation links had been improving between Port Hardy, southern Vancouver Island and Vancouver. A tri-weekly bus service linked Port Hardy and Victoria, with regular stops at camps and towns, and flag-down stops en route. One could board the bus at Port Hardy at 8 a.m. and be in Vancouver by 9:45 p.m. Or one could take a ferry from Beaver Cove to Kelsey Bay and then bus to Nanaimo to catch the Vancouver ferry. Better still, one could catch one of two daily PWA flights from Port Hardy airport and be in Vancouver a couple of hours later.

Change was in the wind. Writing in October 1963 to the Missionary Society of the Church in Canada, a mainstay of the Mission since its founding, Ellis gave notice of the radical changes he wished to introduce. Admitting he "must appear as something of an iconoclast trying to smash the image of one of the Anglican Church's most romantic pieces of work," he laid his cards on the table: transfer to the dioceses all holdings of the Mission which were no longer at the cutting edge of missionary work. The CCM would cease to be a mission area, but would become "a series of mission parishes and eventually self-supporting parishes." Ellis regarded his task not as one of destruction, but of consummation. Indeed, "it is my hope that in a short time the Columbia Coast Mission, as such, will comprise only the spiritual and medical work being done by the MV *Columbia*." In doing so, he aimed to "build firm foundations of faith in places where we can concentrate our preaching and teaching, and that therefore we should not dissipate our energies and effectiveness by trying to visit every nook and cranny all the time."

Without a word of explanation to the public, the eight-year-old mission ship *John Antle* was declared surplus late in 1963. The Mission was unable to find someone with a master's certificate to run her. Besides, the Mission's Kingcome operations, which the *John Antle* served, had been taken over completely by the Diocese of New Westminster, which had already assumed responsibility for St. Mary's Church and the Aged Folks' Guest Houses at Pender Harbour. Listed for sale in *The Log* at the end of 1963, with photograph and vital statistics, the *John Antle* was sold in the spring of 1964. Proceeds from the sale covered the purchase of the nineteen-foot catamaran *Che-Kwa-La* for shallow-water river service in Kingcome Inlet. At about the same time, the Mission launched its "radar fund" for the *Columbia*, a move that at least suggested continuity. Nonetheless, major changes continued. When Captain Bill Nicholson resigned in 1964 after five years as *Columbia*'s skipper in order to work for BC Ferries, he was succeeded in command by Charlie Dick, a Native fisherman who had previously served as the ship's relief skipper. Then, St. Mary's Hospital, Pender Harbour, closed—with serious implications for the Aged Folks' Guest Houses. With the transfer of all hospital services to Sechelt, it was no longer practical to provide accommodation for the elderly in Pender Harbour. New residents did not move in to take the place of those who died or moved out. Bit by bit, it seemed, the Mission's traditional operations were slowing down.

Exploring new directions, the Mission espoused the ecumenical movement then capturing the religious imagination of the 1960s. More pragmatically, perhaps, it simply recognized that ecumenism in general—and cooperation with the United Church in particular—seemed the best approach to optimizing the Mission's resources. In fact, St. Peter's, Campbell River, had broken new ground as early as 1941 by welcoming joint use of the church by Anglican and United Church congregations. Indeed, the rector had announced at the time that "it was open for public worship for all recognized Christian communions." Then, in 1964, the Mission undertook unofficial exploratory discussions with the United Church to review the requirement for Christian mission in the region comprising the northern half of Vancouver Island. In an effort to avoid all "useless duplication," an early meeting laid the groundwork: common Sunday Schools and common use of each other's church buildings. As Ellis reported in 1965: "We are very happy with the understanding that has been reached between us, and hope that continued co-operation will enable us to provide the best possible service to Our Lord and Master."

How best to deliver that service in an increasingly secular world was an ongoing issue in churches across the land. The effects of urbanization and secularization provoked vigorous debates in theological circles, leading many church people to reassess the meanings of biblical tradition. This was the decade of the so-called Secular City debate, in which many Christian thinkers celebrated the emergence of secular urban civilization and the collapse of traditional religious culture. It was a time of ferment, when the progressive bishop of Woolwich, John A.T. Robinson, sparked widespread theological reflection in Britain and North America by arguing that the church might perhaps be experiencing "the new Reformation." Some churches sought renewal in the "secular meaning of the Gospel," while creative thinkers in the area of social and intellectual processes coined slick new phrases that were open to misinterpretation. Debate ensued under a variety of banners: "God is Dead"; we are "living in accelerated change with a static theology"; and "secular man needs a nonreligious interpretation of Scripture." Reflective churchpeople everywhere were drawn into the debates. Some found them profoundly unsettling, others liberating. Everyone had to wrestle with the question society at large was asking: "Can a truly contemporary person be a Christian?"

This ferment triggered questions about the relevance of the Mission's mandate and operations, and seemed particularly timely. The theme was addressed by Cecil FitzGerald in the Golden Jubilee issue of *The Log* celebrating "sixty years of dedicated service to the isolated people along the B.C. coast." In his final editorial after six years as editor, FitzGerald summarized key points in the Mission's history and considered what might lie ahead. He concluded that the Mission of the past had indeed been relevant:

> Here was the Anglican Church keeping pace with the times and speaking to the people of the day in terms which could be understood. For in receiving care when it was most needed, many a rough logger, who knew

nothing of theology or doctrine, came to know the love of God. Here, too, was a field where priest and layman found a means of expression for their faith, and over the years a great host of people across the country have had a hand in the ministry of the Mission.

With regard to the present, FitzGerald reminded his readers that adaptability had been a keynote of the Mission through two world wars and a Depression. The Mission's leaders adapted themselves to external circumstances in order to pursue their principal goals: medical service had been the medium of delivering the Gospel during the John Antle phase, while social service had become the medium with Alan Greene. The medium was indeed the message under both superintendents. The 1965 Diamond Jubilee year found the Mission at what FitzGerald defined as "another cross-roads of decision." It would have to address the question not only of whether the church, through the Mission, was keeping pace with the times, but also whether the church's language was still intelligible to the modern world.

Not convinced that the present medium was as effective as it had been in the past, the board had begun restructuring the Mission with diocesan support. The resulting closures, and the transfers of administrative and fiscal responsibilities, were far reaching. The *John Antle* and *Rendezvous* had been sold; St. Mary's Hospital at Pender Harbour had been closed; St. George's Hospital at Alert Bay passed to a private corporation; and the Diocese of New Westminster had assumed responsibility for the mission at Kingcome Inlet. Now, the Diocese of British Columbia took over the northeast coast of Vancouver Island, as well as Cortes and Lasqueti Islands, all of which would be administered and financed as part of its missionary area.

For Ellis, the term "missionary area" referred to a financially dependent region requiring external assistance in order to maintain its pastoral services. Pragmatically, he viewed a mission as an operation designed to address a specific problem, and he readily accepted that it would close down once the problem had been solved. Having succeeded in establishing parishes, the Mission should hand them over to the appropriate diocese and turn its energies elsewhere. Eventually, this meant declaring his own office and position redundant. In the meantime, Ellis found support for the notion that work "be carried out by the regular settled Diocese, and that the Columbia Coast Mission continue to operate as a frontier enterprise." Endorsing reorganization, Cecil FitzGerald concluded his Golden Jubilee editorial on a note of exhilaration. "This is growth," FitzGerald explained. "This is keeping pace with the opening up of communications in these parts of the Province; this is the beginning of the consummation of the work begun sixty years ago."

Ultimately, restructuring left the *Columbia* operating as "a special form of ministry" in isolated areas. This left the *Alan Greene*, with layreader and skipper Don Maclean, to carry out its usual patrols from Lund to Port Neville, and the northern half of Quadra Island to Kelsey Bay—except for areas with road connections to Campbell River. Maclean's report for July 1965 describes some conditions he encountered:

> . . . we have some fifty-three camps [in the mainland area] with a population of approximately 1,000 men, very few women and children. The turnover in this population is approximately three times each year as men are coming and going in the various camps. We have nearly the same conditions on the Islands and Vancouver Island which gives [about] 6,000 loggers, many of whom we hope we are "reaching."

The rather tentative conclusions about the effectiveness of such patrols suggest Maclean was not convinced of success, however he might have measured it. But for FitzGerald, the situation as a whole was positive. "The Columbia Coast Mission is not finished, but [by reorganizing] is taking one step towards its fulfillment in order to help the advance of the whole work of Christ's Church. The only thing that passes out of existence at this time is the office and headquarters of the Superintendent."

Patrick Ellis left the Mission in 1965 on completion of a five-year appointment during which "the groundwork was difficult and the

The Reverend John W. Forth, MBE, CD, DD, who succeeded Patrick Ellis with the
new title of Supervisor (1965–70).

spade work frustrating." Certainly, his tenure as superintendent was marked by the general ferment of the times. For some, he had shown himself to be "first and foremost a man of God" concerned with updating the Mission effectively, streamlining its operations and maintaining personal, collegial relations throughout the Mission family. Others saw him as intent on scrapping the Mission altogether rather than transforming it. Either way, what he called his "five hectic years" of restructuring a mission in need of redirection were not easy. He was succeeded in September 1965 by the Venerable John W. Forth, under the new title of Supervisor. An experienced administrator and churchman, Forth had served as chaplain in the Canadian army from 1939 to 1960. He had landed in Normandy on D-Day with the Cameron Highlanders of Ottawa. Awarded the MBE for bravery and devotion to duty during the invasion, he had continued with the Third Canadian Division for the remainder of the campaign. He brought to the office of Supervisor of the Columbia Coast Mission a much broader concept of Canada and the church than his predecessors had espoused.

Forth's first article in *The Log* as both supervisor and editor announced that "a new day dawns," for he had succeeded in finding not only a chaplain, but also a medical doctor for the *Columbia*. Significantly, neither were local. The Reverend Ivan Futter was from England, and Dr. Fred Wiegand from Montreal. Forth's article signalled a "new plan of operations" in which Futter would serve both as "supervising chaplain of the *Columbia*" and as priest-in-charge of the churches on Cortes Island, Quadra Island and in Sayward. That essentially meant two weeks ashore (covering the area previously handled during the past four years by lay reader Don Maclean in the *Alan Greene*), and two weeks afloat aboard the *Columbia*. Declared redundant and taken out of service on 30 June 1966, the six-year-old *Alan Greene* was sold at the end of January 1967. "Diminishing returns and increased costs" made it uneconomical to operate the vessel any longer.

This rationalization was supported by the new secretary-treasurer of the Diocese of British Columbia and of the Columbia Coast Mission, Lieutenant Colonel D. Stewart Mitchell:

The venerable Ivan Futter, Columbia's chaplain 1965–67, at the eagle lectern in St. George's Church, Kingcome.

The increased ferry services and rapid road development have made these changes possible, and it is felt that the work of the Mission can now be carried on more satisfactorily by the resident priests in both Dioceses and, where necessary, regular visits by priests using air transport.

Although layreader Don Maclean left the Mission, he continued to live in the now vacant Whaletown rectory. One of the Mission's final links with medical care, the Whaletown clinic continued to provide monthly medical and dental service. But like the *Columbia*'s medical mission, it too, was nearing its end.

"The last sea-going chaplain of the Columbia Coast Mission," as Ivan Futter once described himself, arrived in 1965. An officer in the British merchant marine prior to entering the ministry, Futter was first attracted to the Mission in theological college, after reading an article about Trefor Williams. Later, a sequence of fortuitous events after his ordination made him "sit up and take notice." First, a fellow priest returning to England showed slides and discussed the fascinating work of the Mission based in Whaletown. Then, a former Mission nurse joined Futter's parish and spoke glowingly of her experience. Finally, an interview in the Royal Naval College (Greenwich) with the Chaplain to the Missions to Seamen based in Vancouver, convinced Futter and his wife Brenda of the merit of their new venture. "My wife and I both felt we were on the edge of something big; we didn't know what it was." With their three children and family dog, the Futters emigrated for what they saw as no more than a five-year contract. "For me it was just another trip, for I had been a sailor most of my working life, but for my wife it was a movement to another country, another way of life." Despite some understandable culture shock, the family settled in very quickly, and "fell in love" with Canada where they remain today.

The Futters stayed first in Campbell River where the *Columbia* was then based. Her patrol cycle kept her away three weeks out of four. The ship's patrol area had expanded considerably, always taking up the slack when smaller ships were sold off and the Mission reorganized. In summer, the patrol covered the area from Kelsey Bay, north to Smith Inlet, and in winter as far as Pine

Island, the northernmost lighthouse before Queen Charlotte Strait. While Alan Greene had needed to steam no more than two hours between stops, Futter now had to steam eight. In short, the Mission continued its ministry to logging and fishing camps, settlements and lighthouses, but largely without its former medical dimension. The ship's new doctor, Fred Wiegand, had scarcely settled in when he observed that "the days of requiring a doctor on board have drawn to a close inasmuch as the doctoring service has become a mere convenience rather than a necessity of the people served." Having served only four months, he left the Mission to practise elsewhere. The *Columbia* was doing little more in the way of medicine than delivering the provincial public health nurses to Indian villages and picking them up on the way back. Residual health care was now fully covered by the province's public health service, and regular float plane service to the cities and towns with doctors and hospitals. Once again, the secular world was replacing the church-based medical mission.

As for Ivan Futter, he was happy with an operation virtually independent of any "head office." Except for the annual general meeting and rare briefings in Victoria, he was left entirely on his own. In keeping with Mission tradition, "they trusted me to get on with the job." His first time on his own in the *Columbia* was an adventure, even though he had no nautical responsibilities. Layreader Charlie Dick of the Kingcome Indian Reserve was still the captain, assisted by his fellow villager, Jimmy Willie:

> But really Charlie Dick and Jimmy the deckhand and myself were the [whole] Mission out in the boat. And I really appreciated having the time, being in such close contact with the two Indian people . . . It was through them that I got to know and to be accepted by the Indian people and began to understand a whole different way of life and culture to what I was used to . . . One of the things the Mission taught me was to be adaptable to circumstances. It broke me out of the mould in which I'd been poured when I went to theological college and gave a freer [approach]. You know, it's a very awe-inspiring experience to celebrate Holy Communion on

the back deck of the *Columbia* with a five-thousand foot mountain as your reredos to the altar behind you—a very moving experience.

Gradually, Futter's duties as priest-in-charge of the shore parishes claimed more of his time and energy. Facing increasing difficulty in juggling his responsibilities between ship and shore, "my time in the Mission began to get shorter and I began to fly more, meeting the boat at some outlying point, spending some time [aboard] and then coming back and doing church work at all the different points" ashore. Besides the usual ministrations such as baptisms, weddings and funerals, he found himself drawn into "counselling, particularly with young wives that the loggers had married in Vancouver and brought up and stuck in the middle of the wild in a camp." Life in the bush could still be terribly isolated and rugged. And while aircraft permitted easy access, Futter still regarded the mission ship as the best vehicle for pastoral care:

> . . . the advantage of a boat is that you can bring it in and tie it up alongside and you can stay there, but you weren't dependent on the hospitality of the people. And, to the people who live on the coast, an airplane is [solely] a means of transport, whereas with a boat, it's part of their life. They all have boats, and if they want to talk to you they'll come onto your boat. So in a sense you take them out of their environment and into another; and then they talk freely that way.

Appearances to the contrary, Ellis himself had regarded the effect of aircraft on the Mission as a mixed blessing. While a plane gave the impression of covering the whole territory, it had "no sooner dropped into a community than it would depart." Boats at least gave the impression of greater commitment by tarrying a while, even if the skipper-chaplain did little more than anchor or tie up for the night. Ellis saw the mere presence of the mission ship as providing "a sort of spiritual uplift."

For Futter, the ideal combination was one he shared with the United Church minister, the Reverend Peter Newberry, who flew

Reverend Ivan Futter with Columbia's hand-carved thunderbird flag staff.

the United Church aircraft out of Alert Bay. Theirs was an example of successful ecumenical partnership. The *Columbia* would transport aviation fuel to a rendezvous point, where it would serve as operations base for the aircraft that could reach out into isolated pockets. Both chaplains rode the aircraft, and both shared the hospitality of the ship as an itinerant parish church. Being able to share his floating rectory confirmed Futter's view that "the boat was the answer; the plane only did part of the job."

This perception seemed confirmed on an occasion in 1966, when thick fog shut down flying operations and only the *Columbia* could answer an emergency call to pick up a seriously ill woman on Gilford Island and bring her to St. George's Hospital in Alert Bay. Leaving night anchorage in Echo Bay, the *Columbia* undertook a hazardous journey that not even a seiner with local knowledge wanted to undertake. What made it possible for the mission ship to respond so promptly was the recent installation, at Futter's recommendation, of a new Decca radar. Although not budgeted for, and therefore a bone of contention, it proved the key to the operation's success. Having reached Gilford Island and taken the patient aboard, Futter described the journey back:

> Well, the *Columbia*, besides being a fine sea boat captained by a man of great Christian understanding, is also a ship of faith, and we got underway with as much speed as the weather would permit. Once clear of the dock, we couldn't see a thing. Going at slow speed, we crept toward the main channel along the course that the captain and I had already plotted—followed by the seiner that hadn't wanted to take the patient himself. Once there we encountered a fairly large ground swell, and it was blowing. This was strange as you do not usually have any appreciable wind with fog. But this all added to the problems of navigation. Here we added to our little convoy: another fisherman who had heard that we were in the area and attempting to make the "bay." He radioed us to put on all our deck lights so he could pick us out in the glow and, once joined up, follow us in. He was lost. Well, we made Dodman Point, and crept around it before heading on a straight course for Cormorant Island. The course should have been easy from there, but those of you who know the waters there will know all the many hazards. Feeling our way into port, we finally caught our first glimpse of shore—the lights of somebody's bedroom window flickering through the fog.
>
> When one takes into consideration the factors of human life involved in this episode, [including] the cost of the *Columbia* and the other vessels, the price for the Radar is far from exorbitant.

In the fall of 1967 the Mission reported what it called a "successful year—with the exception of finances." (It had been running a deficit since 1961.) The much-touted reorganization Ellis had begun was nearing completion. But, despite $10,000 in proceeds from the sale of its ships, and two bequests with a total value of $32,000, the Mission continued to operate at a considerable deficit. Its reserve fund had been reduced to $18,000. Encouraged by successful downsizing, Supervisor John W. Forth reaffirmed the will to continue work. "The Columbia Coast Mission testifies to our Church's determination that no person is so isolated that he is beyond the reach of the ministration of the Church. If such persons cannot be reached by land, they will be reached by sea or air."

Pondering the future, the board of directors looked not only toward its own effectiveness, but to the Mission's as a whole. For some time it had felt the need to appoint new members who were resident in, or at least active in, the areas served by the *Columbia*. This obvious change was long overdue. The new members included Chief Jimmy Sewid, the first Native member of the board. As Sewid's autobiography reveals, the church had played an important role in the Kwakiutl culture of Alert Bay: "the Anglican Church was there for us and we were all baptized and confirmed there and married there and when we die we are going to be buried there. They have done very well for us."

Following the principle of centering its resources in the area it served, the board shifted *Columbia*'s home port from Alert Bay to Port Hardy, and likewise moved the Futters' residence there from Campbell River. But the future of the seventy-two-foot hospital ship was under review. The board found her considerably larger than required, maintenance was expensive—$8,000 the previous year—and federal government regulations required that a vessel of her size be crewed by staff with recognized marine qualifications. A smaller vessel would skirt the regulations.

The board therefore began mulling over the prospect of acquiring a forty-two to forty-five-foot diesel-powered, radar-equipped displacement hull that could cruise at about twelve knots and cope comfortably with the waters in *Columbia*'s territory. Such a ship would cost considerably less for maintenance, insurance and staff. Seeking to make even greater use of the ship, the board appointed a Church Army officer to the Mission's pastoral staff. Captain Tom Armstrong's appointment to the Mission's pastoral ministry began on 1 September 1967, scarcely three months before the *Columbia*'s demise. The board considered other options as well. Impressed by Ivan Futter's "ideal combination" of linking the Mission ship with a United Church aircraft and pilot, members seriously entertained the notion of getting their own plane to supplement the ship. Yet, on 5 December 1967, the *Columbia* was paid off in Vancouver and put up for sale on the understanding that her name would be kept for a successor. Her captain, Charlie Dick of Kingcome, was retired from the Mission, and the X-ray equipment returned to the Tuberculosis Society which had donated it. With little fanfare, an era had come to an end.

As a counterpoint to these events, in the late autumn of 1967 the Reverend Ivan Futter flew with the United Church's aircraft *George Pringle*, piloted by the Reverend Peter Newberry, to a rendezvous in Port MacNeill with the United Church's new mission ship *Thomas Crosby V*. Named after missionaries famous throughout the coastal communities, the aircraft and the new one-hundred-foot ship were continuing a ministry parallel to that of the Columbia Coast Mission. Based on a Norwegian trawler design, *Thomas Crosby V* was built by Star Shipyards of New Westminster where some of the Mission's ships had also been built. Her patrol area lay north of *Columbia*'s in the zone beyond Pine Island, and her task followed that of her four predecessors, bringing both medical and pastoral care to isolated coast dwellers regardless of their church affiliation. Given the Columbia Coast Mission's downsizing, Futter must have wondered at the luxury of the United Church's ship: large living quarters for the crew, and a spacious chapel area that could serve for both worship and meetings. With bunks built into the bulkheads and sides of the chapel, the space could easily be transformed into sleeping quarters. Futter found in Jack Gosse, the captain, a man who shared his own enthusiasm for the region and the people to whom he ministered. More particularly, Goss had "a remarkable grasp of the problems that this kind of ministry involves, and it was a great pleasure to discuss common problems and to gain valuable information from this inspiring personality."

While *Columbia* lay alongside in Vancouver during the winter of 1967–68 awaiting a buyer, the Mission tried its hand at chartering

*Ecumenical visits in Mission territory aboard Canadian destroyer HMCS
Columbia. (l. to r.) Commander Trevor Shuckburg (commanding officer), the
Right Reverend Remi De Roo (Roman Catholic Bishop of Victoria), and Most
Reverend Harold Sexton (Anglican Bishop of BC).*

a replacement. The arrangement did not prove satisfactory. Not
only was it difficult to find something suitable, but the outward
appearance of the rental boat marked a break with the Mission's
traditional image. In terms of public relations, all the trust associated
over the years with the character and distinctive colours of the
mission ships were lost. As John Forth said, nothing about the
charter boat reassured those seeing it that "the Columbia Coast
Mission is still active in serving Christ's flock." Chartering therefore
proved an interim measure which left the Mission in the spring
of 1968 without an operational hull. To remedy the situation, the

The cabin of the fourth Columbia. *(l. to r.) a visitor, Reverend Ivan Futter, and skipper Dave Willie.*

Mission ill-advisedly accepted the gift of a totally unsuitable boat whose commissioning the Victoria *Daily Colonist* announced under the headline: "Racy Chapel to Ply Coast." Forty-feet long and capable of over eleven knots, the *Columbia IV* was dedicated by Bishop Godfrey Gower on 17 June 1968. Her engine was in poor condition, and her hull unable to handle the often rough waters of the northern patrol. When she was sold off a year later, the Mission's marine service came at last to a definite end.

The sale of *Columbia IV* was but one outcome of a study begun by a special committee of the Mission in 1965. Submitted in 1969, its report urged a radical shift in both style and aim. Deeming the Mission to have now fulfilled the purposes for which it had been founded, the committee tendered some drastic proposals. First, the Mission should phase out all operations by June 1969, second, it should transfer all capital assets to a trust fund known as the Columbia Coast Mission Trust, whose mandate would be to assist any parish in the Mission district unable to support itself; and third, it should explore the possibility of sharing the United Church's aircraft. Pending a decision on the first two recommendations, the

Mission, under its chairman, Bishop Roy Gartrell, committed itself in 1970 to a feasibility study of an airborne mission as the way of the future. This took place in the fourth year of Ivan Futter's five-year contract. He was the last seagoing chaplain, and his ship had already been sold.

Some years later, the Mission's downsizing triggered the anger of Alan Greene's widow, who claimed the Board had willfully liquidated its assets without regard to their real value or the purposes for which the Mission had been established. These charges were repudiated not only by Cecil FitzGerald, a long-time member of the board, but also by Ernest Antle, the founder's son. Where FitzGerald argued that the Mission was "not dead, but in a state of transition," Ernest Antle defended it as a financially responsible organization responding to change. "My father, were he alive today, as well as Alan Greene, would have a sense of great accomplishment, and [would] be . . . happy and gratified to see that the reasons for the existence of the Mission have been gradually resolved, and permanent establishments created."

The Mission's first pilot-chaplain, John Mellis, was recruited in 1971 to assess the new enterprise. An American citizen, he learned about the Columbia Coast Mission from the Reverend John Lancaster when both were studying at Princeton Theological Seminary. Lancaster, it seems, "had kidded me about coming to Vancouver Island" and was ultimately instrumental in helping Mellis immigrate to Canada and establish himself in the Mission. Mellis had a strong desire for parish ministry combined with an abiding interest both in flying and in cross-cultural work. His father had been a missionary bush pilot and Mellis' own flight training prepared him for a similar ministry. Bishop Roy Gartrell hired him for what would ultimately be an eight-year appointment.

Arriving in Canada on 4 July 1971 with his wife Dana, Mellis was ordained at Nanaimo and on his way to Port Hardy within the week. He remained there until November, working with the incumbent United Church minister-pilot, Al Shaw, out of Alert Bay. For a brief, intense period he set about "surveying the entire area that the Mission covered, getting to know the camps that were there, the villages . . . and coming up with a plan whereby we could work together." Shaw had been flying on the station

"Mission on Wings," an ecumenical ministry. (l. to r.) Anglican pilot-chaplain, Reverend John Mellis, and United Church pilot-chaplain, Reverend Allan Shaw, with the United Church's Cessna 180 in 1973.

for a little over a year. Three months after Mellis's arrival, he resigned to take a parish in Saskatchewan, leaving Mellis to fly in the company of his wife. During the summer of 1972, the Mellises flew into camps, performed baptisms and weddings, counselled and carried out educational programs similar to those of the old *Columbia*. Using film from the *Davy and Goliath* television series produced by the Lutheran Church, and taking advantage of a couple of itinerant singing guitarists, they laid the basis for Sunday School training by entertaining children. Mellis's ministry was a symbiotic relationship in which the United Church provided the plane, and the Anglican Church the pilot. Theological students sometimes assisted him during the summers and he was joined by United Church minister Clare Holmes in a team ministry.

The combined district of the two churches, which included the west coast of Vancouver Island as well as the traditional Mission regions, turned out to be too large for two men and a single aircraft. Mellis later recalled that he and Clare Holmes "were finding ourselves increasingly going in opposite directions." Even if both were pilots, it was wearing and counterproductive to drop off one colleague at one camp and then continue on and cover a couple of places with the one plane before returning to pick up the partner. Yet both John and Dana Mellis approached the job "with a great deal of youthful enthusiasm and excitement." Mellis quickly became aware of "just how close people lived to tragedy in living and working [near and] on the water, in isolated areas both in logging and fishing."

Mellis expected to be working among backwoods people, in fishing villages and logging camps, but he admitted years later that he really had no idea what that might mean except "probably rough cut people, and in that I was not disappointed." In many respects, his ministry echoed the experience of his predecessors. Often mooring his float plane to float houses, he came to know a mixture of loners and recluses, including "some really hard nuts, the old-time loggers on the coast, who had no use for religion." Like everyone else who ever joined the Mission, he brought his own cultural baggage. Working in Canada, he discovered the opportunity of "experiencing how the Gospel feels in another culture [and] not just in terms of the Native community people." In confronting the "sub-culture of logging and the sub-culture of fishing," he found himself obliged to explain theological principles and Bible stories in ways he had never experienced. He also encountered social changes which underlay the reasons for the Mission's decision to switch from ships to planes:

> . . . the handloggers and that whole way of life was on its way out, and so the kind of boat and nautical orientation of the previous years was already rapidly disappearing, and the new way of life was much more oriented around air travel and larger camps.

Equally striking was just how well developed many of the logging camps had become:

Divine worship on the beach in 1974, with a "little Jimmy"-type portable organ.

During the '70s companies were moving into the heads of inlets where there were vast amounts of timber and they were setting up camps with thirty or forty families and people were bringing in their trailers and families, and there were schools and teachers and community services. Sometimes swimming pools, and in a few cases some of the men had airplanes and would widen a road and put in an airstrip. For all of this I was unprepared, and the net effect was it meant civilization was a lot closer to the hinterland than what I had imagined . . . Airplanes were as much a way of life as boats had been.

As chaplain of the Mission, and indeed its sole itinerant missionary, Mellis shaped his own patrol patterns. They were largely seasonal. During the summer, roughly April to October, he visited each of the eight patrol areas he had identified. Each "natural community" had its own focal point: a post office, a general store, a fuel depot

275

or a combination of all three. Spending about a week in each area, Mellis shaped his ministry according to local needs. Not being tied down to a parish (as his United Church partner was), he enjoyed the advantage of flexibility, remaining just as long as there was work to be done, and moving on whenever the weather was favourable.

During the period November to March, flying conditions were generally poorer and the days shorter. The plane was at hazard when left unattended at temporary moorings, where it could ice up or capsize in heavy snowfalls. In the winter, though flying whenever possible, Mellis tried to concentrate on the camps that were accessible by road, or took a company boat or water taxi from Port Alice. In all, this meant there were some sixty or seventy locations he could serve. For example, he could head up the Nimpkish Valley to the Nimpkish Lake, Woss Lake and Vernon Lake camps. These were large camps with schools and stable populations that generally remained in place even during the winter shutdown. Woss Camp, which Mellis regarded as the centre of Nimpkish operations, consisted of some eighty or one hundred families for whom he established a regular wintertime Sunday School. In carrying out his ministry, he would travel either by scheduled air carriers, or by his own plane, which he had converted from floats to wheels, making it possible to land on the dirt airstrips of different camps. But the turnover in the logging community made his work frustrating. "The average family stayed about two years, and the average single person about six months. And that certainly affected church life where I was always having to meet new people." As his United Church colleague, Clare Holmes, said: "If I really didn't think that we were in the business of training first class lay people for the rest of the Canadian Church, I'd go crazy."

The ministry itself was as varied as one found in an established parish. In some cases, it entailed little more than providing parents with Christian education materials for their children and encouraging them in their role as educators. In others, it meant "listening to people's problems in a particular camp or village [and] doing some mediation or counselling, trying to help people reconcile their relationships." Some adults requested marriage counselling and

Bible studies. There were Sunday Schools to be organized and the general nurturing of parish life by constant personal contact. Mellis found himself often drawing on Lutheran materials, books, pamphlets and films. There was little room in all this for preaching, which had never been a mainstay of the Mission. The best he seemed able to offer were "meditations" in his monthly bulletin.

Like Antle and Greene before him, Mellis took his illustrated lecture tour "to the East" in 1973 to raise funds. Badly arranged by the Mission, the lecture tour was virtually useless. Although the milieu was the same as in the era of Antle and Greene, the atmosphere was decidedly different: "we got the definite impression people didn't want us to make any kind of appeal from the pulpit, [so] I would end up plugging mission in their own Diocese." Nor was the Mission able to attract funds from other customary sources. In the fall of 1974, for example, traditional church gifts such as the General Synod's grant had ceased, and the board made a general appeal for $3,000 to avoid another deficit year.

As chaplain-pilot of an ecumenical ministry, Mellis served two quite different masters, each with its own system and expectations. Years later, he confessed to having "found the supervision and accountability of the Anglican Church far easier to deal with because they weren't looking at the dollars and cents as the bottom line; and they weren't trying to measure out the money available to so many different projects." Less the astute business managers, the Anglicans seemed to him to be saying "if the work needs to be done, we do it; we'll find the money—it will come." However, the United Church's mission remained economically viable whereas the Anglican's often did not.

Mellis's own sense of accountability had less to do with managerial or financial considerations than with evangelism. His sole measure was the "effect the Gospel is having on the lives of the people to whom I was ministering." But by his own admission, this "varied from person to person, and from camp to camp" and was no more quantifiable as justification for the work than anything else the Mission had done. Yet the Board was clearly convinced it was getting value for money. In 1978 the Mission bought its own plane, a Cessna 180.

Significantly, the new plane was named neither "John Antle"

The CCM's pilot-chaplain in 1978, Reverend John Mellis, with The George Pringle II, the Mission's own Cessna 180. Note fuselage lettering: "Working Together for Christ—Anglican and United Churches of Canada."

nor "Alan Greene" in the tradition of CCM ships, but *George Pringle II*. The name reflected the status of the new "flying ministry," as it was called in brochures and reports, an extension of the Anglican-United Church partnership the Mission continued to endorse. As the Mission president expressed it, there were now two pilots and two planes working in support of the joint mission. Equipped with STOL (short takeoff and landing) gear, *George Pringle II* was based at Nimpkish Lake where retired RCAF pilot and lay worker Bill Eliason lived in a trailer near the docking site. The construction of an "Alaskan float" for mooring the plane during the winter ensured it could remain in the water year round and be ready for constant service. The aircraft was financed through a $31,000 interest-free loan from the Diocese of British Columbia, an amount the Mission's president, Bishop Roy Gartrell, saw as a $3,100 annual grant from the diocese towards Mission operations.

He nonetheless appealed to potential donors in December 1978 to help him retire the whole loan within a year.

Throughout his ministry, Mellis remained convinced the Mission was better served by aircraft than by boats. The advantages seemed obvious: rapid access to remote areas and relatively short 'hops' between stations, which allowed a missionary to enjoy a regular family life at home. For Mellis, the plane cast him back upon the goodwill of those to whom he ministered; in this he saw a link with early Christian tradition:

> . . . it meant that I had to stay with a family in a camp when I did spend the night. In many respects, most . . . itinerant missionaries down through history have been dependent upon the hospitality of those among whom they've ministered. In a similar way Jesus and his disciples were dependent upon the hospitality of others and didn't have their built-in accommodation. I would have to use facilities in the camp like cook houses, or homes or community halls in order to hold services. But that's not bad either; it brings the church a lot closer to the people.

Relieved only briefly by Anglican pilot-priest Gerald Kaye, the incumbent at Alert Bay who had experienced Native ministry in the Kewatin diocese in Ontario, Mellis flew the Mission's aircraft regularly until 1980, when he submitted his final report. The year had been "a good one in many respects." He had been to Kingcome once a month "for the Eucharist and visitation," had the services of a student minister during the previous summer, and was deeply involved in continuing education and in Bible Study groups in the camps and Sunday Schools in the settlements. Overall, he sensed an increased interest in religious matters in his patrol area. The aircraft, however, needed upgrading with a $900 transponder, which would soon be required by major airports like Vancouver, and a single sideband radio for reliable air-ground communications. More seriously, Mellis foresaw the need for a $10,000 major overhaul of the aircraft's engine. Once again, the Mission would have to weigh the question of value for money carefully.

After Mellis's departure, the flying ministry continued with the Reverend Gerald Kaye at the controls until health reasons grounded him in April 1981. As the Mission's last pilot-missionary, he submitted a highly critical report to the executive committee on the "aims, objectives, methods, achievements and prospects of the Mission into the 1980s." More a sweeping argument than an analytical study, it pleaded, among other things, for new inspired leadership such as the Mission had found in John Antle and Alan Greene. "We have lost the sense of divine mission [and] there is no real vision for the Mission." Convinced of the continuing need for the CCM's services to "a population of 1,000 scattered people [who] will never be a financially viable parish," he sought financial backing, prayer and "the right man for the job." Ultimately, the Mission board disagreed. Describing itself euphemistically to the 1982 Synod as "at a cross-roads," the Mission reported that it had discontinued aircraft mission work. The expense of the venture had been "too great to be justified by the results [and] was seriously eroding our reserves."

Yet in remote coastal areas, there still remained both a residue of human need and a staunch loyalty to the Columbia Coast Mission. Writing at about this time from "Beaver Creek, Blind Channel, BC" to the Rector of St. John's, Quathiasiki Cove, migrant parishioner Don Startin spoke for many:

> Just in case you are beginning to wonder where I am, you should know that I've decided to work for the above homestead for a while. I will be the carpenter and handyman here. So please pass my name on to the Anglican Mission Boat so that I can go to a Sunday service being held close by, or perhaps take Communion on the boat if they come to Beaver Creek.
>
> Tell them we are on the north side of Beaver Inlet. My small cabin is in the yard behind the A-frame house. Beaver Creek is at the mouth of Loughborough Inlet. See East side of chart 3595, also chart 3555. Approx coordinates 125 36W + 49 31N.—Heck, they'll know where it is . . . I look forward to hearing from you soon or receiving a visit from the Mission.

Transmitted to the Synod Office in Victoria for a reply, the letter bears lean secretarial notes for an uncompromising response: "no boat—plane is being sold—don't expect anyone for awhile."

With the passing of its aircraft ministry, the CCM's operational life ceased, leaving the Mission nothing but a bank account and a budget. The board of directors "ordered that the 1982 net income be divided 50-50 between the two dioceses [of British Columbia and New Westminster], to be utilized in such a way as to carrying out the originally contemplated work of the Mission." In practice, this meant sponsoring more viability studies and providing cash subsidies to financially dependent parishes. For all practical purposes, John Antle's vision had fulfilled its purpose.

Could the Mission have continued? In retrospect, John Mellis thought not. "There were fewer and fewer people in the '80s in those camps. It is questionable how long we could have continued the operation with the airplane, what with the recession at the time. But during the '70s it was an ideal opportunity." For himself, the Mission had meant an opportunity for spiritual enrichment, a chance to experience "the applicability of the Gospel to the lives of almost any kind of people."

Those who doubted the purpose of the Mission, he later recalled, misunderstood the role of ministry. "I always felt they underestimated the effect that the Mission had on the lives of individuals who later would become active in other parishes, and who through the Mission really got their first start in understanding . . . what the Christian faith was about." Seen in this light, the Columbia Coast Mission had been the leaven in the bread of secular life, and its ministry would now live on in other forms. Meanwhile, the Mission could look back with pride. Its itinerant, seaborne medical chaplaincies played the catalyst in bringing health care, medical health insurance, social welfare and workmen's compensation to the British Columbia coast. Its seaborne and airborne pastoral care reached into the lonely outposts of a rugged coast and formed the basis of a caring community of concern and, ultimately, of faith.

Epilogue

T HE COLUMBIA COAST MISSION no longer survives as a
seagoing institution. Overtaken by time, technology and the trans-
formations of a secular world, its ships and aircraft no longer patrol.
Its missioners and seafarers have all gone on to other things; some
to "higher service." The demise of the Mission may well be as
much cause for celebration as regret, for as the *Columbia*'s last
doctor noted in the autumn of 1966, "the goal of every medical
mission is to work itself out of a job." Certainly, the medical side
of the Mission did just that, leaving its legacy to institutions outside
the church. More subtle still are the traces of spiritual ministry
which, like the leaven in the bread of which the missioners often
spoke, touched isolated human lives in the profoundest and most
deeply personal ways.

For many people, the Mission and its ships constituted a vehicle
for spiritual life. Echoing testimonials from a broad spectrum of
coast dwellers, the Reverend Ivan Futter recalled in 1989 that the
community embraced not only those who already had a tradition
of faith, but "those with no affiliations to any church, and without
interest in establishing such connections." The links were lasting,
if often difficult to define. By the very nature of their work, the
missionaries lacked any objective means for measuring what they
had accomplished. Yet, as Dr. Daryl Hanington put it in 1940,
the Columbia Coast Mission was "one of the best examples of a
real Social Service, combining as it does medical aid with sympathy,
personal contact and a religion which is always at hand, and yet

unobtrusive. It has become an institution recognized throughout Canada as outstanding in its unique usefulness."

Confiding to his memoirs just what that experience meant to himself as chaplain-skipper, Rollo Boas wrote:

> When I think of those ten years operating that boat, summer and winter, fair weather and foul . . . I marvel at the parts of my life that were affected. Every day of those ten years I faced the physical dangers of the sea. I laid my life on the line so often that I cannot count the number of times. Physically, and as a seaman, I stood alongside seasoned boatmen and acquired a reputation as a reliable skipper. Even now, after all these years, I can picture in my mind most of the names of the islands, points, reefs, coves and rocks in that 500 miles of coast-line. It was so important to survive, so important to conquer the task of boatmanship, that every fibre of my being was used. I gave it all I had in a dimension never before demanded of me. All this was doubly important because, by choice, my wife and two girls travelled with me for the first five years . . . My vocation in these years was stretched to the limit.

The Mission Boat Homecoming in Pender Harbour in August 1994 was an occasion for many to experience some measure of that achievement. The event celebrated a rich legacy of seagoing missionaries throughout the British Columbia Coast. Focussing on the ninetieth anniversary of the Anglican Church's Columbia Coast Mission, the homecoming also saluted the shared tradition of service with the ships and sailors of other missions: the Shantymen and the United Church of Canada. The reunion of classic vessels conjured up a fascinating heritage of seafaring with its fine craftsmanship, salty yarns—and old diesel engines. In gatherings ashore in the former St. Mary's Hospital and Chapel (now the Sundowner Inn), mission lore was remembered and re-enacted. When the participating ships flew the Columbia Coast Mission flag and conducted their sailpast throughout the anchorage from Hospital Bay, to Garden Bay, Gerrans Bay, and outbound past Irvines Landing, they too triggered residual memories and affection, and wide recognition of the fact that the missions had met real needs throughout coastal society. The long line of ships reminded us that history is not a past but a process: the former Anglican vessels *Columbia* (ex-*Columbia III*), *Chelsea II* (ex-*John Antle V*), *Veracity*, and *Montserrado* (ex-*Alan Greene*); the former United Church ship *Argonaut II* (ex-*Thomas Crosby*), and the former Shantyman *Messenger III* sailed by. Representing the Columbia Coast Mission, the sloop *Peregrine* brought up the rear as a reminder that the Mission had not lost its interest in the coast.

From its founding in 1904, the Mission coped with enormous difficulties. The venture strained both human and fiscal resources. It gave many missionaries cause to wonder which direction to take, or if it was even wise to continue. They, too, were part of the coast; they, too, experienced the coast's brooding grandeur and storm-whipped seas, moments of tough physical challenge followed by fjord-locked tranquility. Like those to whom they ministered, they experienced loneliness, discouragement and perhaps even moments of self-doubt. On the long hauls between ports of call, they had time for reflection. So it was when the Reverend Trefor Williams single handedly took *John Antle* to sea in 1960, and meditated on the meaning of mission:

Is it worth travelling all this way, eight or nine hours? Are the mission ships too slow? What results do I see for my work? Do the people understand what I am trying to put over? To a non-Christian mind many of these questions would have remained unanswered, but I turned to my Bible, or I read in the lessons which come in the daily office which a priest has to say, and there I find how St. Paul travelled on foot often for hundreds of miles, or took a ship, the old Mediterranean grain ships which could not sail less then six points into the wind and would sometimes have to tack for days to round a headland. No mention is made by St. Paul of the long hours, or of the slow travel. He did what he could and left the results in the hands of God.

Ships and Boats
of the Columbia Coast
Mission

Alan Greene. Built for CCM in 1959 by Bissett's Boatbuilding Yards, North Vancouver. 35 feet LOA, 13 tons, 65-hp Perkins Diesel, cruising 8 knots. Sold 1967, renamed *Montserrado.* Later owned by Réjean Rois and Doreen Richards.

Che-kwa-la. Kingcome Mission catamaran. Donated 1964.

Columbia (I). Built for CCM in 1905 by Wallace Shipyards, Vancouver. 60 feet LOA, 38 tons, 20-hp Union gasoline engine. Sold 1910.

Columbia (II). Built for CCM in 1910 by Dawes Shipyard, New Westminster. 100 feet LOA, 106 tons, first diesel replaced by 140-hp Atlas Diesel. Sold 1957 and renamed *Wayward Lady.*

Columbia (III). Built for CCM in 1956 by Star Shipyards. 67 feet LOA, Gardner Diesel, cruising 9 knots. Sold 1968. Renamed *Columbian.* Later owned by Bill McKechnie as *Columbia.*

Columbia IV. Built 1952 at Pender Island. 42 feet LOA, 24 tons. Donated to CCM by owner in 1968. Sold 1969.

Eirene. Loaned by owner for summers of 1911 and 1912. 30 feet LOA.

Fredna. Built 1912 for private owner by W.R. Menchions, Vancouver. 30 feet LOA, 6 tons, Scripps gasoline engine. Loaned to CCM in 1930. Sold 1934.

Governor Musgrave. Small launch on loan from owner and operating out of Vananda (1914–19) and Alert Bay (1925–28).

Gwa-yee. Launch, 24 feet LOA, operating in Kingcome, 1945.

John Antle (I). Built 1921 by Thornycrofts, Hampton-on-Thames, as luxury yacht *Syrene.* 75 feet LOA, 67 tons. Donated to CCM in 1933 by BC and Yukon Church Aid Society. Sold in 1936 and renamed *Syrene I.*

John Antle (II). Built 1926 at Houghton, Wash., for Nitinat Packers Ltd. as *Florida V.* 60 feet LOA, 28 tons. Sold to CCM in 1936 and renamed *John Antle.* Sold 1945.

John Antle (III). Built 1932 by Vancouver Shipyards for private owner. 25 feet LOA, 17 tons, Gray Marine gasoline engine, cruising 7 knots. Sold to CCM 1945, redesigned and renamed John Antle. Renamed *Laverock II* in 1956, donated to Diocese of Caledonia 1957.

John Antle (IV). Built 1940 by Edward Wahl's Shipyard, Prince Rupert, as *Western Hope* for Diocese of Caledonia. 45 feet LOA, 19 tons. Rebuilt 1947. Donated to CCM 1953 and renamed *John Antle.* Renamed *Rendezvous* in 1957. Sold 1962.

John Antle (V). Built for CCM in 1956 by Star Shipyards, New Westminster. 44 feet LOA, 9 tons, General Motors Diesel, cruising 9 knots. Sold 1964 and renamed *John Antle II.* Now owned and operated by Nils Lovenmark as *Chelsea II.*

Laverock. Built 1904 by John Antle, Vancouver. 16 feet LOA, 2.5- hp Bull Pup outboard and sail.

Laverock II. See *John Antle* (III).

Makehewi. Built 1910 for private owner as *Charlotte S.* 35 feet LOA, 14 tons, Union gasoline engine. Rebuilt and renamed *Makehewi.* Sold to CCM 1920. Sold to private owner 1924.

Rendezvous. Built in 1924 for CCM by Hoffar Motor Boat Co., Vancouver. 32 feet LOA, 12 tons, Kermath gasoline engine. Sold in 1955 to Edward C. Tooker as *Tari Jacque.*

Veracity. Ketch, 37 feet LOA. Bought by Ernest Christmas for Kingcome Mission in 1952. Later owned and operated by Becky Beaton.

Notes on Sources

Researching the Columbia Coast Mission presented special problems, the major ones being lack of substantive narratives and some serious gaps in chronology. What one finds beyond the usual files on management and administration are scraps of repetitive anecdotal information, and an extensive collection of middling quality and largely unidentified photographs. It also seems that the Mission's second superintendent, the Reverend Alan Greene, removed some records on his retirement in 1959 with a view to writing his own history. Whether these "Greene Papers" are purely private, or might be of value to the historian, remains unclear. This collection remains in the hands of his legatees and, as such, inaccessible to public scrutiny until deposited in archives.

A major key to interpreting the Columbia Coast Mission is its journal and news magazine, *The Log*. As John Antle expressed its purpose in the first number of the journal in 1906, *The Log* was to "stand for the social, moral and religious interests of the people of this district." Reflecting the Mission's perspectives, tenets and times, it frequently published correspondence and internal reports that can be corroborated in archives. Irregular in its publication history, and inconsistent in numbering its issues, *The Log* offers a wealth of material, but should be read with caution. In the course of my research, more material came to light—the Boas papers, for example, which the Reverend Rollo Boas entrusted to my care before he died, and a few occasional letters from the private collection of Catherine Greene Tuck. Any new collections I acquired have been deposited with the Provincial Synod Archives, at the Vancouver School of Theology.

In short, the records of the Columbia Coast Mission provide no closely knit history, as can be found of the Grenfell Mission of Newfoundland

and Labrador, with which the CCM is so frequently linked in the popular mind. Grenfell himself left a remarkable legacy of literate documents. As a medical doctor and principal driving force, he was the central personality in the medical mission. Skipper-chaplains of the Columbia Coast Mission, by contrast, have left few significant written records of journeys, sermons, reflections or letters. John Antle sketched notes that barely cover the early years, and provided only hints of a trail that ultimately fizzles. The oral record as well, preserved in the memories of those who knew the Mission, plays but a few basic variations on a narrow canon of scenarios.

This doesn't mean that a fully fleshed profile cannot be built on scant clues and circumstantial evidence. Much like a detective, the historian makes assumptions about pattern, purpose and process, thereby developing a context into which a variety of clues can be viewed. By assuming, for example, that these Christian missionaries were motivated by an abiding faith and a commitment to the Social Gospel, I gained a context in which I could view the most disparate material. As obvious as this approach might seem, it has been overlooked by others when recounting the CCM story.

The primary unpublished documentation for the Columbia Coast Mission is deposited in two sources. The principal repository is the Archives of the Ecclesiastical Province of British Columbia, Anglican Church of Canada (at the Vancouver School of Theology). It is referred to in my chapter notes as the Provincial Synod Archives, and covers the breadth of ship's logs, financial accounts, correspondence, diaries, boat-building and maintenance records, aircraft acquisition, and of course annual reports and minutes of all meetings. The second repository is the Archives of the Diocese of British Columbia in Victoria, which contain, in addition to microfilm copies of most of the material transferred to the Provincial Synod Archives, a number of tapes and transcripts covering interviews with former missionaries. The Provincial Archives, Victoria, are of course central to basic research into British Columbia themes.

Richard John Lonsdale's unpublished MA thesis, "A History of the Columbia Coast Mission" (University of Victoria, 1973), pioneered studies in the CCM. Doris Andersen's *The Columbia is Coming!* (Sidney, BC: Gray's Publishing Ltd., 1982) provided many anecdotes and yarns, as well as a useful appendix on the histories of the Mission boats; Margaret Craven's novel *I Heard the Owl Call My Name* (Toronto: Clarke, Irwin and Co., 1967) popularized the story of the Reverend Eric Powell, a CCM missionary at Kingcome village.

In preparing this history I have consulted everything in the Provincial Synod Archives pertaining to the Mission, though I make only selective references in my chapter notes. I have consulted supplementary material in the diocesan archives in Victoria.

Chapter One
Maverick Minister

The principal sources for these early years are John Antle's draft of an autobiography in the Provincial Synod Archives, Vancouver School of Theology. One is an unpublished typescript entitled "The Memoirs of John Antle"; the other consists of pages in Antle's hand. Both are in the uncatalogued "Boas Papers," which also contain drafts of a biography on Antle, whom Boas had known. These papers include Antle's "Report of a Visit of Investigation among the Logging Camps and Settlements on the North East Coast of Vancouver Island and the Islands Adjacent Thereto, during the month of June, 1904." Under the rubric "Birth of an Idea," Antle published retrospectives on the period in the The Log of the Columbia, vol. 1 (New Series), nos. 9–10 (Feb.–March 1931), through vol. 2 (NS), no. 3 (August 1931); he continued under the title "The Idea Grows" in vol. 2 (NS), no. 4 (September 1931). Seven cassette recordings of "Conversations" with the Reverend Alan Greene, made in 1969, are held in the Provincial Synod Archives. The earliest study on the period is J.H. MacDermot, "The Early Medical History of the B.C. Coast," read before the Vancouver Medical Association, 3 November 1935, and published in The Bulletin, 5; BC. Not easily traced, it is found in file "Yukon Church Aid Society, I B37," at the Provincial Synod Archives. MacDermot's manuscript fragment "Makers of Canada" in the Boas papers is also significant. It is perhaps noteworthy that John Antle and his wife separated during the founding of the Mission, leaving him to lead a bachelor's life. She died in Toronto in 1943.

Chapter Two
Launching a Dream

Vignettes on CCM operations are found in the first issues of The Log, vols. 1–4 (April 1906–June 1909), after which the journal ceased publishing until 1930. Antle continued the story of these years in the series "Birth of an Idea" (see notes on Chapter One), and in The Log, vol. 2 (NS), no. 12 (July 1932). Stories on the opening of St. Mary's Hospital, Pender Harbour, are found in The Log, vol. 2 (NS), nos. 1 and 4 (1930). These are supplemented by Antle's unpublished memoirs, together with drafts of a biography in the Boas Papers. Essential for the period are the

Mission's annual reports, the tapescripts of "Conversations" recorded by Alan Greene in 1969, and Greene's article "Twenty-Three Years," in *The Log*, vol. 4, no. 11 (May 1934). Local newspapers are also helpful. For example, the *Daily Colonist* (26 January 1930) published an important article "The Story of BC Hydrographic Surveys," reprinted in *The Log*, vol. 1 (NS), no. 5 (October 1930); and the *Vancouver Province* (21 July 1906) on the sinking of the *Chehalis*. For the account of the Hallidays, I have drawn on Gilean Douglas, "The Bible Barge to Kingdom Come," in *Raincoast Chronicles*. The Provincial Synod collection on the British Columbia and Yukon Church Aid Society contains letterbooks of correspondence; see especially letters no. 22 and 44. Mrs. Catherine Greene Tuck kindly offered copies of the following correspondence: TALC [Thomas A.L. Connold], to Alan Greene, 16 October 1937; and Jack Stanforth, to Tuck, March 1973.

Chapter Three
The Dirty Thirties

Primary documentation in the Provincial Synod Archives includes the correspondence with the British Columbia and Yukon Church Aid Society, in particular that between Jocelyn Perkins and Alan Greene, and the annual reports and correspondence of the CCM. Three numbered boxes containing subdivided files of Alan Greene's correspondence and memorabilia are found in the Synod's "Greene A." These sources are supplemented by *The Log* for the period 1930–1937. Greene's "The Skipper Soliloquizes" in issues of July 1930 and January 1931 gave insight into his early thoughts, as do the taped "Conversations" of 1969. See also Ralph R. Burry, "The Columbia Coast Missions [*sic*] and their Postal Service," *Newsletter*, British Columbia Philatelic Society, vol. 40 , no. 3 (April–June 1991), 4. From the private Catherine Greene Tuck collection I have used the following letters: TALC [Thomas A.L. Connold], to Alan Greene, 16 October 1937; Margaret E. Daniels, to CGT, February 1975; Gilbert Thompson, to Tuck, 29 November 1979. Some reflections on this period are found in the cassettes and transcript "Eric Powell, interview with Ian Sutherland, 5 July 1989."

Chapter Four
The Greening of Columbia

In addition to primary archival sources, I have consulted *The Log* (1937–45). Alan Greene's retrospective "The Skipper Soliloquizes" (March–May

1936) and Heber Greene's reflections in the series "A Landlubber Afloat" (March–April 1943, and May–June 1944) are noteworthy. For biographical sketches of Heber Greene see *The Log* (April–October 1958, and July–September 1962). See also the three boxes of Alan Greene's correspondence. Ian Sutherland's recorded interview with the Reverend Eric Powell, 5 July 1989, is a helpful source, as are Greene's recorded "Conversations" of 1969. Mrs. Catherine Greene Tuck offered the following letters from her private collection: Alan Greene, to Rt. Rev. Sir Frances Heathcote, 3 December 1942; John Antle, to Alan Greene, 4 September 1944.

Chapter Five
Rendezvous Patrols

The uncatalogued "Boas Papers" are essential. For an insightful retrospective in this collection, see Boas letter of 18 January 1954, to Archdeacon A. Hendy, Chairman of Survey Committee, Columbia Coast Mission. *The Log* (1944–55) provides useful anecdotal information as well as briefs on the work of CCM, as do the annual reports and related correspondence. *The Campbell River Courier*, as well as other newspapers, provide background on the issues of the day. See, for example, the *Vancouver Sun*, "Last Rites for Rev. John Antle" (9 Decmber 1949), and Gilean Douglas's "This Minister's Putting the Church on Skids" (*Family Herald and Weekly Star*, 26 April 1951). Ian Sutherland's taped interview with the Reverend Rollo Boas on 16 June 1989 documents important aspects of the *Rendezvous* patrols.

Chapter Six
Medical Pioneers

J.H. MacDermot, "The Early Medical History of the B.C. Coast," read before the Vancouver Medical Association, 3 November 1935 (noted under Chapter One). For correspondence with individual physicians and pastors, see the three "Greene, A." boxes in the Provincial Synod Archives. *The Log* provides sporadic converage of this theme in anecdotes and brief reports. See, however, Florence L. Nichols "First Impressions of a Woman Doctor," vol. 12, no. 6 (Nov.–Dec. 1944) and vol. 13, no. 1 (Jan.–Feb. 1945); and Fred Wiegand, "History of Medical Service Here" (Thanksgiving 1966). From the private collection of Catherine Greene Tuck, I have consulted TALC [Connold], to Alan Greene, 16 October 1937, and Ella Johnston, to Tuck, 4 May 1975.

Chapter Seven
Potlatch and White Man's Prayers

There is a wealth of published and unpublished material on the complex themes of this chapter. While I have consulted widely, convenience prompts me to list very little. William B. Henderson's "Indian Act," in *The Canadian Encyclopedia*, (2nd ed. vol. 2, 1052) provides a useful synopsis. For a detailed account see Richard H. Bartlett, *The Indian Act of Canada*, (Saskatoon): University of Saskatchewan, Native Law Centre, 1980. Useful background is given in James Spradley and James Sewid, *Guests Never Leave Hungry: the Autobiography of a Kwakiutl Chief*, New Haven: Yale University Press, 1969. Other helpful sources are in the bibliography under Boas, Bolt, Collison, Jonaitis, Patterson, Walens and Wolcott. *The Log* published regular notes on the mission to Native peoples under such rubrics as "News from Kingcome Inlet Indian Reserve," "News from Kingcome" and "Kingcome Indian Mission Notes." See in particular Rene Duncan, "Potlatches: A Plea for the Modification of the Law Prohibiting Potlatches," vol. 2 (NS), no. 8 (February 1932). For other CCM involvement, see the three numbered boxes entitled "Greene, A." Of special significance is Alan Greene, Superintendent of the Columbia Coast Mission, to the Chiefs of the Kwakewlth Tribes, 29 February 1944, Box 984–42 (Columbia Coast Mission—Eric Powell), file: church government, potlatch. Ian Sutherland's recorded interview with the Reverend Eric Powell, 5 July 1989, is helpful. For criticism of the *Columbia*, see Diocesan Archives, "Columbia Coast Mission: Notes, Correspondence, Printed Matter, 1941–44."

Chapter Eight
Two-World Tensions

Issues of *The Log* (1944–63) provided considerable anecdotal evidence, which one must read against the background of relevant files in the Provincial Synod Archives. Heber Greene covered selected conventions of the Native Brotherhood in *The Log*, vol. 14, no. 2 (Mar.–April 1946) and vol. 19, no. 5 (Oct.–Nov. 1950). Ian Sutherland's interview with the Reverend Eric Powell, 5 July 1989, was helpful. See also, Powell's "Kingcome Comments" (*The Log*, vol. 24, no. 3, July–Sept. 1955) and "Christmas Greetings from Kingcome Indian Mission" (*The Log*, vol. 26, no. 7, Oct.–Dec. 1957); and his *Speaking Personally*, Division of Missionary Education, MSCC, Toronto, no. 5 (October 1960). For the *Willis Shanks* incident, see "Greene, A., box 2, file 2.5 'Medical Ship Willis Shanks.'"

Ian Sutherland's interview with the Reverend John Mellis, 30 June 1989, sheds light on his experience of BC Native peoples.

Chapter Nine
Overtaken by Time

Issues of *The Log* (1954–62) provide anecdotal detail, as do transcripts of three interviews: Ian Sutherland with the Reverend Joe Titus, 3 August 1989; Sutherland with the Reverend Patrick Ellis, 19 June 1989; and Sutherland with the Reverend Eric Powell, 5 July 1989. Important insights are afforded by Greene, to the Reverend T. Clough Williams, 29 October 1957, in "Greene, A., box 2, file 2.11, Correspondence with Trefor Clough Williams," and "Diary of Elizabeth Goudy, 8 March–11 April 1958," CCM: 987-29, box 1/1. See in particular Cecil FitzGerald, "Welcome New Superintendent," *The Log*, vol. 28, no. 14 (April–June 1960); Trefor C. Williams, "Report from the *John Antle*," vol. 31, no. 3 (July–September 1961); and "Reverend Trefor Williams Bids Farewell," vol. 31, no. 4 (October–December 1961). The account of the Sullivan Bay wedding is taken from Gilean Douglas, "The Bible Barge from Kingdom Come," *Raincoast Chronicles*. Concerning building a church at Sayward, conflicting evidence suggests that the property had originally been donated by Anna and Louis Sacht, long-time residents of the area. For the later development of the property and buildings, see *The Log*, Summer 1968.

Chapter Ten
Mission on Wings

The Log (1962–71) provides important information. See in particular, P.R.E. [Ellis], "Wings to the West Coast," vol. 32, no. 2 (April–June 1962); Rev. J.D. Addison, "St. Peter's Is Consecrated," vol. 10, no. 4 (May–June 1941); Cecil FitzGerald, "An Editorial," Autumn 1965, 4–5; I.P. Baird, "A Farewell to Patrick R. Ellis," Spring 1966; Fred Wiegand, "History of Medical Service Here," Thanksgiving 1966; John W. Forth, "Successful Year Reported," Fall 1967. Ian Sutherland's interviews with Ivan Futter, 7 July 1989, and with John Mellis, provide important detail. Administrative files of the CCM document this period well. See, for example, the "Reorganization" files in CCM: 987-29P, box 5/5, which contain "Minutes of Special Committee Meeting," 10 January 1963. The Provincial Synod Archives holds correspondence files "Correspondence to Patrick Ellis," as well as "Futter Corresp. 1965–66"; and "Ivan Futter Correspondence 1968," and "Mellis, 1973–80." For aircraft see "Aircraft

Information—Correspondence 1960–64," as well as "Aircraft: 1982 and prior." Files on CCM operations and reports are the basis for this discussion.

The New Reformation, Secular City, Death of God debates of the 1960s are documented by a significant body of literature. But see, for example, Paul M. Van Buren, *The Secular Meaning of the Gospel* (1963); Harvey Cox, *The Secular City: Secularization and Urbanization in Theological Perspective* (1965); Paul Tillich, *Theology of Culture* (1959, 1964, 1967); and John A.T. Robinson, *The New Reformation?* (1965). *The Log* joined the discussion in 1966. See, for example, "Is God Then Dead?" (Summer 1966). The venture was short-lived as the editors probably felt the theme exceeded their readers' interest or grasp.

Epilogue

Heber Greene died on 31 May 1968 at the age of eighty. E.A.C. "Ed" Godfrey, skipper of *Columbia* for ten years, died on 19 March 1972, aged seventy-nine. Alan Greene died on 10 October 1972 at the age of eighty-three. Rollo Boas died on 4 June 1993, aged eighty-two. Attributions are from the following: Ian Sutherland's interview with Ivan Futter, 7 July 1989; Dr. D.P. Hanington, "Greetings," *The Log*, vol. 9, no. 4 (May–June 1940); Rollo Boas, "Laying it on the Line," unpublished autobiography, Provincial Synod Archives; and Trefor C. Williams, "The John Antle," *The Log*, vol. 29, no. 14 (July–September 1960).

Selected Bibliography

Andersen, Doris. *The Columbia is Coming!* Sidney, BC: Gray's Publishing Ltd., 1982.

Antle, J[ohn]. *Christmas on the 'Columbia'.* [Vancouver: Columbia Coast Mission, 1928].

Ballentyne, Gordon and Paul Stoddart. "They don't make 'em anymore" [The early days of air transport on the BC coast], *Raincoast Chronicles*, no. 12 (1990):, 64–76.

Bartlett, Richard H. *The Indian Act of Canada*, [Saskatoon]: University of Saskatchewan, Native Law Centre, 1980.

Benson, Don. "Voice from the Inlet" [BC Tel cable-laying and telephones], *Raincoast Chronicles*, no. 15 (1993): 28–37.

Boas, Franz. *The Religion of the Kwakiutl Indians*, 2 vols. New York: Columbia University Press, 1930.

Bolt, Clarence. *Thomas Crosby and the Tsimshian: small shoes for feet too large.* Vancouver: UBC Press, 1992.

Carrington, Philip. *The Anglican Church in Canada.* Toronto: Collins, 1963.

Collison, W.H. [William Henry]. *In the Wake of the War Canoe.* edited and annotated by Charles Lillard. Victoria, BC: Sono Nis Press, 1981.

Corbett, Shirley. "Lund: the beginning of the road," *Raincoast Chronicles*, no. 11 (1987): 25–29.

Craven, Margaret. *I Heard the Owl Call My Name.* Toronto: Clarke, Irwin and Co., 1967.

Day, J.F. *Our Church in British Columbia.* Toronto: Church of England in Canada, 1933.

Douglas, Gilean. "The Bible Barge to Kingdom Come," *Raincoast Chronicles*, no. 10 (1983): 4–10.

Greene, Alan. "Marry'n and Barry'n Logger Style," *Raincoast Chronicles*, no. 3 (1974): 24–26.

Grove, Lyndon. *Pacific Pilgrims*. Foreword by Godfrey P. Gower, prepared for the Centennial Committee of the Diocese of New Westminster. Vancouver: Fforbez Publications Ltd., 1979.

Healey, Elizabeth. *History of Alert Bay and District*. Alert Bay Centennial Committee, n.p., n.d. [1958].

Hilson, Stephen E., ed. *Exploring Puget Sound and British Columbia*. Holland, Mich.: Van Winkle Publishing, 1975.

Holecka, Jackie. "Pender Harbour: A Steamer Stop," *Raincoast Chronicles*, no. 1 (1972): 24–30.

Howard, Oliver. *Godships*. Toronto: The United Church Observer, 1984.

Iglauer, Edith. "Bella Coola," *Raincoast Chronicles*, no. 12 (1990): 23–28.

Johnson, Louise. *Not Without Hope: the Story of Dr. H.A. MacLean & the Esperanza General Hospital*. Matsqui, BC: Maple Lane Publishing, 1992.

Jonaitis, Aldona, ed. *Chiefly Feasts: the Enduring Kwakiutl Potlatch*. Vancouver: Douglas and McIntyre, 1991.

Kennedy, Liv. *Coastal Villages*. Madeira Park, BC: Harbour Publishing, 1991.

Kopas, Leslie. "Growing up in Bella Coola," *Raincoast Chronicles*, no. 4 (1974): 18–23.

Lambert, Gertie. "Cortes Island Back Then," *Raincoast Chronicles*, no. 13 (1991): 41–44.

Lawrance, Scott. "Sointula: Saltfish and Spuds Utopia," *Raincoast Chronicles*, no. 4 (1974): 12–17.

Longstaff, F.V. "The Story of B.C. Hydrographic Surveys: And a Good Case for an Additional Deepwater Surveying Vessel." *Daily Colonist*, 26 January 1930. Reprinted in *The Log*, vol. 1 (NS), no. 5 (October 1930): 8–9.

Lonsdale, Richard John. "A History of the Columbia Coast Mission," unpubl. MA thesis, University of Victoria, 1973.

MacDermot, J.H. "The Early Medical History of the B.C. Coast," a paper read before the Vancouver Medical Association, 3 November 1935, published in *The Bulletin* of the Vancouver Medical Association, 1935: 3–13.

McKervill, Hugh W. *Darby of Bella Bella: Wo-Ya-La*. Toronto: Ryerson Press, 1964.

Moffat, Flora C. "Hospital Life at Bella Bella," *Raincoast Chronicles*, no. 11 (1987): 51–55.

Murray, Peter. *The Devil and Mr. Duncan*. Victoria, BC: Sono Nis Press, 1985.

National Film Board of Canada. *Mission Ship*, Film in the series *Canada Carries On*, 1953.

Patterson, E. Palmer. *Mission on the Nass: the evangelization of the Nishga (1860–1890)*. Waterloo: Eulachon Press, 1982.

Paynter, Margaret. *Miracle at Metlakatla: the inspiring story of William Duncan, a missionary*. St. Louis: Concordia Publishing House, 1978.

Peake, Frank A. *The Anglican Church in British Columbia*. Vancouver: Mitchell Press, 1959.

Pringle, George C.F. *In Great Waters*. Toronto: Ryerson Press, 1928.

Rompkey, Ronald. *Grenfell of Labrador: A Biography*. Toronto: University of Toronto Press, 1991.

Rushton, Gerald A. *Whistle Up the Inlet: the Union Steamship Story*. Vancouver: J.J. Douglas, 1974.

S., E.W. "On Board the 'Northern Cross'," *Across the Rockies*, no. 2 (1938), 12–13. Provincial Synod Archives, Greene, A., box 1, file 1.5.

Spilsbury, A.J and Howard White. "Float Planes and Snow," *Raincoast Chronicles*, no. 8 (1979): 3–9.

Spilsbury, A.J. "Logging on Savary Island," *Raincoast Chronicles*, no. 12 (1990): 1–7.

Spradley, James P., ed. *Guests Never Leave Hungry: the Autobiography of James Sewid, a Kwakiutl Indian*. New Haven: Yale University Press, 1969.

Tickner, Florence. "The Float House," *Raincoast Chronicles*, no. 13 (1991): 5–6.

—————. "Alert Bay," *Raincoast Chronicles*, no. 14 (1992): 77–78.

—————. "The Handlogger," *Raincoast Chronicles*, no. 14 (1992): 10–11.

Walbran, John T. *British Columbia Coast Names*, [1906] Vancouver: The Library's Press, 1971.

Waldie, Adam C. "Summer Intern at Bella Bella," *Raincoast Chronicles*, no. 15 (1993): 37–47.

Walens, Stanley. *Feasting with Cannibals: An Essay on Kwakiutl Cosmology*. Princeton, NJ: Princeton University Press, 1981.

Wallas, Chief James, and Pamela Whitaker. *Kwakiutl Legends*. Vancouver and Blaine: Hancock House Publishers, 1981.

White, Howard, ed., *Raincoast Chronicles*, nos. 1–15, Madeira Park: BC Coast Historical Society, 1972–93.

White, Howard. "Bringing the Indians to their Knees: the coast's first Christian missionaries in Metlakatla," *Raincoast Chronicles*, no. 4 (1974): 24–37.

—————. "Minstrel Island," *Raincoast Chronicles*, no. 11 (1987): 35–50.

White, Howard and Jim Spilsbury. "Q.C.A. The Accidental Airline," *Raincoast Chronicles*, no. 9 (1981): 41–50.

Wild, Pamela. "Fire in a Finnish Colony: Sointula," *Raincoast Chronicles*, no. 13 (1991): 58–63.

Wolcott, Harry F. *A Kwakiutl Village and School.* New York and Chicago: Holt, Rinehart and Winston, 1967.

Index